FIGHTERS

The Lives and Sad Deaths of
Freddie Mills and Randolph Turpin

James Morton

timewarner
paperbacks

A *Time Warner* Paperback

First published in Great Britain in 2004
by Time Warner Books

This edition published in 2005 by Time Warner Paperbacks

Copyright © James Morton 2004

The moral right of the author has been asserted.

A CIP catalogue record for this book
is available from the British Library.

ISBN 0 7515 3321 1

Typeset by Palimpsest Book Production Limited,
Polmont, Stirlingshire

Printed and bound in Great Britain by
Mackays of Chatham Ltd, Chatham, Kent

Time Warner Paperbacks
An imprint of
Time Warner Book Group UK
Brettenham House
Lancaster Place
London WC2E 7EN

www.twbg.co.uk

Contents

Introduction

Once upon a time, when I was young, I used to beg my parents to allow me to listen to the boxing commentaries on what was then called the wireless. Since they started after my bedtime, permission was seldom, if ever, granted, but a note would be left by my bedside so that when I awoke I would know the result. This may have been self-preservation on the part of my parents, who would otherwise have been disturbed by my waking them. In any event, it was how I came to learn that first Freddie Mills and then, five years later, Randolph Turpin had won their world titles.

At school at the time there was a craze for sending off to Pinewood and Ealing Studios to get the autographed photos of stars such as John Mills and Patricia Roc. I wrote, I believe to Solomons' Gymnasium, or it may have been to the restaurant in the Charing Cross Road, for a picture of Freddie Mills, and back it duly came with the address in his handwriting and 'Best o' Luck, Freddie Mills' as the inscription. I have lost it now, but I had it for certainly forty years.

In those days there was a maximum of eight world boxing champions at any one time, and not the alphabet boards of control who offer titles as though they are handouts in a supermarket promotion. In the late 1940s and early 1950s Britain had three of those title-holders, all of whose lives ended tragically. This book is about two of them: one was among the bravest men ever to go into a ring and the other was one of the most talented.[1] Mills held the light-heavyweight title for almost exactly a year and a half;[2] Turpin the middleweight for a mere sixty-four days. There are great similarities in their lives and deaths. During the periods of their success and, particularly in Mills' case, for long afterwards, they were fêted as the heroes they undoubtedly were. Both, however, faded from public view and lost money in a series of business ventures. Each died in circumstances that have never been fully explained. There are many who believe Mills was murdered, and a case has been advanced that Turpin, who seemingly committed suicide, was in fact also killed.

This book does not, however, tell their stories alone; it is the story of boxing in the immediate pre- and post-war years; when there were only eight recognised weights; world championships were contested in major arenas – Harringay, Kelvin Hall, Madison Square Garden – and not in hotel rooms and leisure centres; when there was a colour bar against black boxers fighting for British titles; when the promoter Jack Solomons ruled the roost; when men took contests at a moment's notice and, having taken a savage beating from a heavier man, boxed again within a matter of days against another heavier man and took another savage beating.

One of the most important players in the stories of both

---

[1] The third title-holder was the Scot, Jackie Paterson.
[2] The terms light-heavyweight and cruiserweight were interchangeable at this time.

Mills and Turpin, and indeed of Paterson, is the British Boxing Board of Control, which could be considered the grandson of that wild and woolly outfit, the Pelican Club, which reached its nadir with the so-called Battle of Bruges.

Strictly, prizefighting has always been illegal and the great days of the prize ring, with its bouts lasting a hundred rounds and three hours, really came to an end in Britain with the 1860 Heenan v Sayers contest. Then it went even more underground. The Railway Act in 1868 prohibited the railway companies from carrying spectators to prize fights, but it was still possible to purchase tickets for special trains known as 'There and Backs', where the fancy could watch bouts of over fifty to one hundred rounds. The length of the contests, and how many there were on a card, often depended on how long it took the authorities to break up the meeting. Usually there was the main event and possibly one or two subsidiary contests. If necessary the main event could be continued over a period of days and certainly in a number of different counties.

In London the home of the prize fight was the celebrated Pelican Club, which opened its doors in Wardour Street in 1887, before moving to nearby Gerrard Street.[3] Generally, the wealth and rank of its members kept the fights safe from the prying eyes of the police. One intruding officer was told by Sir Robert Peel, 'My father did not invent you to interfere with me.'

One of the club's protégés was Jem Smith, the All-England Heavyweight Champion, who fought a 106-round draw with Jake Kilrain. Shortly after that, he was matched on the club premises in a glove match with a black American, Peter

---

[3] The club took its name from a stuffed bird which was kept proudly on display, along with a stuffed flamingo. See Douglas Sutherland, *The Mad Hatters*.

Jackson. Smith was badly beaten at the time when he was disqualified for trying to push Jackson out of the ring. The club members lost heavily on the result and had to recoup. Smith's next contest was promoted by 'Squire' George Alexander Baird at the tennis court of Atkinson Grimshaw, a retired major in the Cameron Highlanders, in Bruges, Belgium, on 21 December 1889.[4] This time he was matched with the Australian Frank Slavin, known as 'The Sydney Cornstalk'. The club's members had cleverly backed Smith 'not to lose' and they were determined their man should have the best possible support.

Smith's party turned up accompanied by what were described as thirty or forty of the roughest villains that ever disgraced creation. They swarmed round the ropes forming the ring and with bludgeons, knuckledusters and knives, attacked Slavin whenever he came within their reach. It was reminiscent of the days of the former prize-fighter Bendigo, whose Nottingham Lambs behaved in a similar fashion towards his opponents and supporters when their man was in trouble, or simply to intimidate them.

Nevertheless, Slavin punished Smith so badly he was insensible at the end of the fourteenth round and it was thought he would not come up for the fifteenth. It was then that Squire Baird led the charge into the ring. Slavin was defended by Lord Mandeville with a Bowie knife and, to the delight of the members, the contest was declared a draw. Now the police arrived and the Mayor of Bruges applied to

---

[4]   The heir to a shipbuilding fortune who squandered millions on the prize ring, racing and women, Baird was a throwback to Regency days. He died in New Orleans in 1893 at the age of thirty-one. He had gone on the town after Bob Fitzsimmonds had defeated Jem Hall, whom he seconded. His body was dressed in full evening clothes, placed in a coffin and returned to England. See J. B. Booth, *Old Pink 'Un Days*.

the military for support. The principals were jailed.[5] Baird was brought before the committee of the club under the chairmanship of Lord Lonsdale and was expelled. It was the beginning of the end of the Pelican Club.

Earlier in 1889 the last heavyweight contest under prize-ring rules was held between John L. Sullivan and Jake Kilrain at Richburg, Mississippi. The next year the first world title to be contested with gloves was the Canadian George Dixon *v* Nunc Wallace at the Pelican Club. In 1891 it closed its doors and the National Sporting Club (NSC) was born. Until then professional boxing, even with gloves, was regarded as an illegal occupation. Thursdays, and later Mondays, were fight nights and were financed by backers who put up their prize-fighters in contests for wagers running into the thousands.

The NSC was effectively a middle-class version of the Pelican Club, but this time it was scrupulously well conducted. It was there, however, not to promote the sport but to act as a betting establishment, pure if not simple. The old Marquess of Queensbury would have nothing to do with it, but the presidency was accepted by Lord Lonsdale for the good of the sport. It was there also to clean up professional boxing. It tried to draw lines both under and over its members. Out went the bohemian artists, but there was no entry for the stockbroker who caught the suburban 8.37 train each morning.

Betting establishment it may have been but, nevertheless,

[5] J. B. Booth, *'Master and Men': Pink 'Un Yesterdays*. For an account of the prize ring in its heyday, see Tony Gee, *Up to Scratch*, and for Bendigo's career see J. P. Bean, *Bold as a Lion*. In 1846 the Irish prize-fighter Peter Rafferty was convicted of the murder of Brian Patrick Daley following a four-hour bout in Limerick. Sentenced to death, he was reprieved and transported to Australia. On the voyage he saved the captain's daughter from drowning and, on condition Rafferty never returned to Ireland and changed his name, the man agreed to smuggle him back to England. Joe Robinson, *Claret and Cross-buttock*.

it was the first of the controlling bodies to govern British boxing and, by 1909, the original eight weight divisions had been established.

The NSC lost its control as the organising body because other promoters appeared on the scene who offered bigger purses for top heavyweight contests. In 1909 *Sporting Life* began a campaign for international control of boxing. A proposal by Paul Rousseau, the president of the Fédération Française des Sociétés de Boxe, put forward a series of proposals for world-championship bouts. They were to be of forty-five rounds' duration; doping was to be forbidden; gloves would weigh four ounces and the contests had to be refereed by someone recognised by one of the countries forming the Board of International Control. It was partly because of the NSC's intransigence over the constitution of the new board that it was recognised there must be an independent board of control for British boxing.

In 1919 the National Sporting Club relinquished control of boxing to the newly constituted British Boxing Board of Control. But a decade later it was felt that the board was still too closely associated with the NSC, at least in the minds of the public, and on 21 December 1928 the Earl of Lonsdale chaired a meeting at Australia House in the Strand to announce the reconstitution of the board.

Gradually, over the next fifteen years, the new and improved board assumed control of all involved in the sport, issuing licences in various categories – boxers, trainers, managers, referees, promoters and so forth. In 1933 it survived a sustained attempt to unhorse it and the Southern Area Council, which included Ted Broadribb, later to become Mills' manager, voted to leave the board. For a time there was talk of a rival governing body, but the stewards, with

Lord Lonsdale firmly in place, regained control. Now, the country has been divided into areas, each with its own council able to make independent decisions but accountable to the board to whom appeals can be made. Some of the areas are run by non-financially interested councils, whilst some run by the licence holders themselves. As for appeals from the board, these are made to Appeal Stewards, comprised mostly of independent lawyers.

Apart from numerous newspaper and magazine articles, there have been four books written about the death of Mills, and two about that of Turpin. Peter McInnes, who had known Mills in Bournemouth and who wrote extensively for *Boxing News*, wrote one on each, of which the one on Turpin leans heavily on the earlier biography written by journalist Jack Birtley, who also wrote about both boxers. Tony Van den Bergh wrote one on the death of Mills, and the fourth was by a former estate agent Bill Bavin, who handled Mills' property investments for some time after his retirement from the ring. In his introduction he wrote: 'Every page of the original manuscript for this book was vetted and approved by the boxer's widow, its story being based on a close personal friendship that lasted twenty years.'[6]

My particular thanks are due to J. P. Bean, who has been a continuing source of information, advice and help. My thanks are also due to many who have asked not to be named, as well as Harold Alderman, Gilbert Allnutt, Tish Armstrong, Jeremy Beadle, Simon Block and the stewards and staff of the British Boxing Board of Control, Barbara Daniel, Wayne Bridges, Adrian Bush, Ray Clarke, Stan and Linda Cullis, Stan Davies, Angela

---

[6] Bill Bavin, *The Strange Death of Freddie Mills*, p. 9.

Deacon, Joe D'Orazio, Ed Reid, Peter Fay, Elizabeth Finn, Daniel Flusfeder, Bruce Forsyth, Frank Fraser, Tony and Hazel Gee, Jeffrey and Shirley Gordon, Sid Green, Ernie Halford, Mike Hallinan, Terry Hicks, Noel Higgins, Catherine Hill, Jan Howard, Brendan Ingle, Jimmy James, Dea Langmead, David Leigh, Chick Linton, Danny McAlinden, Paul McCarthy, Brian McConnell, John McDonald, Peter McInnes, Dennie Mancini, Maurice 'Mosh' and Maria Mancini, Jean Maund, Thomas Mellis of Horsham, Bill Mills, Douglas Mitchell, Bob Monkhouse, John Morris, David Nash, Ron Olver, R. E. Oxford, Gordon Petrie, Eddie Phillips, Fred 'Nosher' Powell, Tom Price-Davies, Leonard and Pat Read, Judith Rollestone, Robert Rossi, John Sandow, Bill Sheeran, Linda Silverman, Dennis Slade, Garry Stapleton, Cecily Stroud, Jack Taylor, Jim Taylor, Jeff Tite, Jackie Turpin Snr, Bill Tunney, Derek Whitfield, Professor David Wingate and Orig Williams.

As is always the case with my books, this could not have been undertaken without the constant encouragement, support and help of Dock Bateson.

1

Freddie Mills Meets the Turner Brothers and Gypsy Daniels

If the boy wore a dressing-gown on his way to the ring in the middle of the ice-rink on 12 February 1936, there is no record of it. It is much more likely that there was a towel draped around his shoulders, and that he wore a pair of ordinary shorts and plimsolls. Those were the days when a boxer could turn up at a tournament with a pair of shorts and hope to get a fight. He'd be told to see the doctor and pay the inspector five shillings. And he fought. There was no real medical. No trial to see if he could look after himself. If a boy looked useful, the inspector would follow it up.[1] And that was if it was a licensed tournament under the supervision of the British Boxing Board of Control.

---

[1] Ray Clarke, former General Secretary to the British Boxing Board of Control, conversation with author.

This boy had been to the boxing at the Westover Ice-Rink in the centre of Bournemouth before. Some years earlier, he and a friend had climbed a ladder up the side of the building and sat on the slats on the glass dome to watch the boxing, seemingly miles below in the ring. The visit ended when he and his friend had been seen by the promoter and chased away.

Now, at least, the boy had Gordon Cook, the former light-weight champion of Wales, in his corner.[2] The promoter at the rink, the man who had chased him away years earlier, was Jack Turner. He was running a novices' competition. Novice competitions as supporting contests for the main events were very popular at the time, and for many years afterwards. Apart from anything else they were cheap to run. The first two or three rounds would be boxed on the first or second night, with everything leading up to a grand final and a small trophy.

The boy, who had given his place of residence as Parkstone, in an attempt to fool his parents, had already been to see the promoter and had been told to turn up in shorts and socks. He was due to box another young local hopeful, Syd Jones of Wareham. After a few swings, the other boy went down. There was no applause or cheering. Gordon Cook tapped the boy on the shoulder and told him to leave the ring so the next fight could take place. Nevertheless, he was elated when he was told to come back in two weeks' time. Freddie Mills had won his first bout.

Born on 26 June 1919, Frederick Percival Mills was a late

---

[2] A chronic gambler, Cook was still boxing in the fairground booths at the age of forty-two. By now he had a glass eye, which he would keep in a handkerchief during the bout, using a towel as cover to slip it back at the end. Few in the crowds seem to have noticed. Harry Legge, *Penny a Punch*.

foal, the fourth and last child of Tom and Lottie Mills, who lived not far from the pier in Terrace Road, Bournemouth. His father was a scrap dealer with his own horse and cart. His mother had not worked since the First World War when, with her husband serving in the army, she had been a maid in the local hotels. Mills' eldest brother Jim was born in 1907, his brother Charlie two years later and his sister Hannah, known as Cissie, in 1911.

Described as shy but also in continual mischief, at the age of five, Mills went to St Michael's Junior School near the top of Commercial Hill, Bournemouth, some two hundred yards from the sea. At the age of ten he appeared in the local juvenile court after he and a friend broke into an empty house and stole a pair of roller skates, which he sold for a shilling. This success did not last long. Within a day Freddie was denying to the local police officer that he had ever seen the skates. He held out in the subsequent questioning, but his partner in crime did not. After a lengthy hearing Freddie was found guilty, fined a pound and placed on probation. Until the week before his death that was his only appearance in the criminal courts.

After the court case, he joined a local youth club run by a man with a wooden leg who taught him to box, although by then his brother Charlie had already introduced him to the sport. Charlie went to the bouts at the Westover Ice-Rink and was determined to be a professional. He had some contests, but he never really made the grade. He was, however, the foundation stone of Mills' career. Reluctantly, Freddie's parents had given him a pair of boxing gloves for a birthday. When he left school at the age of fourteen, they found him a job as a gardener. He lasted all of one week, before finding himself his second job with the local milk company. He was sent to Westover depot and put under the supervision of Percy

Cook, Gordon's brother. Mills would groom the horse after the round and, with luck, he could fill the hour before the second round sparring with the other boys, and later the roundsmen themselves. By the time he was fifteen he could hold his own with Cook. In the meantime he supplemented his income by selling the Bournemouth *Echo* in the evening and working on a Saturday in a local grocers. Then it was off to Sandbanks to dig for lugworms to be sold to local fishermen. No one could ever accuse Mills of being lazy.

Mills boxed again in the tournament on 26 February and knocked out a boy named Barfoot, again in the first round. Reg Davis would be his opponent in the grand final two weeks later. Mills had 'weight and reach advantage which he used to good advantage', said the local paper, when Mills knocked Davis out in the third round. There was even a short write-up in the trade paper: 'A promising local boy in Freddie Mills was presented with a handsome silver cup after winning a talent-finding competition by knocking out his opponent Reg Davis (Bournemouth) in the third round. Throughout the competition this 16-year-old novice has removed all opposition by the k.o. route.'[3]

Mills went home and found his parents by the fire reading and darning. By now they were well aware that Freddie Mills of Parkstone was their son, and that he was sneaking off at night to box. His mother kept the silver cup as a treasured possession until she died in 1975. Years later Mills would thank her 'for stoically knitting so many sweaters to relieve her tension on the nights her son was partaking in a sport she never really liked'.[4]

---

[3] Bournemouth *Echo*, 26 March 1936; *Boxing*, 1 April 1936.
[4] *Sunday Graphic*, 26 October 1958.

It was back to the dairy the next day, but a few nights later Jack Turner came to his home to ask if he would like another contest. If so, Mills would have to train properly. According to his memoirs, Mills wanted to know who his opponent was and where the bout would be. He was told he would be fighting George Heskett at Weymouth. He jumped at it. He went to train at a public house in Lower Parkstone, run by Turner's brother Bob. But Mills is wrong in his recollection. In fact his first professional contest proper came a month later on 20 April when he drew with Stan Nelson at the Parkstone Conservative Club, where Jack Turner promoted Friday evening tournaments.

After Mills' death Jack Turner remembered his early training. At the gym they put the gloves on and Mills tore into him. 'I'd had enough and really trounced him,' said Turner. 'I told my wife, "If he comes back tomorrow we've got a good fighter." He did come back the next day for more – and just apologised for being late.'[5]

Given that Mills was only just seventeen in the autumn of that year, what followed might be described as working a novice hard.[6] However, not that many of his contests lasted too long. The first of the new season came on 14 October, when he defeated Jack Scott, an American living in the West Country, twice in the same night. In the first bout Mills

[5] *Daily Mail*, 26 July 1965.
[6] In fact Mills had it easy. 'Nipper' Pat Daly, managed for much of his career by Professor Andrew Newton, who ran the Empire Academy of Arms in the Marylebone Road, became a professional at the age of eleven and was finished at seventeen, having fought a hundred contests, including five with British champions. He was sixteen when he was knocked out by the British featherweight champion Johnny Cuthbert in nine rounds in 1929. He turned to all-in wrestling. Newton's son Andrew Jnr was a professional boxer, who lost the sight in one eye after his bout with Len Harvey, and the sight in the other following a contest with the Frenchman Marcel Thil. Nevertheless, he continued in the sport as a trainer and writer.

knocked him out in the first round, but the crowd took the view it had been a quick count by Gordon Cook, who was refereeing for the evening, and the pair were rematched as the last contest. Almost at once Scott went down under a hail of punches and Mills had won for a second time. 'Out cold,' said the Bournemouth *Echo*. His record, however, shows only the one win. Now *Boxing* described him as a 'find'.[7] A fortnight to the day, he was matched in a return with Stan Nelson and knocked him out in the second. On 11 November he met 'Slogger' Wilson from Southampton, who lasted until the seventh before being knocked out. The Slogger 'entirely failed' to live up to his name, according to the newspaper reports. The surprising thing was that he lasted so long.

Six days later Mills went to Weymouth to draw over six rounds with George Heskett. This must be the contest which he has confused with his first in his memoirs. It was the first time he had worn a gum shield and he also bought himself a pair of shorts. His purse was nineteen shillings. A week after that, back in Bournemouth, he knocked out Fred Lennington.[8]

In his last contest of the year, on 9 December, still boxing as Fred Mills (Local), he 'caused a sensation' when he defeated George Bradby, knocking him out in the first round of what was for Mills ten two-minute rounds. It was the first time he had appeared on the bill proper: 'The 17 year old boy who in the opinion of sound judges of the fistic game is the most

[7] Bournemouth *Echo*, 15 October 1936; *Boxing*, 21 October 1936. It was not all that uncommon for a boxer to have two bouts on one evening. Jackie Binns boxing in Luton defeated Ken Vass in the third round and then, when the scheduled opponent failed to appear, boxed Johnny Boyle, winning on a disqualification in the fourth. (*Boxing*, 12 May 1936.) It was, happily, quite unusual for a boxer who had been knocked out to be required to box a second time on the same bill.

[8] His name is sometimes given as Sinnington.

promising youngster yet produced in Bournemouth.'[9] It had been a good start: eight contests, six wins – all inside the distance – and two draws, one of which he had already avenged.

There were two quick wins in January 1937. Billy Brown was knocked out in the first round and, a fortnight later, Teddy Warren lasted only into the second. Mills was now starting to get noticed and 'The Watcher' from *Boxing* magazine promised to go to one of Jack Turner's promotions, if only to see Mills in action.[10] At the beginning of February, Mills retired Harry Frolic, who had a badly cut mouth, in the seventh round. Then came a more serious test. On 17 February he was paired with the well-thought-of and skilled Irish middleweight Jack McKnight over twelve rounds, again at the ice rink. It was widely believed that Mills might have been overmatched against a man who had been boxing for seven years, and who had met many of the top middleweights. McKnight apparently thought so, laying a bet on himself that he would stop Mills.

The contest showed up Mills' inexperience and limitations. Kept at bay for long periods by McKnight's left hand, Mills knocked him down in the fourth, but was unable to do so again. As the contest progressed he became increasingly frustrated and took to charging across the ring with his head down. It was not a tactic which pleased the crowd, but his determination and strength eventually overcame the Irishman, who was driven about the ring in the last two rounds. It was a grandstand finish which earned Mills the verdict, though the crowd, thinking he had been fortunate, booed the result. Nevertheless he had come through a stern test.

[9] Bournemouth *Echo*, 8 December 1936; *Boxing*, 16 December 1936.
[10] *Boxing*, 20 January 1937.

By now, Mills was working in Jack Turner's boxing booth, as well as at the dairy. The car which Turner drove was unreliable and Mills found himself dozing in it waiting for repair work to be done, then going straight into work the following morning. Two days after the McKnight contest both the Turners came to see him and suggested that he turn professional full-time in contests and at the booth. The thinking was that working at the dairy was interfering with his training. This would ensure there were enough fights to cover his lost dairyman's wages. Mills obtained his mother's reluctant permission and went off to the funfair at Chipperfield's Circus, opening in Exeter the following week. Pay would be £2 5s a week, almost double his earnings in the dairy. There would also be the chance of regular 'nobbins', the money shared between boxers after a well-fought bout, either thrown into the ring or carried in a bucket through the crowd.

For the better part of two centuries, boxing booths at fairs were part and parcel of the sport.[11] One of the most enduring booths was the Hickman Boxing Show. The bare-knuckle fighter Tom Hickman, known as 'The Gas Man', was one of the finest champions of the prize ring until he was crushed to death in a coach accident on 10 December 1822 at the age of twenty-seven. Boxers who knew Hickman collected sufficient money to buy his wife and child a booth and agreed to fight there without fee for the next year. It remained in the family: by the 1930s the heavyweight Charles Hickman

---

[11] In their heyday, there were probably over a hundred touring booths, but by the mid-1990s the last boxing booth in Britain was the Excelsior Pavilion, run by Welshman Ron Taylor. His great-grandfather started the business in the 1840s and he took over in 1936 when his father died. (Michael Prestage: 'Last Boxing Booth Fights to Stay off the Canvas', in the *Guardian*, 22 February 1994.) It was still functioning in the summer of 2003.

Jnr was both boxer and proprietor. The booth lasted until the end of the twentieth century. In these booths it was a matter of pride if a man stood up for his allotted three rounds against a boxer who later became a champion. Matt Queenan recalled his bout: 'In my youth I went three rounds with Randolph Turpin in a bet organised by promoter Pat Collins where people were bet a pound for every round they stayed standing.'[12]

Garry Stapleton remembered: 'I heard from my mother that my granddad Jack who was built like a barn door once fought Freddie Mills in a boxing booth somewhere in Middlesex. My granddad went the distance but suffered a broken jaw and always swore blind that there was something in Freddie Mills gloves; i.e., a horseshoe possibly.'[13]

Perhaps, or Mills hit even harder than some thought possible.

John Sandow recalls the days of the booths in the West Country:

> There were two booths. There was the West of England Boxing Academy and there was Sam McKeown's. Bernard, Sammy's son, was the barker and he never dressed up, but Mickey, who ran the West did: dinner jacket, bow tie and patent leather shoes. I was a gee man in the crowd at two pounds a night. I had a day job but at night and at the weekends I travelled to the fairs from Whitsun onwards – Truro, Helston, Barnstaple, all over Cornwall for the season. When the genuine challengers had been put away I was in the

[12] Birmingham *Evening Mail*, 11 July 2000.
[13] Garry Stapleton, letter to author, 24 March 2003.

crowd calling out. Would I stay up for three rounds?
Of course I did and I'd be saying, 'Give me another
round and I'll knock him out.' But of course I never
did. There was a lot of hitting with the inside of the
glove, which made it sound good to the crowd. Then
we'd go round the crowd afterwards with buckets for
the nobbins. You got good boxers – Boswell St Louis I
remember was one. I think he fought five British champions, including Bobby Johnson and Pat McAteer. Those
days the professional season ended with Jack Solomons'
show on the eve of the Derby, which they ran on a
Wednesday then, because the boxers wanted to work
during the summer.[14]

Stan Cullis, who boxed for the British light-heavyweight title
twice, remembers his booth days with some affection: 'I
boxed on booths at the age of fifteen. At first I was a gee
in the crowd. The gees would use names like Wacker
Williams and older ones would be Sergeant Something. Of
course, the governor knew who you were and so did some
of the crowd, but they never said anything. Then when I
was a bit older I moved to the Top. I did the early booths
at Easter and I was first on the Top [outside the booth, chal-
lenging the crowd] in the Midlands. They were all gees. You
got some straights [real boxers] at Helston because of the
navy.'[15]

Freddie Mills' first full day at a boxing booth was a painful
one. One of the fighters was Gypsy Daniels, now ten years
past his prime. Born Daniel Thomas in Llanelli, his path to

[14] Conversation with author.
[15] Ibid.

the top had been a struggle. He had begun boxing in 1914 and in the 1920s he had beaten many of the top boxers of the era, including Phil Scott, at the time a leading heavyweight contender. In 1927 he outpointed Tom Berry in Holland Park over twenty rounds for the British light-heavyweight title. Although he was never regarded as a big puncher, the following year he knocked out Max Schmeling, then the European light-heavyweight title-holder, in the first round in Germany. He found it difficult to get bouts in Britain, so for some time he boxed in America, which was where he became 'Gypsy': to try to promote a more colourful image he was taken to a shop off Broadway, where his ears were pierced and his head wrapped in a bandana. From then on he was the 'King of the Gypsies'. Now, with over 130 recognised contests behind him, he was well on his way down. But he was more than a match for the likes of young Mills.

That first night Mills was in the crowd as a gee. There was, of course, the usual repartee designed to wind up the punters: 'Here's a young man. They say he's got a knock-out punch. Gypsy, will you accept the challenge?' Of course he would. Daniels told the crowd he would 'eat him', and once in the ring assured Mills that he should take it easy and things would be all right. Mills, giving away four stone, recalls he took more punishment than he had ever known and ended with a splitting headache, being sick at the back of the marquee.[16] Is it fanciful to think his later troubles may have started there and then?

It was the Gypsy who later gave Mills his cauliflower left ear with a swinging right-hand punch. There was a recognised cure for this injury prescribed by Professor Andrew

---

[16] Freddie Mills, *Twenty Years*, p. 24.

Newton: the ear should be lanced and then bathed in boiling water. A pad of borassic lint soaked in surgical spirit should be laid flat to the ear and a small piece of plywood put over the lint and bandaged in place. It was thought that however painful it became, the patient should lie on the injured ear. The next morning it had to be bathed in hot boiled water and washed again with surgical spirit before the pad was replaced. Andrew Newton Jnr, former boxer and manager, recalled that his father had received over fifty letters from non-boxers asking how they could acquire this badge of courage.

It may be that Mills did not follow Newton Snr's advice to the letter. Surgical spirit and boiling water were no doubt in short supply at the fair. Mills left the booth for the evening and tried a variety of remedies, including hot milk, and leeches – also recommended – from the chemist: 'These were no better than the milk had been and my next remedy was anti-phlogistine. Still the ear would not go down and after three days in sheer desperation I put an empty match-box on top of the anti-phlogistine against the ear and bandaged it as tightly as I could to the side of my head,' he recalled.[17]

Too late. But he was boxing again within the week. Shortly after that his mother paid a surprise visit to the booth and was not pleased to see her handsome son disfigured by the professional trade mark; nor his black eyes from other Daniels' punches. To his credit, the Gypsy was suitably sheepish about the mauling he had given Mrs Mills' ferocious lamb and she accepted her part in the disfigurement of her son. After all, she had given him his first gloves.

Years later in a radio interview with Dr Edith Summerskill

---

[17] Ibid., p. 28.

on the dangers of boxing, Mills claimed his cauliflower ear had come from playing rugby.[18] He also claimed that he knew only one punch-drunk boxer and he was not British. But Mills was surely being economical with the truth. When Mills began his career, punch-drunk boxers littered the halls and booths. Back in 1933 *Boxing* had tried to bring what it saw as rogue managers to book, saying, 'Some managers . . . only qualification is that of a term of imprisonment . . . I could name at least a dozen lads whose careers have been ruined by such imposters whose one thought is how much can be made out of a lad before he is too punch-drunk to fight anyone and in consequence is discarded to make room for some other deluded youngster.'[19]

Mosh Mancini, who later worked on Griffith's Boxing Booths with Randolph Turpin, thought, 'The best time to catch the punters was after lunch when they'd come out of the pub. Occasionally you had a good one but it was rare.' The only difficulty was that if the men had had too much to drink they could cause trouble in the booth, and so keep away the crowds, who would not want to get caught in a fight in the audience. In an evening some booth owners would shut them down before the pubs closed to avoid trouble.

In the early part of the summer Freddie Mills had something of a scare in a booth of a fair being held in a disused quarry in Cornwall. Mills took a challenge from a man who had been making a nuisance of himself. Jack Turner told Mills to give the man a good hiding and Mills set about his work, catching him with a left hook. The man hit his head

[18] Tony Van den Bergh, *Who Killed Freddie Mills?*, p. 114.
[19] Editorial, *Boxing*, 3 October 1933.

on the boards and had to be carried out of the booth, bleeding badly.

In the 1930s there was then no likelihood of a prosecution after a death in a British Boxing Board of Control-sanctioned contest. The case of *R v Roberts*, heard on 28 June 1901 following the death of a boxer at the National Sporting Club, had effectively put paid to that. It is instructive to look back at the summing-up of Mr Justice Grantham: 'If . . . you think it was simply a case of boxing or sparring with rules proper for the purpose of preventing men going on until exhaustion ensued or injury resulted, and with the desire to make it a pure question of science and as little injurious to the individual as possible, then Gentlemen, your verdict will be Not Guilty.' The jury considered their verdict for two minutes before acquitting the defendants.

Booth fights, however, were another matter entirely. Rules did not count for much. Mills was right to be scared. Gerard Fook, who boxed as Jerry Wang, was at this time facing a manslaughter charge following the death of a Joseph Kehoe after a booth fight, which was described by one witness, admittedly Kehoe's brother, as a 'spite fight'. Kehoe had gone to a booth in Bootle, where Fook was refereeing a contest in his dressing-gown. Kehoe twice took hold of the gown, tore it, and Fook then threatened him. It was agreed that the two should meet over three rounds and if Kehoe was still standing, he would receive ten shillings. Kehoe had drunk fourteen half pints of beer that evening and when Wang knocked the man down with the first punch, he hit his head on the boards. He was revived by ambulance men and went home, but had started to vomit the next morning and died a week later. The court was told that he had a skull half as thick as a normal person and that he could have died in any sporting activity.

The judge stopped the case against Fook, but said it was perfectly proper that one had been brought.[20]

Back in Cornwall, no doctor was called and there were no ambulance men. Mills thought that he also might be heading for the courts because it was over an hour before the man started to come round. Now the relieved Mills said to the man he should keep away from boxing booths, which were dangerous places.

Mills returned to Bournemouth to fight more or less every fortnight. Red Pullen was defeated over twelve rounds on 3 March and Mills won the return with Jack McKnight exactly a month after their first contest. On 14 April he beat Jack Alder, and a fortnight after that he beat Harry Lister. On 5 May he defeated Albert Johnson. All were points victories and all were over twelve rounds. That was the end of his season and for the rest of the summer it was the booths or nothing. Freddie was seventeen.

After a couple of months Jack Turner decided to leave Chipperfield's and go back to Bournemouth. As far as he was concerned, anyone who wanted to go to Sam McKeown's booth was welcome to do so. It seems incredible nowadays that a fair could support two boxing booths, but from time to time McKeown's had been in opposition to Turner's, and Mills, who knew and liked McKeown, now joined him. Gypsy Daniels, who had been Mills' roommate in their lodgings, did not.[21] Bob Turner also remained with the booth.

During the summer, Mills returned home with a bad case of dermatitis, no doubt brought on by the lack of hygiene on the booths. Now Lottie Mills took the opportunity of

[20] *Liverpool Echo*, 15 July 1937.
[21] Jack Birtley wrote that the pair sometimes shared a bed at their various digs. (*Freddie Mills*, p. 39.)

trying to persuade her son to get 'a proper job'. He began as a trainee mechanic at the Westover Garage opposite the ice-rink. Within a week, however, he had jacked up a car incorrectly and had managed to ruin its petrol tank. With his mother's blessing, it was back to the booth, now at Brixham.

In August Bob Turner matched Mills with George Davis from Notting Hill at Poole Greyhound Stadium. Davis was another fighter who had beaten many of the top welterweights and had now moved up a division. Mills reckoned he was fit from working on the booths and he went to the match full of misplaced confidence. In the second round Davis put him down with a body shot, but Mills recovered and gave a fine display until, in the tenth and last round, he was floored by another body shot. Mills' corner claimed it was a low blow, but the referee continued counting and this time Mills did not get up.[22]

Booth boxing was all very well, but it was no proper training. As Stan Cullis says, 'A booth was a holiday. It was keeping you active, but if you got three straights in a season with anyone who could box, it was rare.'[23] After his loss to Davis, despite some mocking comments by the other fighters, Mills began to put in daily and essential roadwork, as well as work on the bag.

The free and easy life on a fairground suited Mills. Chipperfield was not even particularly annoyed when he and another boxer, Jack Thompson, took a week off unannounced to stay in Southampton on a houseboat owned by Thompson's

[22] This open-air promotion on 14 August 1937 drew some 13,000 spectators. Mills boxed in the second contest. The three main events saw Larry Gains, the great black Canadian heavyweight, knock out Bert Ikin in the first round; Jack 'Kid' Berg draw with Jack Lewis; and Johnny King being outpointed in a non-title match by George Mardsen.
[23] Conversation with author.

parents. A similar incident occurred towards the end of the summer when the fair was at Devizes. One night, the canvas top of the booth collapsed on the ring in a gale. When no lodgings could be found, Mills told McKeown he was going home. McKeown replied that by the time Mills reached Bournemouth his cards would have beaten him there. But off Mills went. After a week, when the cards had not arrived, Mills went to see Bob Turner's wife to find out the fair's next venue. This time he was welcomed back with open arms. This was a pattern for Mills. He was apt to make seriously important decisions on the spur of the moment without any real thought of the consequences.

Mills did not return to the ring proper for two months after his defeat by Davis. Then, on 8 October in Paignton, he beat Harold 'Kid' Anthony readily enough, knocking him out in the first round. Now it was Davis who was signed up for a rematch over twelve rounds. Mills started slowly and the far more experienced Davis outboxed him with clean, crisp punching. Despite stinging body attacks as the fight progressed, Mills was unable to make up the ground lost at the start and Davis kept his lead to the end, a good winner on points.[24] The pair never met again.

The rest of the year continued well enough. The Bournemouth heavyweight Billy Fuller was knocked out in seven; there was a draw with Jim Greaves from Leicester, and Fred Clements retired with a damaged hand at the end of the sixth round. That was probably a question of hastening the inevitable. Mills had been getting up steam in the last couple of rounds and Clements had more than enough trouble keeping him at bay.

[24] By now Mills' contests were being given good space in the reports from around the rings. The fight with Davis was reported in *Boxing*, 27 October 1937.

Then came a step up in class and distance. On 15 December Mills met Jack Lewis, the vastly experienced Bournemouth middleweight who had boxed Kid Berg earlier in the year. This time the bout was over ten three-minute rounds. It was the first time Mills had boxed that distance, and he was outpointed. There had been queues outside the ice-rink hours before the doors opened. *Boxing* thought that both had boxed at their best, with Mills earning a slight lead before being defeated by the accurate punches of Lewis. Two days later Mills was back in the ring to draw over twelve rounds with Ginger Dawkins in Paignton.

He had little rest over the Christmas period and 1938 started well on 5 January with a return against Dawkins, who this time was stopped in eight rounds. Dawkins had been scheduled to fight Jim Greaves, who was himself due to meet Mills in a return a fortnight later. Now the Leicestershire man was injured in a car accident and Mills, who had simply gone to the tournament as a spectator, stepped in. This time he was far too much for Dawkins, winning after eight one-sided rounds. In his turn Greaves was duly beaten on points in Mills' next contest.

1938 was a year of almost unbroken wins, mostly on stoppages. Victims included Harry Vine, later to become the chief inspector of the Boxing Board of Control, who was stopped in nine; Jack Lewis, this time beaten on points; Charlie Parkin, the Northern area champion, who was beaten twice in a fortnight; and the very useful Ernie 'Butcher' Gascoigne. Mills received a Certificate of the Month from *Boxing* for his second contest with Parkin. In all, until the last bout of the year, Mills' record was fifteen wins and no losses. Nine of the opponents had failed to last the distance.

There was some controversy over his win in an open-air promotion against Moe Moss from Camden Town, who had considerable Jewish support. In the fifth round Moss knocked Mills down, but instead of going to a neutral corner he half turned his back. Mills, then on one knee, sprang off the canvas and hit Moss on the ear, knocking him out. There were vociferous complaints from the Moss supporters.

Mills was certainly making serious progress, but there were some doubts when he was matched with the experienced Canadian, 'Yorkie' Bentley, who had lost a very close decision to the highly talented Ginger Sadd, and another to Dave McCleave.[25] Mills knocked him out in six rounds. Then, on 7 December, came the match with Ernie 'Butcher' Gascoigne, which Mills won on points over twelve rounds: 'He hit me in the fifth round on the side of my head and again in the eighth round in the body and on each occasion I just did not know what had happened for the rest of the round.' Mills clearly did not remember much of the contest, despite his book of cuttings, because in his memoirs he wrote that the bout had been in the September.[26]

A week later, on the last Westover card of the year, he met Dave McCleave, who had beaten Ernie Roderick, Charlie Parkin and Butcher Gascoigne. It was thought this would be a real test for Mills, but the bout was the classic match between boxer and slugger. Mills was outboxed by a man

---

[25] Arthur 'Ginger' Sadd fought over two hundred contests in a career that lasted over twenty-nine years, winning the Eastern Area middleweight championship in 1935 and again in 1948. He fought twice in final eliminators for the British middleweight championship, losing on both occasions. In recent years only Peter Buckley has fought over two hundred contests, reaching that mark in April 2003. To put matters in perspective many of Buckley's contests have been over four rounds, whilst after his first five contests Sadd never boxed over less than eight, the majority being ten rounders.

[26] Freddie Mills, *Twenty Years*, pp. 51–2.

with adroit footwork. The vastly more experienced McCleave opened up a lead and, although in the later rounds Mills scored with heavy body shots and seriously troubled McCleave with a right hand to the head in the ninth, he was 'quite unable to wipe out the deficit'. Nevertheless *Boxing* was very pleased with him: 'Mills has no cause to feel discouraged by his defeat at the hands of a master boxer like McCleave and deserves a compliment for the magnificent display he gave against his most formidable opponent to date.'[27]

Yorkie Bentley opened up Mills' campaign for 1939. 'This match will provide thrills from gong to gong' said the posters. But this time Bentley was stopped in seven rounds. The fight had been little more than a maul and Bentley was cut after a clash of heads.

Then came a landmark in Mills' burgeoning career. On 18 January he was scheduled to box the Canadian champion Paul Schaeffer. The BBC wanted to broadcast the contest. Schaeffer, who was a genuine contender for the British Empire title, was so confident of victory that he put up a £100 side stake that he would knock out Mills.

Twelve days before the contest, Mills went down with influenza and spent a week in bed. There was, however, no question of calling off the bout or seeking a postponement. Mills was in bed for eight days and his training for the last four days before the fight was simply walking along the promenade to at least get some sea air. Remarkably, Mills won a comfortable points decision. But the local paper was not completely satisfied: 'If Mills is going to get right to the top of the tree he will have to do more than swing heavy

[27] *Boxing*, 21 December 1938.

punches.'[28] It was to be a recurring criticism of his boxing throughout his career. On 1 February, relegated to the under-card, he defeated Johnnie Blake, who took heavy punishment and retired with a badly damaged face at the end of the sixth round.

In his contests up to this point, Mills had boxed outside the Bournemouth area on just four occasions, travelling only as far as Paignton. He did not seem to travel well and there was a setback when he journeyed to Great Yarmouth on 20 February and lost over twelve rounds to Butcher Gascoigne. It was a poor contest, with the crowd singing 'Dear Old Pals' as the pair mauled together.

The pattern of boxing and booths continued in the last year before the war. In Exeter Fair Week Mills boxed a twelve-round draw in a booth match with Jim Gayford.[29] In the licensed ring Eddie Maguire was beaten on points in Bournemouth and Mills once again demonstrated his seeming inability to travel when he drew in Plymouth with Nat Franks. Not that he improved in his next contest: on 12 April back in Bournemouth Elfryn Morris from West Bromwich beat him on points. He defeated Charlie Parkin, again over ten rounds, a fortnight later and then at the beginning of May knocked out Dave McCleave in the first round back home. He lost to Ginger Sadd on points on 14 June, and knocked out Charlie Parkin in the first round on a rather more successful visit to Plymouth on 21 July. He had a break until he defeated the unfortunate McCleave, knocking him out on 28 October in

---

[28] Bournemouth *Echo*, 19 January 1939.
[29] Gayford, who also boxed as Young Tucker, Gunner Bennett and Jimmy Bennett, began his career at the age of thirteen and defeated Dave Penfield on Jack Solomons' first Devonshire Sporting Club show. After the Second World War he was heavily involved with amateur boxing, both as a referee and in setting up a number of clubs. He died in August 2002 at the age of eighty-nine.

three rounds in Southampton. There followed a win on 7 November over Eddie Maguire, again in Southampton, but a fortnight later he could only draw with him in the same ring.

Mills' last fight before he was called up to the RAF was on a Boxing Day morning promotion, when he again fought Elfryn Morris in Bournemouth. 'Freddy Mills last appearance in the ring at Bournemouth before joining the RAF. Elfryn Morris will definitely arrive in Bournemouth on Christmas Day,' screamed the poster. The pair weighed in at the Norfolk Hotel and Mills thought he was in good condition, for he had been using a pick and shovel at a military camp. Instead, he found himself muscle bound and by the end of the fourth round he was tiring. There had been a clash of heads in the opening round and both men had taken and given a good deal of punishment when, in the sixth, Morris came out of his corner head down and fists flying. Mills ducked and there was a serious clash of heads. Morris went to the canvas; Mills, helpless on the ropes, stayed upright whilst the Welshman was counted out. 'Mills apparently had the harder head,' said the Bournemouth *Echo*. The 3000-strong crowd was not pleased.[30]

Five days later Mills went off to war. Up in the Midlands Randolph Turpin was just eleven years old.

[30] Bournemouth *Echo*, 27 December 1939.

2

Randolph Turpin and the Wathen Road Gang

Freddie Mills had an easy childhood compared to Randolph Turpin's. It might be thought that as the only black family in Leamington and Warwick in the 1920s, the Turpins must have suffered a good deal of racial abuse, but that seems not to have been the case. In fact the Turpins suffered not particularly from being black but from being poor.

'That racial hatred only came after the war,' remembers Bill Mills, who grew up at 24 Wathen Road in Warwick and recalls Turpin standing shyly on the doorstep on the day the family moved into the street. 'The only coloured people we saw then was when the Indians came round once a year in their turbans flogging chains and ties.' Years later Danny McAlinden, the former British heavyweight champion, recalled how in the 1960s there were signs on the windows and doors of lodging houses and pubs in Coventry saying, 'No Irish, no blacks, no dogs'.

Randolph Turpin's brother, Jackie, recalls the 1920s, however, as a time of condescension, but little racial abuse. None of the children of his age treated him differently: 'It was all very different in those days. The town was full of retired colonels and the like. They used to offer to adopt us. I think they liked the idea of having a little houseboy.'[1]

Once, on a walk with his sister Joan, Jackie felt ill and they had gone to a house to ask for water. They were given a jug filled with ice cubes, which neither of them had ever seen before. There was some sort of party going on and the pair were invited in and patted on the head because the guests wanted to see how their hair felt. The greatest insult Jackie suffered was from a boy known as Banjo because of his bandy legs. When goaded beyond endurance the boy retaliated by calling Jackie, 'Cotton Hair'.

In Warwick there were fights between the boys from Wathen Road and Pickard Street, with broom handles being the weapon of choice. But there were never any serious injuries and, 'It seems like a world away from now when people use knives and get really brutal.'[2]

The Turpins' father, Lionel, had been the first black man to arrive in the area. A merchant seaman, he and his ship-mates arrived in Britain from British Guiana and he decided to join the forces, signing up with the King's Royal Rifles during the First World War. For his pains he was badly injured in a mustard-gas attack during the Battle of the Somme. Sent to a hospital in Warwick, whilst recuperating

---

[1] Conversation with author.
[2] Leamington *Morning News*, 28 August 1990.

he fell in love with Beatrice, a local girl whose father, Thomas Whitehouse, had been a bare-knuckles fighter. They had five children; the eldest, Lionel Cecil, was known as Dick, then came Joan, Jackie, Kathy and Randolph, who was born on 7 June 1928. Lionel, who never really recovered from his gassing, died within twelve months of Randolph's birth.

The family lived in a damp basement flat in Willis Road, Leamington, a few hundred yards from the Royal Pump Rooms with its hammam bath, and a million miles away in terms of luxury. There was very little money in the house. Beatrice worked as a cleaner at the Shire Hall and could more than stand her ground against any insults or sneers she might get. 'She could hold her own with an Irish navvy,' recalls Tom Price-Davies, who knew the whole family. But there was less than £2 a week coming into the house. Worse, Turpin was a sickly child, regularly ill during the winter. Maurice 'Mosh' Mancini, Turpin's lifelong friend, remembers Beatrice telling him how, when Randolph contracted double pneumonia at the age of three, the doctor gave up on him. 'He won't be here in the morning, Mrs Turpin.' 'He will,' came the reply and he was, sitting up in bed. But he was ill with a chest complaint for the next two winters.

Shortly after that the family split. Dick went to live with Beatrice's mother; Joan went to an 'auntie' in Wales. Ethel, Beatrice's sister, had Randolph and Jackie; only Kathy remained at Willis Road with their mother.

By 1931 Beatrice Turpin had moved to Warwick, renting a flat over a fish and chip shop. That year she married a local man, Ernest Manley, who worked as a foreman at a large local scrapyard. The family, together again, moved to Wathen Road. Theirs was one of the first council houses in the area. The rent was seven shillings and sixpence per week. Ernie

Halford, who grew up in the street, recalls: 'Even at that price it was a struggle for most of our parents, no work and, but for the outbreak of war, many of us would have finished around the corner at the local workhouse where, for a few hours work daily, we would have enjoyed three square meals a day and a change of corduroys every month.'[3]

Bill Mills, who lived in the same street, confirms the degree of poverty: 'We had bread and milk for dinner and my Christmas lunch was a sausage. We had cardboard in our shoes and when it rained we walked on our heels. The Turpins were as poor as everyone else.'

At the age of five Randolph went to West Gate Council School, where six teachers had control of three hundred boys.

Mills remembers: 'Randy used to sit near the front of the class and he'd write on a piece of paper and send it down on the floor to you. When you looked it would say something like, "Tell me the answer to no 6 or I'll give you a beating afterwards."' He was also said to have passed a lemonade bottle around the class, telling the other boys to 'Fill 'er up.'[4]

By the time he was twelve years old, Randolph could out-punch, out-run or out-climb any boy in the school. His prowess as an athlete and fighter soon had him tagged 'Licker', a nickname he carried throughout his subsequent boxing career.[5] 'He liked being called Licker. It was never Randy. It was "Call me Licker,"' says ex-boxer Stan Cullis.[6]

No other boy of his age could match him for speed, indeed he was so superior to his schoolmates that one year he was banned from taking part in the school's annual sports day.

[3] Letter to author, April 2003.
[4] Jack Birtley, *The Tragedy of Randolph Turpin*, p. 18.
[5] Ibid., p. 16.
[6] Conversation with author.

Physically, it seemed he could do anything, including leap-frogging over an unbroken line of nine or ten boys. The teachers would stand and watch as: 'His school friends would line up, bend their heads forward to waist level and Turpin would then sail over the line with one gigantic leap.'[7]

Turpin was a good swimmer, going underwater for long distances, which may have damaged his eardrum and led to his increasing deafness. There is also a story that he was trapped in some reeds in a local lake. Although he extricated himself, there have been suggestions that perhaps it was this that caused the damage.[8]

Turpin became a fitness fanatic and more or less remained one throughout his life. He designed exercises to build up his body. At first there was skipping outside his house with his brother Dick. There was also swinging from trees. Any exercise others could do, Turpin had to do more repetitions. If someone did forty he would have to do fifty. Bill Tunney, who wrestled him on a number of occasions in later years, remembers his strength: 'He was one of the most naturally fit men I ever met. He always looked fantastic, whatever he ate. Three hamburgers and chips never seemed to matter. He had tremendous sinew strength. If he held out his arm parallel to the ground you could neither push it up nor pull it down.'[9]

This strength was apparent early in his life, for instance when Turpin challenged Peter Price for leadership of the Wathen Road Gang, and knocked him down with a two-fisted blow. Nevertheless they remained friends throughout Turpin's life.

---

[7] Jack Birtley, *The Tragedy of Randolph Turpin*, p. 16.
[8] Ibid. Gwen Turpin does not mention the incident in her interview in the *Sunday Mirror*, 29 May 1966, attributing the deafness to swimming generally.
[9] Conversation with author.

In Wathen Road Randolph Turpin met 'Mosh' Mancini: 'I met him when I was a little boy. I lived at the top of the road and he and Jackie would wait to chase me on the way to school. We became blood brothers, we cut our wrists and rubbed the blood in. They were the only coloured people in Warwick but they could look after themselves.'

Blood brothers or not, Randy could be moody with his friend: 'He would come and collect me to go to the pictures, but he wouldn't speak to me on the way there or back or during the show. Sometimes I'd call and he'd say he was going to bed. He was never a good conversationalist.'[10]

Randy and his friends were not all that popular, and some remember him as something of a bully in his young days, a complete contrast to his elder brother Dick. Nor was being a blood brother or sister an exemption from a beating. As far as Dick was concerned Randy was, 'What you call a likeable bully, because although he bullied you, you went back with him. He was just the boss of the gang.' It was the same with the rest of his family. His elder sister Joan remembered: 'He could be so lovable. He'd break your arm one minute and mend it for you the next. He was that type, you know. We was all pretty violent come to that. He blacked my eyes for me twice. Once for my birthday and once for telling my granny tales about him.' His sister Kate recalled: 'If you didn't do what he wanted he'd clank you for it. He'd squeal to me mother if you hit him back and if you did anything he didn't like he came in and smashed all my dolls. I had some little black celluloid dolls and he'd put his foot on them and break them.'[11]

---

[10] Ibid.
[11] Dick, Joan and Kate Turpin talking in the television film, *64 Day Hero*.

Others recall him at the age of ten or eleven having a victim held by others whilst he hit him. But he could be generous: 'After he had started boxing and won a few shillings in amateur contests he would buy sweets for everyone.'[12]

All the Turpins could stand up for themselves. Tom Price-Davies remembers being at a fête in Stratford after the war. He and Jackie Turpin were walking towards a marquee, when out staggered a man, followed by another, with Kathy Turpin at their heels telling them they should not call the Turpins 'black'. 'She'd fisted the pair of them.'

As a teenager Randolph was not the flavour of all the town: 'People would step off the pavement into the roadway to avoid contact with him. He was always regarded in Warwick as what we today call a Yob. My most vivid memory of Randy was when I visited the County Cinema in Warwick; the cinema was very crowded except for a circle of empty seats around one person. It was Randy sitting all alone with his feet up on the back of the seat in front smoking and eating chips. The management was too intimidated to interfere.'[13]

Randy Turpin's ring career really began when his brother Dick first boxed. The eldest Turpin was born on 26 November 1920 and became fascinated with boxing after going to the booth at Warwick Mop as a schoolboy. He was enchanted by the shouted offers of one pound to last three rounds and gripped by the fact that any local boy could have a friendly spar and 'no liberties taken'.[14] Dick began turning up at the gym at the Warwick Corn Exchange. To get rid of him, the boxers would give him a penny to go and get some chips,

[12] Bill Mills, conversation with author.
[13] 'A Warwickian', letter to author, 21 March 2003.
[14] 'A Credit to his Race', *Boxing News*, 24 November 1948.

but he always returned. At the age of fifteen he had made such progress that the local boxer Mick Gavin took him to Charlie Hickman's booth and put him on the front. Within the year he had his first contest, fighting Jack Trentfield in a booth at the Hay Mills, Birmingham. He would say later that it was one of the hardest of his career.

Then a local street bookmaker and owner of a corner shop, George Middleton, started to put together a school of professional boxers. Middleton would go on to manage all three of the Turpin brothers and, much later, would be alleged to owe money to Randolph and have mismanaged his affairs.

Dick started boxing professionally in 1937, winning seven out of eight bouts. A handsome youth, he also used to appear in local carnivals as 'The Black Prince'. The next year he won thirteen bouts, drawing and losing one. In 1939 his record was twenty-six wins against three losses and a draw.

Meanwhile, his other brothers had been making their way in the ring, at first in so-called exhibitions as 'Moses and Alexander', with small gloves, dressing-gowns, boots and shorts. Jackie Turpin recalled: 'Then Mr Middleton had the idea that I and Randy should box exhibitions on the bills when Dick was topping them. We'd go round with fire buckets and we got more than he did for topping the bill.'[15] Randolph did not have such a happy recollection of the contests: 'Jackie used to thrash me and I'd cry my eyes out.'[16]

In 1940, before Dick Turpin joined the army, he racked up twelve wins, one draw and two losses. On 16 December that year he fought Ginger Sadd, who had three times

---

[15] Conversation with author.
[16] Later, as adults, there were countless family exhibitions. As a variation on a theme, on 23 April 1948 at West Bromwich, Dick boxed Randy in an exhibition with Jackie as the referee.

opposed Freddie Mills. Turpin had previously beaten him, in Nottingham. There were now complaints that Turpin was being passed over for Empire honours, but *Boxing News* pointed out that the lesson he received from Sadd showed he was not up to a title match. Sadd, never a heavy puncher, knocked him down in the sixth round and in the seventh Turpin, anticipating Roberto Duran by many years, lifted his arms and cried 'enough'.

George Middleton was quick to defend his man, writing that Turpin had been engaged in war work and, like so many, had difficulties in training. He had also had a three-month lay off. 'Let's get the Big Fight over and give the boys a fair chance.'[17]

Dick Turpin then fought in the 'Big Fight' with the Desert Rats in Italy. Jackie served on the Russian convoys and the Turpin sisters entered the WRAF. This left Randy as the only one at home.

In 1942, with the intention of keeping local boys such as the Wathen Road Gang off the streets, John Gibbs, a local police inspector, introduced boxing at the Leamington Spa Boys' Club. Randolph was an enthusiastic member. On 19 March 1942, guided by Gibbs and coached by Ron Stefani, a former British welterweight champion who became head coach at the club in 1941, Randolph made his ring debut proper. It was not all that an auspicious beginning. He was outpointed by evacuee Harry Shord from West Ham in a tournament at the Ford Motor Company. But Turpin lost only twice more as an amateur. The first was when he was knocked out in thirty-five seconds by Coley Fowler from Birmingham. The second, as a senior, came when he was outpointed by Johnny Ryan, a stylish army boxer.

[17] *Boxing News*, 2 and 9 January 1941.

The loss to Fowler, whom he had already beaten, is both explicable and shows the lack of medical supervision of amateur boxing in those days. Turpin had been working for a local builder Bill Tarver when he left school, and a brick had fallen on him as he leaned out of a window. Turpin sustained a large lump and a headache to go with it, but he still went in the ring.

In short order Turpin acquired a huge local following. With little professional boxing available to fans, he became a name to watch, and queues formed when he was due to appear at an amateur tournament. Trophy followed trophy, to the mixed delight of sister Kate: 'I used to love it. He'd bring his cups home and he'd let me have the privilege of cleaning them for him. He was a bully but I don't think I'd have had him any way else.'[18]

In 1943, Turpin won the Junior 'A' class seven-stone championship. The next year it was the nine-stone-seven Junior B class and the year after that he was Junior C class champion at ten stone seven pounds. Twenty-three days later he won the ABA senior welterweight title at the Albert Hall, defeating Wally Thom – who would himself have a very successful professional career – in the final. *Boxing News* thought, somewhat tweely, that before the fight Turpin had been, 'A teeny-weeny bit scared, not of his opponents – nothing on two legs would frighten this young man – but at the prospect of boxing for the first time in his life in a rather overpowering Albert Hall.' The correspondent was sure his eyes had 'goggled', something which happened to those of his opponents in slightly different circumstances.[19] He

[18] *64 Day Hero.*
[19] *Boxing News*, 4 July 1945.

remains the only boxer to win both junior and senior national titles in the same season. He won the title in 1945 and was then beaten in a close decision over six rounds by Johnny Ryan, whom he had previously knocked out. A third contest was arranged at Stourbridge over four three-minute rounds, conditions which were thought to favour Ryan, but he did not appear. This was not uncommon at amateur shows. One tournament of the period began forty-five minutes late 'for circumstances beyond our control'; the circumstances were that only half the boxers had turned up.

On 12 December 1945 Randolph joined the Royal Navy for his National Service and was sent to the training ship, *Royal Arthur*. He had tried to sign up a year earlier when his friend Mosh Mancini had joined up: 'He came with me to sign up so he could be on the same ship. But he was too young and was told to go away.' In theory on the *Royal Arthur* he was an assistant cook but, as with many sportsmen and women, much of his time was spent training and appearing for the Services in charity tournaments. Heavyweight Dennis Slade, who sparred with Joe Baksi, was with Turpin in a combined Army and Navy team against the Royal Air Force and Royal Marines at Chatham. 'We both won our bouts. Turpin won his by a knockout and he really laid the fellow out.'[20] During this part of his career, the papers were full of joking threats that if he did not knock out his opponents it would be back to spud bashing. 'So what could a poor cook do?' queried *Boxing News*.[21]

For the fight on 13 March 1946, the ABA's match against France, Ryan was picked in preference to Turpin.[22] Gibbs

[20] Conversation with author.
[21] *Boxing News*, 5 June 1946.
[22] Ibid., 6 February 1946.

wrote to *Boxing News* suggesting that there may have been a hidden agenda behind the decision. Turpin was to be in the reserve contests, which would not count for the match, but with a proviso – if he could make the weight. He could not. He did, however, box a draw in the return match in Paris later in the spring.

But before that came the 1946 ABA championships. Turpin had apparently looked tired at the end of his contest for the Inter-Services Championship when he beat Bob Parker on points in Brighton. There were suggestions that Turpin's naval service was the cause and that the decision might have even gone against him had the contest gone another round. Afterwards Parker went to hospital with an eye injury. Before the contest he had been suffering with a bad cold. Then his eye haemorrhaged when he blew his nose violently, and the final damage had been a first-round punch from Turpin. He retired in May 1946, not having boxed again.

Even before the ABA finals Turpin had been in some trouble in the courts. On 17 March he was found collapsed on a sofa at home after drinking liniment. He had had a row with his girlfriend, Mary Stack, on the day he was due to return from his leave. Her family was from Cork and her brothers Willie and Mick were more than fair boxers themselves. Willie was an international amateur, Mick was a not quite top-class professional middleweight. Over the years he would spar with Turpin and these turned out to be fierce fights. It is said that boxers can leave their fight in the gym and it is sometimes said that Michael Stack, who topped a number of bills around the country, did not progress further in the ratings because of his gym wars with Turpin.

That would, however, be years in the future. Now a doctor was called and Turpin appeared to be incapable of answering questions. Taken to Warwick Hospital, he escaped in his pyjamas and was later found by the police at his home. This time he climbed out of a back window, partly dressed. He was eventually found in a telephone box on 20 March. He told the police that once free he would attempt suicide again – suicide was then a crime. Asked if he had intended to kill himself with the liniment he replied, 'That's right. I was fed up. That's why I took it.'

That morning he appeared, handcuffed to a police officer, at Warwick Magistrates' Court. He was remanded until the Monday. By then the defence team was out in force. The liniment drinking had been accidental and he had no more thoughts of suicide, if he had ever had any (which, as lawyers say, is denied). William Tarver, his former employer, was in court to say how sorry he had been to lose Turpin to the navy, and that he had an excellent character. David Ashdown from the Boys' Club was there to give an account of a shy boy, unspoiled by success and not one 'whom one would have thought would do this sort of thing'. An officer from Portsmouth, Lieutenant R. M. L. Ray, was present to say the navy wanted him back, that he had been a good lad during his short period of service and, most important of all, that he was due to box at Wembley in the ABA championships the following Saturday. The bench decided it would be lenient. Turpin was bound over to be of good behaviour for two years.[23]

As with Freddie Mills' earlier indiscretions in the RAF, the incident was overlooked. After all, Turpin was bringing fame and fortune to the navy in tournaments against the other services. As it turned out, the escapade clearly did him no

[23] Warwick and Warwickshire *District Advertiser*, 22 and 29 March 1946.

harm. In the semi-final and final Turpin had Ian Mitchell on the floor five times and then stopped Ian Walton, who was knocked down twice in the second round and twisted his ankle.

Turpin's last fight as a member of the British ABA team was on 29 May 1946 in a match against the United States. Now he had moved up to middleweight and was due to meet Harold Anspach, a marine who was regarded as a banker for the Americans. Turpin knocked him out in ninety seconds. Anspach managed to get up after the first knock down, but not the second. For the record, rather unexpectedly, the British side won the match 5–3.

Turpin continued to box for the navy throughout the summer of 1946 and then in August announced he was turning professional, a decision which did not please the amateurs, nor indeed some of the boxing writers, who thought that he might have been better waiting until he had completed his National Service.

3

Freddie Mills' War

Freddie Mills' war began at Padgate, a camp in the New Forest, where he swiftly contracted pneumonia, losing a stone and a half in the process. Once he had finished his sick leave he was offered a place on a physical training course at Uxbridge, along with Ted Drake, the Chelsea footballer, and Sam Bartram, the Charlton Athletic goalkeeper, whose speciality was to play halfway up the pitch and then run back, hoping to get to his goal before the opposing forwards. As far as Mills was concerned, the best news was that his friend, the boxer Tom Reddington, was also on the course.

Even then, however, Mills was showing signs of insecurity. He did not like the parallel bars, the rings or the wall bars. After a week he wanted out. It is amazing that a man with such physical courage in the ring should show fear at exercises any schoolboy of the period would have taken in his stride. "'They'll have me breaking my neck next," I told some of the other men. "This is too dangerous a life for me.""[1]

Off he went to see the Squadron Leader, who told him to complete the day's training. Half an hour later he was taken to one side and spoken to by the Middlesex cricketer R. W. V. Robins who explained the facts of the RAF to him.

Apart from boxing Mills always suffered this curious fear of pain. R. E. Oxford remembers playing cricket with him as a boy on the Bournemouth sands when the tide was out: 'If the tennis ball went into the sea it became wet and, covered in sand, was as hard as a stone. Freddie used to say, "Don't bowl too hard, don't hurt my leg."'[2] After his retirement, Mills spoke to the boxing writer George Whiting about these fears: 'Deep down inside I have to fight myself first before I can fight anyone else, and it's been that way since I started in the booths right up to the time I beat Gus Lesnevich for the title.'[3]

Meanwhile, in the evenings he sparred with Reddington and went to a tournament at Wembley between the French and English amateurs, where the great Ted 'Kid' Lewis pointed out the well-known manager Ted Broadribb to him. He also boxed for the RAF against the navy, knocking out his opponent with a blow to the solar plexus.

On the professional front, in March 1940 Mills was rematched with Ginger Sadd in a charity tournament at Coventry. It was an event of which Mills' commanding officer approved, and he was given special leave to train along with Reddington. Mills was fortunate to have such a commanding officer. Not everyone could get leave, and whole bills could

[1] Freddie Mills, *Twenty Years*, p. 63.
[2] Conversation with author.
[3] *Evening Standard*, 26 July 1965.

be ruined at an hour's notice when it became apparent that the main event was going to have to be rescheduled. Not surprisingly, there were complaints from the punters, who were paying up to a week's wages for tickets.

When it came to it, however, Sadd developed influenza and Mills boxed a southpaw, Jim Berry, instead. Curiously, since he had by now had over fifty professional contests, it was the first time in his career that he had faced one. He won well enough, beating Berry from North Shields on points. Sadd had recovered by April, when Mills beat him on points over ten rounds in Eastbourne. He was in the ring again the next week when, weighing twelve stone, the heaviest he had ever been, he boxed the Jamaican middleweight Stafford Barton at a promotion at Walthamstow. It was Mills' London debut and for once he was receiving weight. Barton retired with a damaged hand after the sixth round. He had been knocked down in the second, but Mills had been unable to put him away.

Mills next fought on 22 May, when he met the hard-punching Ben Valentine at Bournemouth's Winter Gardens. The Fijian was a well-ranked man, who had drawn with Ginger Sadd, defeated a number of Mills' other opponents and was rated as a contender for Jock McAvoy's Empire title. Despite the fact that Mills was receiving twelve pounds, it was thought to be another big test. After the fight Councillor Frank McInnes, now Mayor of Bournemouth and a long-time friend of and adviser to Mills, presented him with a gold watch, subscribed for by local boxing fans, and announced that he would finance a Mills shot at McAvoy's British middleweight crown. The fight itself was disappointing: Valentine was badly cut early on and retired at the end of the third round.

Then came the news that on 8 August there was to be an overweight match with McAvoy at Liverpool's Empire Stadium, known as the Graveyard of Champions. Mills' purse was to be fifty pounds. He and his friend, fellow boxer Duggie Bygrave, travelled there the day before and, according to his memoirs, watched the wrestling at the stadium, which had a hole in its roof blown in by an incendiary bomb.[4]

McAvoy, known as the Rochdale Thunderbolt, was widely regarded as being far too experienced for the Bournemouth man. Now aged thirty-one, he had held the middleweight title after outpointing Len Harvey in 1937 and had taken the light-heavyweight title from Eddie Phillips. McAvoy had toured America where, in perhaps his finest bout, he had knocked out Babe Risco, then regarded as the world middleweight champion. But he had also lost on points to John Henry Lewis for the world light-heavyweight title. McAvoy was another who constantly fought heavier men. In 1939 he had lost on points to Jack Petersen for the British heavyweight title.

The fight took place before a crowd of 7000, and when Mills was tiring in the fifth round McAvoy, recognising talent when he saw it, encouraged him, saying, 'Come on son, keep punching.' In the sixth the older man injured his thumb and faded over the later rounds, leaving Mills the clear winner on points. Although it was not for McAvoy's title, another champion had theoretically gone down in the graveyard. In fact there were doubts that McAvoy had trained properly. This was a match at an odd weight and McAvoy was not known to take such contests all that seriously.

---

[4] He and Bygrave must have stayed on, because the wrestling was on the night after Mills met McAvoy. Later in the month, evening boxing at the Stadium was suspended because of the bombing.

The Liverpool *Echo* was quite impressed with the winner: 'Mills believes in hitting hard and often even though many of his blows may not count. It was obvious that McAvoy was not as hard as he might have been.'[5]

The next month Mills was off to Newcastle to box Seaman Ernie Simmons, whom he defeated in six rounds. Now there was talk of a match with Len Harvey, and Bob Turner issued a challenge. A stumbling block was that the BBB of C had announced that during the war no serving champion would be required to defend his crown.[6] No one seriously thought that Harvey would agree to a match without a huge fee. If he did, there would be only one winner and it would not be Mills. There was another stumbling block to that contest, however. Harvey was an officer and therefore a gentleman. Mills was a corporal and, however much of a gentleman he might be, military regulations did not permit officers to fight other ranks.

So, boxing in the year 1941 began on 26 May at Leicester's Granby Hall with a second win for Mills over Ginger Sadd, who this time retired with a hand injury after nine rounds. Mills had missed his train and hitchhiked 150 miles to get to the venue. He also missed the weigh-in, but it was generally agreed he was much the heavier man and also that even if Sadd had not injured his hand Mills was well ahead on points. *Boxing News* was impressed: 'If he will cure himself of his habit of hitting with the inside of the glove – a practice which may entail his disqualification one of these days – he

---

[5] Liverpool *Echo*, 9 August 1940.
[6] In general, it was thought the board was dragging its heels and not doing as much for its sport as were the football clubs. If champions did not have to defend, there could at least be an interim competition with a cup or belt to the winner of each weight division. (Gunner J. Symonds, 'Why Not a Boxing Cup Competition?' in *Boxing News*, 3 July 1941.)

may march forward to championship fame in either the cruiserweight or heavyweight division.'[7]

Mills had heard of a booth promotion at Pontypool and wrote asking if he could be matched. In the bout on 31 May he stopped the Coventry middleweight Trevor Burt in a round. The bell saved Burt but he was unable to come up for the second. Again, Mills had hitchhiked to the contest. Burt had only been married that morning and the evening of what should have been his honeymoon ended with a badly bruised jaw and ribs.

On 8 June, at a Sunday show in Liverpool, Mills met Jack Hyams, the Southern Area cruiserweight champion, who as a younger man boxed as Kid Froggy. The ageing Kid did not last long. When Mills had boxed McAvoy at the stadium the year before there had been a suspicion of his punching with an open glove, but he had clearly read his copy of *Boxing News*, for now there was none of this. It was plain by the end of the first round that it was a question not of if, but of how long Hyams would last. His eye was split open in the fourth, and that was that.

Then came the turning point in Mills' career. He met his future manager and father-in-law Ted Broadribb on 30 June 1941, the night he beat Jack Powell in one round at the Reading Greyhound Stadium for a purse of twenty-five pounds. Powell had beaten most of the leading men at eleven stone six pounds and was a highly rated middleweight contender. Now, conceding weight, he was knocked down for counts of eight and six and, after he was floored again and with his mouth badly cut, the referee stopped the contest.

[7] *Boxing News*, 29 May 1941.

After the fight Broadribb went to Mills' dressing room, patted him on the shoulder and told him that the left hook with which he had knocked out Powell was the best he had seen since Mickey Walker's. Afterwards Duggie Bygrave told Mills that Broadribb had his eye on him and that he hadn't come into the dressing room simply to make small talk. In his turn Mills protested that he was happy with Bob Turner. It seemed Turner was there to stay.

4

Ted and Chrissie Broadribb Meet Don McCorkindale

'Freddy Mills' lucky star bumped into mine,' wrote Ted Broadribb in his autobiography.[1] Certainly, so far as his lucky star was concerned, he is correct. Whether Freddie was quite so lucky is open to question.

Edward Broadribb was a hard man, no doubt conditioned in part by his early life. Born in East Street, Walworth in December 1888, his father George Daniel Broadribb had been a fair but unexceptional bareknuckle fighter and had boxed as Danny Wyatt. He was also a heavy gambler. Broadribb himself started selling newspapers at Ludgate Hill at the age of fourteen and was sacked for fighting with a porter. This set a pattern for a series of jobs until, exasperated, his father

[1] Ted Broadribb, *Fighting is My Life*, p. 104.

took him to a horse-racing agency. Arrangements were made to apprentice him for five years to a trainer at Maisons-Lafitte, near Paris. He was given thirty shillings and put on the train to France.

One day at Maisons-Lafitte he skipped his grooming duties to go to breakfast and when he returned, the trainer thrashed him with a steeplechase whip and then locked him in the horse's box. After dark, the other lads opened the door and advised him to go to the police. Instead he went home to England. There were forty-eight weals from his neck to his thighs. The doctor who inspected him told his father to take action, but the response was that his son probably got what he deserved. Broadribb promptly ran away from home and lived with costermongers, earning his two shillings a week rent by selling bananas, working as a tea boy and helping toe-droppers, men who sold pieces of linoleum smaller than they represented.

He was working on a building site by the time he went to the Canterbury Music Hall near the Elephant and Castle, and saw a film of Jimmy Britt boxing Battling Nelson. He was hooked. He was persuaded to enter a four-boy novice competition at the Cornwall Boxing Club near Waterloo station and he won the cup. It was a hard way of earning a living. After three fights at the old Wonderland in the East End, where he was defeated in the semi-finals of another competition, he received five shillings.

He had decided to box as Ted Wyatt but, when it came to it, his elder brother Bill was boxing as Snowball, because of a patch of white hair, and so in turn he boxed as Young Snowball. He began his career proper in early 1909 and by the October he was a respected contender in the bantam-weight division. He won sixteen fights in a row, nine of them by knockouts; he lost over fifteen rounds to Frank Riches at King's Hall, and then won the next five. After that, he went to the Wonderland in Paris in April 1910 and defeated the new rising star Georges Carpentier. Later, people claimed that Broadribb was a veteran and Carpentier a mere novice, but Broadribb was just twenty-one and Carpentier had by then had nearly thirty fights. Like so many, Carpentier was being rushed and over-matched. Broadribb knocked him out in four rounds.

Like Mills, Broadribb had been in trouble in the army. But in his case he had been on jankers. He had signed up in the King's Royal Rifles in 1905, which required his annual attendance at summer camp, but in 1910, after the Carpentier fight, instead of going to the camp he skipped it to go to New York. On his return he was given twenty-one days' detention.

The camp first showed his acumen with money, something his future son-in-law sadly lacked. Earning sixpences by boxing three rounds, he loaned them out to the boys who had lost their cash playing Crown and Anchor. The camp barber lost so much that he was obliged to take Broadribb in as a partner to pay off the debt. At the end of the summer camp, despite the fact he was fifteen pounds to the good already, it became clear to Broadribb that many of his debtors were not going to pay him, so he took the men's boots.

Broadribb's career in the ring came to an end in February 1911. First, he beat Stoker Allen at the National Sporting Club in Covent Garden, knocking him out in the tenth after both had been on the floor several times. Broadribb knew that 'Peerless' Jim Driscoll was counting the days to the end of his career and now he believed he was in line for a shot at the title. Instead one disaster followed another. He was floored by Wally Pickard at the Holborn Empire. Pickard had put him in a half-nelson and Broadribb's corner, believing the opponent would be disqualified, called him over. Instead the referee counted him out. That was the end of his featherweight championship prospects for the present. He won his last contest when he accidentally butted Charlie Dixon at the Ring, Blackfriars. Dixon retaliated with a butt of his own and was disqualified. Broadribb had done a deal with Dick Burge that he would get 50 per cent of the gate, and he would pay Dixon from it. The net receipts were £240 and he guaranteed Dixon £40, leaving himself £80, less his manager's fee.

After that fight he decided to quit the ring. He had been having trouble with his eyes and when he was punched on the nose, blood trickled from their corners. He knew that the black boxer Andrew Jeptha was going blind and he thought enough was enough. So he took up promoting at the Manor Place Baths, Walworth. One of his early bills featured the great Ted 'Kid' Lewis who said he would box eight rounds for 12/6d, and ten or fifteen for 15 shillings. Broadribb matched him over six rounds. He also took over the contract of the Scot, Johnny Matheson, and was soon getting him over £100 for his contests.

By the 1920s, he was a bookmaker with a pitch at Ascot Races and offices in Camberwell, Camberwell Gate and the Walworth Road. He had also become a manager with a very successful stable of boxers whom he supplied for contests at the Ring, where until 1932 the matchmaking was done by Dan Sullivan.[2] All Broadribb's boxers had on their trunks the

---

[2] Dan Sullivan, in the 1920s a member of the BBB of C, was half Italian and completely illiterate. His failure to keep rudimentary accounts and to pay tax on the profits from the Ring almost bankrupted its owner Bella Burge. After he left the Ring he successfully promoted in opposition to it.

initial S., standing for Snowball. He handled champions at every weight and his knowledge of boxing was without question, but he was an aggressive man, happy, even in later life, to match his words with his fists.

In 1932 Broadribb met up with Mills' predecessor, the South African Don McCorkindale, whom Broadribb described as a man of boundless courage. McCorkindale had come to Broadribb wanting to earn one more fight to pay for his fare back home. The boat fare was £45 and he agreed to box Adolph Pott for £50 on the same bill as Larry Gains v Heine Muller. However, when Muller dislocated his shoulder, McCorkindale was put in against Gains and took £600, as the shrewd manager ensured he was now on a percentage of the gate. They boxed a draw and a rematch was scheduled. At the end of the thirteenth of that contest Broadribb looked in Gains' corner and saw a commotion. For the moment he thought Gains was being retired, but he later learned that his second, Jack Goodwin, had died. The very close decision went to Gains.

McCorkindale boxed Gains for a third time on 12 April 1933, on a Jeff Dickson promotion at the Albert Hall. This time in the last round Gains was floored by what *Boxing* described as 'a vicious left swing'. He was ready to rise at nine, but he miscalculated the count and the verdict went against him. McCorkindale, a man physically very like Freddie Mills, was another of Broadribb's protégés who displayed little defence. Had Gains had anything of a punch he would have knocked him down with the right hands he continually landed on the South African's jaw.

For a time McCorkindale stayed with Broadribb and earned well. He also married Broadribb's daughter Chrissie who, with her sister, worked with their father in both betting and boxing.

Always fiery and controversial, Broadribb resigned from the BBB of C in 1933, saying he would now promote independently. He gave the reason as his difficulty in obtaining fights for his non-Jewish boxers south of the river, which produced a howl of protest and claims of anti-Semitism. But Broadribb, never one to shirk a quarrel, stuck to his guns. A host of Jewish boxers wrote to the trade paper in his defence.

Two years later, Broadribb, his quarrels resolved and now restored to the ranks of the licence holders, met and began to manage Tommy Farr. In Farr he encountered someone as difficult as himself: 'He had a razor-sharp fighter's brain, he was as hard as nails and he feared no man. He was a clever fight tactician, he stayed cool under fire and very few boxers could outthink him in the ring. He was a handsome young man and was popular amongst his own people. He had an excellent singing voice and he made several records. But he also had a very large chip on his shoulder and he was not generally well liked.'[3]

Farr was an enormously handsome man in the fashion of the time, and was also highly intelligent. He was born on 12 March 1913 in Tonypandy, South Wales. He started out dirt poor with little or no education but by the end of his stint in America, which ended with a points defeat over ten rounds by Clarence Red Burman in New York on 13 January 1939, his son says he was 'a man of substance, a maths wizard with a literate mind at ease in the highest company'.[4]

After a very short time in the pits, Farr had worked in Joe Gess's Boxing Booth at Tylerstown, joining it at the age

[3] F. Deakin, *Tommy Farr*, p. 5.
[4] T. Farr, *Thus Farr*, Introduction.

of fifteen as a handyman and progressing to be one of the boxers. He loved it, writing in his autobiography: 'In Gess's booth I found and lived with "white" men, true soldiers of fortune. There is small, if any, place for scallywags in a well ordered boxing booth. I was proud when I was voted big enough and good enough to take a place in Gess's troupe of fighters. As a means to learn the trade of fighting it is beyond price. To every fight-minded youngster I strongly recommend the boxing booth as the best teacher of all.'[5]

A major problem for Farr was that in the early part of his career he was a mauler and a clincher, by no means the fighter crowds wanted to watch. As a result, he received no big purses, which made him bitter. Nor, in his early days, did he take the chances offered to him. He was beaten three times by the Bow fighter Eddie Phillips and by the middleweight Jack Casey, the 'Sunderland Assassin'. Part of his chip was that he believed the establishment in the form of the promoters and the BBB of C were cold-shouldering him. When Farr beat the American Tommy Loughran, he thought, with some justification, he should be matched with Jack Petersen for the British title. Some thought that Broadribb had played a major part in Farr's win. It appeared that the referee Jack 'Manchester' Smith was going to raise the American's hand as a points winner, but Broadribb leaped into the ring, called out, 'Tommy you've walked it' and Smith came to his corner. Similarly, when Nel Tarleton, well ahead on points, seemed unable to come out for the fourteenth round against Dave Crowley at Wembley in 1944, Broadribb gained him a few precious seconds' grace by calling to the referee to wipe the water off Crowley.

[5] Ibid., p. 19.

Being an all-Welsh affair, Petersen v Farr would be a big draw in the open air in Wales. Instead, the BBB of C nominated Len Harvey for the fight, and then ranked Jock McAvoy as the number-two contender. Farr sulked, but continued to fight.

On 28 June 1935 he beat Presido Pavesi over ten rounds in the Palais des Sports in Paris. Then he knocked him out in the fourth round of a rematch on 15 November, again in Paris. After Petersen lost to the German Walter Neusel, Farr was matched with Ben Foord for the British Empire heavyweight title, whom he beat on points in a lacklustre contest on 15 May 1937. Farr, who in his fights invariably bet heavily on himself, then knocked out Neusel in four rounds.

At this time the world heavyweight title was in one of its periods of confusion. In 1936 the undoubted number one was the German Max Schmeling: on 19 June that year, unexpectedly, he knocked out Joe Louis in the twelfth round. Under the rules of the game as manoeuvred, this, however, did not make him the automatic number-one contender for a title. Better to have the title held by an American than a European. James J. Braddock was also in the running. He was scheduled to meet Schmeling but Braddock lodged a medical certificate. Now Louis was matched with Braddock. On 22 June 1937 Louis knocked him out in the eighth for the title. To get the fight he had agreed to pay Braddock money if he, Braddock, lost. Various figures have been quoted, including 10 per cent of his ring earnings for the next ten years. Now, however, the way was clear for Louis to meet Schmeling again. The gift of promoting the world title was effectively in the hands of the millionaires who controlled Madison Square Garden, who worked with the former peanut and lemon-drop concessionaire Mike Jacobs.

Jacobs effectively owned Joe Louis, and Farr first saw him coatless in the intense heat of New York: 'His neck-tie, the noisiest ever, was hit off by a giant safety pin, his false teeth rattled. From his bottom lip a stump of a cigarette dangled. His little eyes winked and danced as "giving me the once over" he guessed, "we better get together".' Farr did not see him as a Czar of the ring, but rather as 'a quaint, waddling, generously nosed little man, dressed anyhow.'[6] Jacobs may have had control over New York boxing but there was considerable resentment over the treatment of Schmeling, and doubt over how many states would recognise Louis as world champion. The English press had it as two.

Meanwhile, the London promoters Sidney Hulls and Brigadier Critchley had what could be described as a loose option on Farr to box the German. Hulls, however, did not have Schmeling under contract and there remained various conditions to be sorted out on the Farr option. Hulls had agreed not to disclose the purse he proposed to pay the fighters, but he leaked it to the press and Farr was infuriated to discover he was getting only £7000, one third of the money to be paid to Schmeling.

Now there were all sorts of suggestions flying about, including one that Louis would make a tour of Europe and fight either Farr, or Len Harvey, or even Max Schmeling himself. Then Braddock was suspended indefinitely for refusing to fight Schmeling. It was difficult to see where Farr might fit into the equation in America but, in boxing, where there is the money and the will there is usually a way. Farr

---

[6]   Tommy Farr, *Thus Farr*, pp. 65–6. Born on 17 March 1880, Jacobs later became the sole concessionaire on the Coney Island boats. He was another who made money out of the predilection of the middle classes to go slumming in safety, taking a fleet of wagons to tour Chinatown. (Daniel M. Daniels, *The Mike Jacobs Story*.)

was not highly rated as an opponent for Louis, and the English correspondent for the influential American boxing paper *Ring* commented: 'There are other heavyweights on our shores. There is Len Harvey, Eddie Phillips and two more who are, like Petersen, Welshmen – Jim Wilde and Tommy Farr. As far as these men are concerned you can put them all, I think, amongst the also-rans, a pretty dreary lot . . . Farr is good up to a point, but he needs more experience. He lacks the killer instinct, but with Ted Broadribb training him he is a likely prospect.'[7]

Scales was correct about Broadribb, who was not only a highly talented manager and trainer but also a fearless and enthusiastic litigator. So far as Broadribb was concerned, Hulls' option on Farr was no sort of option at all. More and more states were recognising Louis as the real champion, so there was no question that the winner of a Farr–Schmeling contest would be recognised as the world champion. The prospect of Schmeling fighting Louis in London came to nothing and Schmeling wanted a 30 per cent share of the gate in New York. In part, the German's thinking had been that when, as he confidently expected to do, he beat Farr, he would be in a position to demand a larger slice of the gate. Instead, Broadribb promptly signed up Farr with Jacobs for a reported guaranteed $60,000, plus 25 per cent of the radio and film rights.

Signing up Farr to fight Louis was something of a cloak-and-dagger affair. Jacobs' representative, the lawyer Sol Strauss, was sent to England and persuaded Broadribb to tell him where Farr was. That night, Strauss received a telephone call to say that if Farr signed the contract, Strauss would have

[7] Ted Scales, 'British Boxers as I See Them', *Ring*, January 1936.

his arm broken. Farr was taken to the George V in Paris and sailed back to America with Strauss on the *Berengaria*.[8] Farr's version is that he met Strauss with Broadribb in Eastbourne, where Farr had entered his luxury motor car, his pride and joy, in a *concours d'élégance*. He says that the deal was done away from prying eyes, in the bathroom of the hotel in which he was staying. He was then flown across the Channel to avoid any legal complications, and Strauss kept him in sight, morning, noon and night.

Hulls promptly went to court in England to try to obtain an injunction against Farr. He succeeded in obtaining a temporary injunction, but failed to have it extended. Mr Justice Bennett, vacating the injunction, said that he saw no term in the contract by which Farr had bound himself not to fight in public prior to the proposed Hulls-sponsored fight with Schmeling in September.

Even then it was not, so to speak, plain sailing. The trip was not a success. Farr objected to Broadribb advancing wages to the party, and Broadribb says he censored the papers and letters to protect Farr from reading adverse reports and hate mail. Farr had been receiving letters warning him to beware, as Louis would have tea lead, the foil used inside tea chests, wrapped in his bandages. When Broadribb appeared in photographs and on film, Farr did not like that. Difficulties between the pair escalated.

There is a story that whilst driving with an American friend, Broadribb and Farr began to argue to such a degree that Broadribb switched off the ignition and leapt out, trying to drag Farr with him. The American calmed things down to the extent that manager and boxer did not actually come

8 Harry Markson, 'The Mike Jacobs Story', *Empire News*, 5 June 1949

to blows, but Broadribb left them with the car and thumbed
a lift for the rest of the journey.[9]

Farr surprised everybody, taking Louis to a disputed points
decision. For his pains he received $36,000, less tax, from
the contest. But after paying expenses and giving Broadribb
his 25 per cent, the purse was very substantially reduced. By
the time of their return to England Farr and Broadribb were
not speaking. Broadribb said he did not want anything more
to do with his boxer, something the Welshman took to mean
his contracts – a fresh one had been signed in America to
satisfy the local boxing commission's requirements – were at
an end. Broadribb would swiftly disabuse him of that idea.

On 13 October Farr appeared in Glasgow at the Benny
Lynch v Peter Kane fight. He made a broadcast and had an
article ghosted in his name for a local paper. Six days later
he was presented with a hundred guineas and a silver casket
in recognition of the effort he had shown to maintain the
standard of British boxing in America. Worse, it was
announced that he had made a contract with a man from
the Ring, Blackfriars to appear in an exhibition bout in
Birmingham for, it was said, the highest purse ever paid for
a man to box in that city. Broadribb not only wanted his 25
per cent cut of the hundred guineas, he wanted to put a stop
to Farr's behaviour. On 20 October he obtained leave to take
out an injunction against him. The application for the injunction was heard on 26 October and it was a knock-down
contest all the way. Broadribb relied on the two contracts,
the first dated 18 March 1935 and due to run for three years;
the second had been signed in New York on 26 July 1937
to run for a year: it was claimed the New York State Athletic

[9] Jack Birtley, *Freddie Mills*, pp. 146–7.

Commission would not allow Farr to fight unless there was a year to run on his manager's contract. That itself had led to a major row in which the chairman of the Commission had joined enthusiastically.

Farr claimed that the contract was one for personal services and that, by his conduct in America, Broadribb had repudiated it: he had appointed himself Farr's chief second and then done everything possible to lose Farr the fight, arguing with his trainer and another member of the party, Job Churchill. Farr's affidavit, drafted of course by counsel, claimed: 'When my eyes were cut he [Broadribb] produced a bottle containing a mixture that was unknown to me, and he had no wadding, with the result that when he applied this mixture from the bottle it fell into my eyes and I was unable to see properly for the next two rounds. The mixture itself was not of any use and almost blinded me.' There was a similar complaint about the gumshield, for which there was no spare: 'Further he allowed this mixture to fall on my gumshield and when he placed the gumshield in my mouth it was covered with the mixture and I was unable to use the gumshield for four rounds.'

In a later round Farr took two hard blows to the chin and, when he returned to the corner, Broadribb said, 'You nearly took a dive,' implying that Farr had been thinking of throwing the contest. It was, said the boxer, not a helpful comment. At the end of the fight, with Farr bloodied and cut, Broadribb had ignored him, instead rushing to congratulate Louis and making adverse comments to the press about his own man. It was left to the trainer to get Farr back to the hotel and when Broadribb finally appeared half an hour later he put an alcohol-saturated sponge on his eyes, which made Farr pass out. In view of all this, before they returned to England, Babe Culnan was appointed manager by Broadribb. Broadribb announced he wanted nothing more to do with Farr.

Naturally, Broadribb denied the allegations, but his counsel argued that even if they were true they were irrelevant. 'This is a case of a boxer and a manager,' said his counsel, Andrew Clark, 'not a nursemaid and child.' 'It is something like slavery,' commented Mr Justice Crossman on the terms of the contracts. By the end of the second day, and following ill-tempered exchanges with Broadribb demanding an admission that the contracts were binding, and agreeing that he would then release Farr from them, the judge declined to give him the injunction. Instead, Farr would pay £500 into court and undertake to give Broadribb 25 per cent of any money earned before the trial. Broadribb had claimed Farr owed him at least £2000.

By the time the trial came on in November, heads had been knocked together and, as Andrew Clark on Broadribb's behalf said, 'As a result of the bloodletting and ventilation of grievances the parties were restored to a more amicable frame of mind.' All was sweetness and light. All allegations and counter-allegations were withdrawn. Farr would pay Broadribb £3000 and his costs. Broadribb would hand over the contracts. Each hoped they would again be friends.[10]

Having Broadribb as a manager could be an expensive treat. In 1944 he took over as manager of Jackie Potts, who trained with Freddie Mills and obtained a contest for him against Jackie Wilson on the Mills *v* Shaw bill at the Queensberry All-Services Club. Potts' purse was £43 5s, but out of that came £5 10s for training quarters, £1 for his

[10] *The Times*, 21 and 27 October; 16 and 18 November 1937. Curiously *Boxing*, the trade paper, carried no report of the legal bout.

second, £5 for the trainer, £3 10s for travelling and a further
£2 10s office expenses. There was no fee to Potts for sparring with Mills. Potts received a gross of £25 15s, before
Broadribb took his percentage of £6 8s 9d, which left the
boxer with under 50 per cent of his purse. When, the next
month, Potts wished to change managers, Broadribb threatened him with an injunction.[11]

This, then, was the man who would guide Freddie Mills
for the remainder of his career and whose daughter, Chrissie,
would divorce Don McCorkindale and marry him.

---

[11] Jackie Potts had been boxing since the 1920s and had 104 bouts, including
one against Ernie Roderick, when the latter was the British champion, for purses
which totalled slightly over £800. His last fight was in 1945. I am particularly
grateful to Derek Whitfield for providing me with his papers.

5

Freddie Mills Meets Len Harvey and Some Others

Within a week of the Jack Powell fight, Ted Broadribb was at Netheravon, where Mills was based, asking him if indeed he was still under contract to Bob Turner. He had been impressed with the Powell knockout. So had Broadribb's daughter, Chrissie, regarded as a shrewd judge of boxers. Shortly after Mills' contest with Tom Reddington on 5 August 1941 at Leicester City Football Club's ground – five weeks after first meeting Broadribb – Mills' contract changed hands. Whilst at Uxbridge, Mills had regularly sparred with the heavier and much more experienced Reddington, who had always held the upper hand in the sessions. This time, however, Reddington had been unable to train properly. He had been unwell and now his wife was seriously ill. All he wanted to do was to get home after the bout. The fast improving Mills outpointed him over ten rounds. Reddington had been ahead in the first few rounds, but once Mills had rocked him in the eighth, the lighter man took control. Reddington was out of the ring almost before the verdict was announced.

Mills had, in fact, still got twelve months left on the Turner contract, but the deal was struck: Broadribb would take over and until the end of the year commission would be split between the managers. In addition Turner, who himself was hoping to get into the Royal Air Force, would receive £200. In any event, he was beginning to realise he could not take Mills much further. At the same time, Broadribb signed up the talented lightweight, Mills' friend, Duggie Bygrave.

Mills and Broadribb began inauspiciously. The idea had been to have a return in Leicester with Reddington, but he was unable to obtain leave. So Mills was matched once again with Jack Hyams. On paper the match was meaningless. Mills had shown three months earlier just how superior he was to the once very useful Hyams. It was unlikely that there would now be a different result. However, the contest in Leicester on 1 September, refereed by Teddy Waltham, who would later become the very powerful General Secretary of the British Boxing Board of Control, ended with the disqualification of Mills for a low punch in the third round. The pair never met again for the rubber match.

The disqualification was shrugged off. Now there were plans to match Mills in what would be his second London contest, this time against the black boxer from Deptford, Tommy Martin. The thirty-four-year-old had moved steadily up the weights and was now boxing as a heavyweight. He had only narrowly been defeated by Jack London and Mills feared he was being taken out of his class. All his protests earned were a good talking-to from Broadribb, never a man to listen to the namby-pamby fears of his boxers.

The bout was to be on 29 September, a Monday after-noon, as a supporting contest for the British welterweight title fight featuring Ernie Roderick defending his title against Alf Danahar. Mills was training at the wrestler Bill Klein's gym in London when there came a near catastrophe. Mills ricked his back whilst warming up for his daily workout and it took all Broadribb's skill to get him in a condition to enter the ring. Even then, Broadribb pulled the ropes widely apart so Mills did not have to duck too low. Broadribb's confidence in his new protégé was justified. For once, this was Mills the boxer, picking his punches as the Deptford man wore himself out and was stopped in the fifth round after taking five counts. Broadribb now announced Mills' new schedule: a contest a fortnight.

The first of these came on 3 November, when Mills met the very useful Welsh heavyweight Jim Wilde, knocking him out in three rounds.[1] Broadribb's game plan was clear; he had his eyes not only on Len Harvey, but on the much more lucrative heavyweight division.[2] So, at the end of the month,

[1] In 1986 at the age of seventy-four, former Welsh heavyweight champion Wilde was set to box Colin Davies of Swansea, then sixty-three, who claimed to be, and no doubt was, the over-sixties heavyweight champion of Wales. Perhaps a little over-optimistically, Davies was hoping to raise £30,000 'for a decent retirement'. The BBB of C refused to allow the contest claiming, with some justification, that it was both ridiculous and dangerous. Wilde died in November 1990.

[2] Although some question it – citing irrelevantly that the bare-knuckle champions rarely weighed more than twelve stone – the general opinion is that at the highest level of boxing the smaller man will not often beat the bigger. On the few occasions a top-class heavyweight has been beaten by a jumped-up light-heavy, there is usually an explanation. One of the best of the light-heavyweights of the late 1960s and early 1970s was Bob Foster, who lasted only two rounds against Joe Frazier and eight against Ali. Some years later, referring to the pressure which a heavyweight can exert in the clinches, he would say: 'It takes a lot out of the smaller guy . . . I hit Ali with two rights back to back. If he'd been a light-heavyweight, I'd have knocked him out. I knew I was in trouble when Joe stuck around because he started putting pressure on me.' Even if it does not become immediately apparent, the cumulative effect of facing up to bigger, heavier men can do long-term damage. Foster quote from *The Times*, 1 March 2003.

on 28 November, Mills had the second of his contests with his old friend Tom Reddington. This was also the second within a month of Mills' contests against much heavier men and it foreshadowed Broadribb's subsequent handling of him, continually pitting him against bigger men with harder punches. This time Mills lost on points. Broadribb's immediate target was the huge, if slow, Jack London. At the weigh-in Mills wrote, 'He had a pair of shoulders that seemed to be wedged between the walls of the room and a back that blocked out the light.'[3] On 8 December he outpointed the Blackpool giant over ten rounds at the Royal Albert Hall.

There was then a break from the ring until 26 January 1942, when it was back to the Albert Hall for a third match with Tom Reddington. It had been rumoured that Mills – which meant Broadribb – did not want any more cruiserweight contests. *Boxing News*, for one, could not understand the reasoning at this stage in his career. The writer could not believe that Mills had put on enough weight to cause him difficulties as a cruiserweight, nor that deliberately bulking him up to fight as a heavyweight would do anything for him. Was it the cold snap which had made him decide to put a bit more flesh on his bones? the paper asked. Surely a hardy RAF sergeant would not feel the cold? It was felt that by moving up to heavyweight he was condemning himself to a period of ring wilderness, whereas he could look forward to topping Johnny Muldoon bills at the Albert Hall as a cruiserweight. Anyway who would fight? The American Billy Conn was named more in hope than expectation. Len Harvey might consent with a view to picking up easy money, but objections to that match hadn't changed from the previous

3 *Sunday Graphic*, 30 November 1958.

year. The current form of both Tommy Farr and Eddie Phillips was unknown, and anyway both had been discharged from the army. *Boxing News* thought that was odd. Surely there were light duties for them there? And if they weren't fit for the army, what made them fit for the ring? Additionally, a number of boxers were discharged as mentally unfit in the first years of the war. The stewards could do well to look at such applications for licences.[4]

This time Mills, as most expected, stopped the heavier man in the ninth round. Reddington had been down for a short count in the first and for one of seven in the sixth. In the eight and ninth he took half a dozen counts of eight. A name of interest on the undercard was that of Bruce Woodcock, the young Doncaster heavyweight, who had stopped stoker Fred Clarke in the third round in his first professional bout. Whilst accepting the blood and guts of it, *Boxing News* was not impressed with the Mills contest, nor with the handling of it by referee Eugene Henderson, who had allowed hitting with the inside and butt of the glove by both men. Mills had also got away with rabbit punches to his opponent: 'He [Mills] is careless and ever has been . . . Freddie is such a busy slammer, launches into such cyclonic attacks, fights as though he sees red all the time, notices an object in front of him and just lets go at it from any and every angle.' In his report of the fight, the boxing correspondent Frank Butler said he asked Mills: 'Why not cultivate that left jab? I noticed you picked this up since your fight with London – an effective constructive punch and worth two of your swings.'[5]

[4] See both the editorial and Andrew Newton Jnr, 'The Heavyweight Muddle', *Boxing News*, 15 January 1942.
[5] *Boxing News*, 29 January 1942; *Daily Express*, 17 January 1942.

There was considerably more praise for young Woodcock, who had dealt severely with the much heavier Clarke. It was noted that if he wanted, Woodcock could easily make the cruiserweight division.[6]

Mills fought Jock McAvoy for the second time on Monday 23 February, again at the Albert Hall, before a crowd of 4500. Again there were doubts expressed whether McAvoy would be anywhere near his peak. The betting was 5–2 on Mills. These did not seem realistic odds to Frank Butler, despite his belief that McAvoy 'has just boarded the toboggan that will take him down hill'. In the event the contest ended most unsatisfactorily in the first round. A few flurries of punches were exchanged to no great effect when, after a left hook to his body, McAvoy stepped back and called out, 'My spine, hold it Freddie. I can't go on. I've hurt my back.'

Despite the urgings of Broadribb to finish McAvoy, since the referee had not stopped the contest, Mills, always the sportsman, did hold back whilst his opponent was helped to his corner. McAvoy had displaced a lumbar muscle when he had slipped in one of the few exchanges.

That, at least, is one account of the brief proceedings. Frank Butler was in the dressing room with McAvoy when Dr Phil Kaplin gave the boxer a shot of Novulex between the spine and left kidney. Two men had to hold McAvoy down whilst the injection was given. However, as is often the case with boxing, no two people seem to have seen the same fight, and *Boxing News* had another, rather ambiguous, view: 'Jock McAvoy who has carried on under the most adverse conditions with a broken hand, with a stitched face and even with an outbreak of erysipelas and who had gone through this first round without

6 *Boxing News*, 29 January 1942.

having received a single punch of any solidity had turned to take his seat at the gong – and had all but collapsed with his face contorted in agony. When he recovered McAvoy said that Mills had caught him accidentally with a hard punch on the back which had caused him to slip. "I didn't feel any pain as I rose but ten seconds later it felt as though red-hot needles were shooting from my spine down to my left leg."[7]

Whichever account is correct, for just under three minutes' work in the ring, Mills had earned a purse of £750, the adulation of the men back at Netheravon and the undoubted right to challenge Len Harvey, if the great man wished to accept. It was left to young Woodcock, conceding twenty pounds to Charlie Bundy, to garner the applause. He survived a pile driving right to the body in the first round and a count of eight in the third, before a series of left crosses carried him to a clear and popular points decision.

Back at the camp there were, however, ominous signs that Mills was again unhappy in the RAF. He was now a PT instructor training Fleet Air Arm recruits. His day ran from 7 a.m. until 10 p.m. It left him little time for what he saw as his own boxing training and, sent on a refresher course at Loughborough, he handed in his instructor's badge. This time there was no attempt to talk him out of it and in short order he was sent back to Netheravon and then on to South Witham in Lincolnshire, where he supervised the loading and unloading of bombs between the local railway station and the storage depot. It was monotonous work compared with Netheravon, but it gave him time to do what he wanted. Now he could train in the evening. He hung a punchbag from a beam in the civilians' mess.

---

[7] *Daily Express*, 23 February 1942; *Boxing News*, 26 February 1942.

In the intervening months there had been talk of banning boxing for the duration of the war. Then Home Secretary Herbert Morrison made a statement in the House of Commons, saying that a certain amount of professional sport would help the health and morale of the general public. The problems of an officer meeting a man from the other ranks drifted away, and on 20 June 1942 Mills boxed Len Harvey for the British light-heavyweight title in an open-air match at White Hart Lane, Tottenham.

The Cornishman Harvey was born in 1907. Aged twelve, he won his first professional contest at the now extinct paper-weight over six rounds for a purse of six shillings. He had weighed in at four stone twelve pounds. By 1933 this enor-mously popular and respected man held three Lonsdale Belts and five championship titles. In June that year he beat Eddie Phillips for the light-heavyweight title but, like Gypsy Daniels some years earlier, relinquished it on the grounds that the purse offer for his defence was too low. Nevertheless, the story is that he fought Jack Petersen for the British heavy-weight title for no purse at all. His wife Florence had agreed that if he was given the match he would fight for nothing. He took the contest and defeated Petersen on points. As a still active boxer he was appointed the matchmaker for Wembley Arena. In 1939, with the light-heavyweight scene in disarray and the American authorities refusing to recog-nise either him or Jock McAvoy as chief contenders, the BBB of C had them matched at the White City in a contest for its version of the title. Harvey won over fifteen rounds.

Broadribb wanted to give Mills the opportunity to accli-matise to the outdoor ring at the Tottenham Hotspur FC ground at White Hart Lane, so some of his training sessions were held in an open-air ring with half a dozen sparring partners at the Airman Public House at Feltham. These were open to the public and the admission charge was donated to the RAF Benevolent Fund.

Although Harvey was now twelve years older than Mills, he was the 3–1 on favourite, and the consensus of boxing writers was firmly behind him. The former world flyweight champion Jimmy Wilde wrote in the *News of the World*: 'I am picking Harvey to win for the following reasons. He is a past master in ring craft, possesses an almost impregnable defence and is seen at his best when opposing less-clever opponents.' Some, including Joe Bromley in the *Sporting Life*, were not even sure that Mills would last the full fifteen rounds: 'Mills has no physical weakness to worry him; his chief concern being the question of how to batter down the champion's defence and open him up for some decisive hitting.'[8] Broadribb, however, was optimistic, predicting Mills would win in the early rounds.

The Dagenham Girl Pipers were hired to escort the boxers to the ring before a crowd of 30,000. They can hardly have left the stadium before it was all over. In the second round Mills and Harvey stood toe to toe, not the tactics anticipated by the critics, who had expected Harvey to hand out a boxing lesson. As they pulled out of a clinch, Mills caught Harvey with a left to the jaw which put him down. He was on his feet at a count of eight, but there was no stopping Mills, who landed another ten lefts and rights to the head. Harvey was completely outgunned. A final punch knocked the champion through the ropes and on to the press benches. He was making a valiant effort to climb back into the ring when he was counted out by the referee, Eugene Henderson. The contest had lasted three minutes and fifty-eight seconds.

[8]   Jimmy Wilde, 'Intriguing Fight', *News of the World*, 31 May 1942; Joe Bromley, *Sporting Life*, 2 June 1942.

Harvey commented wryly, 'It's all part and parcel of the game.' Peter Wilson, writing in the *Sunday Pictorial*, thought, 'Mills did everything asked of him – and more. He is a worthy cruiserweight champion.' Jimmy Wilde nobly ate his words: 'That left hook will in the future be associated with Mills' ring career. He is a great-hearted youngster who will maintain his honours with similar dignity to the man he knocked out last night.'[9]

Everything seemed to be roses. In theory at least, Mills held a version of the World Championship. There were celebrations at Broadribb's home and the villagers near the camp fêted him. It does not seem, however, to have been enough and Mills' first serious recorded bout of depression came shortly after. Mills wrote: 'It took about a week for the excitement to wear off, and then in its place came the worst depression I have ever known. Do what I would, it just would not wear off. I suppose it was reaction, but it got to a pitch when it seemed I could stand it no longer.'

He felt he had not had any proper leave for eighteen months and now he was not off duty until the following weekend, which was five days away. So he provided himself with a series of covers. At first the plan was for a sergeant to cover for him from Friday until Sunday. Then that expanded so that he arranged with a string of corporals and sergeants the cover to grant himself a week's leave from that Tuesday until the following Monday morning.

The flaw in the plan was that he did not himself adhere to the arrangements. He simply took off, hitching a lift to London, where he spent his time visiting St Paul's, the Tower of London and Madame Tussauds. He was now AWOL, something which carried a court martial. Apart from seeing the sights, where he stayed and what he actually did never emerged. His detractors, particularly those who believe he had a closet homosexual existence, suggest, with no evidence to back up the proposition, that he lost himself in the wartime milieu. Whatever is the answer, disappear he did.

Mills wrote: 'I have dwelt on this less creditable week in my career longer than probably the reader is really interested, but to me I can assure you it stands out as the time in my life when I have never felt so nearly at the end of my tether, and when today one still from time to time reads of old desertions coming to life, I really think more emphasis should rest upon the cause which prompted that faraway defection.'[10]

This set the tone for recurring bouts of depression, often accompanied by apparently unrehearsed and certainly unconsidered actions. Life inside the ring was one thing. There was a stability and regulation to which he could and would give his all. Outside the ropes it was a different matter. Leaving the boxing booth unannounced is not that serious an offence – it could be put down as part of fairground life – but it displays the lack of commitment Mills could show if he thought things were turning against him. More serious was the desertion from Netheravon and the second one at the end of the war. Nor, seemingly, could he cope with the requirements of the RAF. Depression followed depression.

For the moment, his commanding officer was sympathetic. He had to be. It would be no good for morale if the reigning British light-heavyweight champion were to be court-martialled. His commanding officer suggested Mills apply for another posting. He tried for London, but instead was posted

10 Freddie Mills, *Twenty Years*, p. 94.

to St Athan in South Wales, where he met up again with
Gordon Cook, now working in a civilian post. Most of Mills'
time was spent in exhibitions and some three months later
he was posted to Upavon, where the CO was the cricketer
A. J. Holmes, who persuaded him to take up PT work once
more.

The year 1943 was a quiet one for Mills professionally, as
indeed it was for boxing in general. There were tournaments
in London, Watford, Oxford, Liverpool, Blackpool and south
Wales, but income tax was now 50 per cent, and with restric-
tions on electricity and heating most shows were promoted
for charity and in the open air.

Mills' career was in something of a bind. There was really
no one for him to box in the heavyweight division except
Jack London. Harvey had retired, and even were he to come
out of retirement and defend his heavyweight title, no
promoter was going to pay proper money to stage the match.
As for the cruiserweights, there was no one much there either.
No one could be sure that McAvoy's heart was in training
any more. Mills had comprehensively defeated Jack Hyams,
and his disqualification in the second contest counted for
little. That left the Welsh boxer Glen Moody, who was also
coming to the end of his career. That proposed match was
promptly banned by the Southern Area Council as a 'criminal' contest and the council indicated they would do the
same for another match with Hyams. Moody was not pleased
and offered a £100 sidestake against any cruiserweight.
Woodcock was having only his third or fourth professional
fight and rightly was being kept well away from Mills.

Similarly, there were no foreign boxers to be brought to
the country, and no real indication that top-quality Americans
would be coming over with the troops. So what did that

leave? It left the very real possibility that Mills might join the roughnecks and for a time become an all-in wrestler. There are suggestions that this was made with his tongue firmly wedged in his cheek, but *Boxing News* for one took it seriously and, whilst deploring the possibility, accepted its financial viability: 'A performer with any claim to public notoriety can be assured of an ample income so long as he is sufficiently intelligent to accommodate his fees to the reasonably estimated gate receipts. In fact, an all-in wrestler with a practical certainty of two or more engagements each week will be far better off than a fistic title holder who may have to wait a year or more before some particular area council permits him to engage in any contest which would not be, in the opinion of the majority of the councillors present, "positively criminal".'[11]

In fact, there is no record that Mills ever entered the wrestling ring. He was scheduled to meet an American wrestler in a contest at an airforce base, but he cried off, leaving his masseur Jock Steele to take the contest and to be tied in the ropes. Mills gave him a pound for his trouble.

The only other possibility was a rematch with Al Robinson. In the time-honoured boxing fashion of making a case where none exists, it was pointed out that he had been doing well against Mills in Manchester the previous year, before he was stopped. A match was made for 22 May in Leeds. Unfortunately for Robinson and the spectators, Jack London got there first, giving him a bad beating in Leicester on 29 March. Making the best of all possible results it was now pointed out that Robinson had knocked London down during the contest. It was all hype.

[11] 'Full Circle', *Boxing News*, 1 April 1943. It cannot have been an April Fool's Day joke because the topic was brought up again the next week.

The Mills *v* Robinson contest, such as it was, was fought in the rain and the useful Don McCorkindale carried Mills piggyback into the ring to avoid the wet grass. The Yorkshire boxer lasted less than two rounds, before going down to a Mills' swing. He had been expected to do better and there was now correspondence about why the traditional straight-left puncher – and Robinson was not the only one – who should be able to deal severely with a roundhouser, clearly couldn't. It was decided that they had no experience of them, whereas men brought up on the booths had learned how to deal with all types of fighter.

And that was the end of Mills' boxing that year. He was matched with London on the evening of the August Bank Holiday at the Aston Villa Football Club's ground, but the Blackpool boxer strained a shoulder. Before their first contest he had suffered a similar injury but now, with a title at stake, he was not going to go in the ring less than fully fit. The contest was rescheduled for 23 September, this time at the Queensbury Club in Soho, but again London cried off. There was a great deal of sympathy for Mills and it was suggested that next time there should be a £500 forfeit clause in the contract.

On 16 February 1944, after a nine-month lay-off, Mills boxed Bert Gilroy at the Queensbury Club. Despite his Irish-sounding *nom de ring*, Gilroy was born as Antonio Rea to Italian immigrant parents in Airdrie in 1915. In March 1940, Gilroy had outpointed the English Eastern Area middleweight champion Ginger Sadd at Newcastle. At the time Sadd was still basking in the reflective glory of having inflicted a defeat on Mills, but he received a boxing lesson from Gilroy. This win made the genial, soft-spoken Scots-Italian the leading contender for the British title held by Jock McAvoy. It was a prospect which did not daunt Gilroy, who recalled: 'McAvoy had given ring greats like Len Harvey fits in the ring, but I thought his rush-in style would have been tailor-made for my own boxing style – and I'm really sorry we never met.'[12]

They never met because Gilroy suffered a serious back injury which put him in a military hospital. For a time it was thought he would never box again. Now, in 1944, he was a blown-up middleweight.

For the contest at the Queensbury Club Mills was 20–1 to stop the stone lighter Gilroy inside two rounds. Mills cut Gilroy and then knocked him down in the first round for a count of nine, but his ring rustiness was showing and his timing was wrong. With Gilroy displaying the courage and ability for which he was always known, Mills could not put him away. Eventually Mills wore him down, but not before he had also knocked over the referee C. B. Thomas in the eighth round, who had got in the way of a wild swing when Gilroy was on the ropes. Mills wrote, 'It was Bert who got the bigger share of the applause from the crowd and he deserved it.'[13]

There were suggestions that Mills had been boxing too many exhibition bouts, which had done him no good. To avoid hurting his opponents he had taken to arm swinging. He was in need of battle practice. Nevertheless, two more exhibition bouts followed on 18 and 20 March. Now there was talk of Mills meeting Joe Louis, who was rumoured to be coming to England with the American Services. *Boxing News* was on hand to offer more advice: 'Mills has a long way to travel before he can seriously hope to have a real

---

[12] Quoted in John Donald's obituary of Gilroy.
[13] Freddie Mills, *Twenty Years*, p. 101.

chance of meeting Louis or even making a respectable showing with him. We hope Mills will either perceive or be persuaded to take on and pursue a course, or system of coaching and practice in comprehensive boxing wherein defensive skill and above all ring craft all receive attention.'[14]

Fortunately, the nearest Mills ever came to Louis was refereeing a three-round exhibition at an army base, when Louis boxed fellow American George Nicholson. Afterwards, Mills thought he had the beating of Louis, commenting that, 'Father Time is against him and he's passing his peak as a fighter.' That may have been true, but it did not stop him beating Billy Conn, Tami Mauriello and Jersey Joe Walcott before he retired for the first time in 1948.

By now, Woodcock had accounted for a number of the better heavyweights, including Tom Reddington. He had already knocked out the Glaswegian Ken Shaw in five rounds at de Montfort Hall in Leicester. This was something noted by Mills' critics, including Frank Butler, who suggested that the coloured Canadian heavyweight Gene Fowler or the Irishman Martin Thornton would be better training for him.

Seemingly Broadribb was content with how his protégé was boxing, for there is no record of *Boxing News'* proposed course of coaching for Mills ever being followed. There is an argument that a man can only fight one way and that to try to turn him into another sort of fighter is self-destructive. Clearly in Mills' case Broadribb was of that opinion. In any event, he wanted the money which went with the heavyweights and was seriously talking of a match with Louis or possibly Lesnevich, although the latter was a light-heavy. (How Lesnevich, then serving in the US Coastguards, was

[14] *Boxing News*, 30 March 1944.

likely to be able to travel was another matter.) In the meantime Broadribb arranged for Mills to box a decent American, Tommy Thompson, at a Muldoon promotion at the Albert Hall. The match never came off. Thompson, who fancied his career in the States, was not willing to risk the decision of a sole referee. He wanted a referee and two judges, and unsurprisingly it was not a proposition that appealed to the BBB of C. For Mills there was to be no battle practice from that quarter. It was back to another round of exhibitions.

Nor was there much battle practice when, on 25 May, despite an eighteen-pound weight disadvantage, Mills gained an easy win over Al Delaney at the Albert Hall, knocking him out in the fifth round. The Canadian had undoubted boxing ability, but two weeks earlier had struggled with Ken Shaw and had only managed to obtain a draw. Although he scored early in the contest against Mills, Delaney soon abandoned any boxing pretences and in a slugging match was simply worn down. As the trade paper pointed out, 'Any heavyweight with the exception of Joe Louis and, let us say, Max Baer as he was when in real form, who seeks to make a slugging bee with Sgt Fred Mills will simply ask for trouble.'[15] Whilst it was regarded as better than countless exhibitions, it provided alarming evidence that Mills still had no real defence.

By now, even Broadribb must have realised that Mills should not be allowed in the same ring as Louis in anger, so it was a question of training for Jack London, rescheduled for 8 August at White Hart Lane. Broadribb decided that Mills' training should be at Upavon. Consequently, because no civilians were allowed on the base, he was restricted to

[15] *Boxing News*, 8 June 1944.

sparring with a number of amateurs in the boxing squad, and fighting a continuing series of exhibitions. He was therefore delighted when he received an invitation to spar with Louis, now touring the American bases with Bob Scully and Leo Mattricciani, the heavyweight champion of the US Airforce.

Traditionally, British exhibition bouts have been boxed simply as that – with no referee in the ring and only the timekeeper to stop the bout if things get out of hand. American exhibition bouts are a very different proposition and are fought as a three- or four-round match, in which there is no scoring, but a knockout is perfectly possible. When it came to it Louis was paired with one of his regular sparring partners, and Mills with Scully and Mattricciani. Now the ex-world champion, the legendary Jack Dempsey, was to referee Mills' bouts. Dempsey controlled the Scully workout, but the Mattricciani bout was very much for real, with the American not pulling his punches and Mills obliged to fight back. At the end Mills accepted that he had received an old-fashioned belting, something he would have to learn to accept from American heavyweights, even those not quite in the top class. Afterwards, Dempsey spoke with Mills for half an hour, saying that he thought whilst he had stamina and a punch and so had a fair chance at the world cruiser-weight title he was simply too small for the heavyweights.

A few weeks later there was another invitation from Mattricciani. Billy Conn had been scheduled to box him, but he had pulled out and Mills was suggested as a replacement. This time Mills knew the unwritten rules of the American exhibition bout and, to the huge delight of the spectators, knocked Mattricciani through the ropes.

A week before the contest with London the fight was called

off 'at the wish of the authorities'. With the announcement, Mills went into another bout of 'deep and soul-destroying depression'.[16] He recovered when it was announced the post-ponement would be short. The contest would take place at the King's Hall, Belle Vue, Manchester, on 15 September. Now the RAF had allowed Jack Robinson and Jackie Potts to train with him at Upavon.

There were 7000 at the King's Hall, including Billy Conn, Louis' first post-war challenger, to see what *Boxing News* described as 'by far the best heavyweight battle witnessed in this country for some years . . . hard fought and even threat-ening', before adding that there was little science to it. Tens of thousands listened on their radios.

Months later, the trade paper wrote that only superlatively fit men could have stood up to the heavy pounding that was dealt out so freely.[17] Mills, who was giving away three stone in weight, had started a fairly hot favourite. It was generally thought that London would have to stop Mills if he was to win. Such science as there was came from the balding giant from Blackpool, who used the straight left to good effect. Mills, still hitting with the open glove, took a series of weak-ening punches below the heart. Nevertheless, it was reck-oned by the end of the eleventh round that he might have been ahead by a point or two.

As an evacuee Bill Norman was one of those listening to the commentary. 'Up to the *Nine o'clock News* I thought Freddie Mills might win, but then the commentary was inter-rupted and they gave the result afterwards as Jack London winning on points.'

[16] Jack Birtley, *Freddie Mills*, p. 93.
[17] *Boxing News*, 9 November 1944.

Mills had been drained by the weight of London's body punching and from the twelfth round on he started clinching, something he had never done before. *Boxing News* thought there was little doubt as to the verdict. Frank Butler praised Mills' courage, but once again signalled his doubts: 'Mills lost because he lacked the class and skill of a good champion. He gave three stone away magnificently and took punishment without flinching. I cannot praise him too highly for his courage. But courage without class is not sufficient to win titles and I would like to see him concentrate on the light heavyweight division in future.'[18]

Meanwhile, the trade paper's favourite, Bruce Woodcock, knocked out George Markwick in the third round on the same bill. Now it was announced that Woodcock, who had the young Frank Ronan as his sparring partner and was said to be doing between twenty and thirty miles a day roadwork – something of which the paper wholly approved – was preparing to challenge Mills for his cruiserweight title as a stepping stone to the larger prize of London's heavyweight crown. 'Nel Tarleton, one of the shrewdest judges has tipped the Doncastrian as a certain winner of both titles whenever he goes out for them,' commented *Boxing News*.[19]

[18] *Daily Express*, 16 September 1944.
[19] *Boxing News*, 9 November 1944. (The late report was because the paper was not published from the June of that year.)

6

Freddie Mills Meets Jack Solomons

After the Jack London bout came another period of inactivity and more suggestions that Mills might take up a wrestling career. There was also talk of him being posted abroad. In February 1945, having been out of the ring for nearly six months with no signs of a return with London, he was matched with Ken Shaw. Apart from the weight disadvantage – Mills weighed twelve stone eight pounds and Shaw fourteen stone eleven and a half pounds – this should have been an easy contest. The former Scottish amateur heavyweight champion Shaw, although a big man, was not highly rated and the relatively inexperienced Woodcock had already knocked him out. Mills, with caution thrown to the winds as usual, and well ahead on points, rushed in during the fourth round and was promptly dropped for a count of eight. In the sixth Shaw was himself dropped and in the seventh his mouth puffed dangerously. Mills, ever the sportsman, seeing that Shaw's top lip was completely split, stopped boxing and called to the referee, who in turn stopped the fight.

Again there were worries about Mills' style: 'One fears that the cruiserweight champion's concentration on attack especially with his semi-circular style of delivery may expose him to very severe punishment and possible disaster when he has to meet straight and more accurate marksmen.'[1] No one could say that Mills and Broadribb were not being regularly warned.

Within a matter of days of the contest, Mills received his orders to go to Morecambe for posting. He was confident this would be to Europe, but when he saw the equipment being handed out, he realised he was on his way to the Middle or Far East. He and his fellow troops left on the *Mauretania*, still unsure of their final destination. Only when the ship sailed through the Suez canal did they realise that it would be India. He was first stationed near Poona, where he was introduced to Chinese food, and he was then posted to New Delhi and attached to the army. Mills immediately lost a stone with dysentery.

In New Delhi, Mills was seconded to the fancily named Inter-Services Sports and Entertainment Control Committee. In the camp were Denis Compton and the Chelsea footballer Tommy Walker. The idea was that they would put together a football team each, and one would tour India and the other the Far East. In the half-time intervals Mills would box an exhibition with Al Robinson.

First, Mills was sent with Compton and Walker on a personality tour in Bangalore visiting the hospitals. Then he

---

[1] *Boxing News*, 14 February 1945.

and Robinson were attached to Compton's squad in eastern India and Burma. Quizzes and chat sessions followed the exhibitions, with a line of questioning coming regularly from the troops about the prospects of Bruce Woodcock.

After VJ Day, celebrated by Mills in Calcutta, he boxed the American Jimmy Rouse in another exhibition. It was then on to Rangoon, where he contracted dengue fever. Whilst he was away he was promoted to Flight Sergeant. Back in Bombay he was co-opted into an ENSA show by Bobby Hines and Harry Goss, where he answered questions and did a little shadow boxing. Then, in 1946, he came back to England, on the same boat as Al Robinson and the lightweight, Tommy Shaw.

Whilst Mills had been abroad, things had changed in the pecking order of British boxing. There was a new major promoter on the scene. His name was Jack Solomons and he would play a significant part in the second half of Mills' career and the whole of Randolph Turpin's.

Israel Jacob Solomons was born on 10 December 1900 in a basement below a fish and chip shop at the corner of Frying Pan Alley in the East End. He had five fingers and a thumb on each hand and already had two teeth. The fourth of a family of seven children of Polish parents, he was the first born in England. He was educated at Old Castle Street School, but aged eight he was already working in the market with his parents. At fourteen he went to Holland and was one of the first to import live fish back to England. When he was ten his sister married Joe Brooks, known as 'Bravado' – not because of his courage but after the famous racehorse. A more than fair boxer, Brooks fought Ted 'Kid' Lewis twice and Seaman Hayes well over a dozen times.

During the First World War there was no money in the fish business so Solomons took a job as night porter in the Bonnington Hotel in Southampton Row. Then it was on to the Imperial Hotel, and later to Bexhill. As a porter, he was in a position to run a book for the clientele. After eighteen months he pined for London and frequented the Ideal Billiard Room in Osborn Street, where he met his future wife Fanny Golding.

A friend of Solomons, Harry Grossman, had asked the promoters at the Ring to have him on the card, but when he was offered a six-rounder one Saturday he did not fancy it, and Solomons took his place. Fighting as Grossman he secured a two-round win over Ted Green. Grossman received another engagement the following month and Solomons turned out again, this time beating Harry Berry in four rounds.

However, his fiancée's family were a cut above boxing and, under pressure from Fanny, Solomons promised to give up his fledgling career. Nevertheless, six months later his brother-in-law Joe Brooks, now in the Royal Army Medical Corps, was to box at a drill hall in Southampton. The promoters were looking for an opponent and Solomons, boxing as Kid Mears to confuse his fiancée, lost to him in five rounds. Fanny Golding found out and was not amused. It was Solomons' last fight. He spent his purse on a reconciliatory present for her and went back to the fish business. Solomons maintained that he was the first person to import carp into Britain. He made a penny a pound profit and imported 16,000 pounds of the fish.

Solomons' first boxing promotion was in 1931. He had been approached by the manager Joe Morris to see whether he would be interested in joining a four-handed syndicate to buy the lease of an old church in Devonshire Street, Hackney, and convert it into a sports arena, which would have boxing on Friday nights and Saturday afternoons, and dancing and cabaret on other days. Whilst the workmen were in, there came the opportunity to promote a British bantamweight contest: Johnny King v Dick Corbett in the open air at Clapton Stadium. Solomons did not see how he could lose, but only the cheap seats sold, and during the show the spectators moved down to occupy ringside. His first promotion cost him a massive £275.

Six months later he opened the Devonshire Sporting Club, a venue which held 1500. But no one came, preferring instead the Ring and the Whitechapel Pavilion. He was also in competition with a whole host of small clubs and promotions, including those at the Stadium Club, Holborn, Mile End Pavilion, Canning Town, Stepney, Hammersmith, Kilburn and Nine Elms.[2] Solomons started Sunday morning shows, the other end of the spectrum to the dinner shows with which he ended his life as a promoter. Now East Enders could sit at tables around the ring and breakfast on kippers. For the first show, with Archie Sexton topping the bill, there was a good house. For a time afterwards the punters turned up, but the novelty wore off.

So Solomons reverted to afternoon shows and by consistently promoting good contests he began to draw the punters and sell out the house. He was the first of the promoters who paid the boxers' claims for a minimum of one pound for six rounds. The quality of his promotions improved and Jack 'Kid' Berg boxed for a share of the gate against Harry Davis. Later, on the advice of referee Jack Hart, he promoted

[2] Charles Hull, 'Devonshire Club Reminiscences', *Weekly Sporting Review*, Xmas and New Year 1948–9.

Eric Boon. Boon cycled down from Chatteris in Cambridgeshire for the contest and became Solomons' first protégé.[3]

At the time, boxers in the preliminary contests, which could last up to ten rounds, were obliged to pay what was known as seconds' money, which the boxers called blood money. Out of the few shillings they earned they were pressed into giving the house seconds a cut. It was a form of black-mail. 'Don't forget the seconds' was more of a threat than a suggestion. If they did not pay up they were unlikely to get further work. Solomons, 'sportsman that he is', announced that the practice would be discontinued at his Devonshire Club.[4]

Meanwhile, he had joined Sydney Hulls and was promoting with him at the Harringay Arena. In February 1939 Boon boxed Alf Danahar for the British title at the venue, winning in the fourteenth round, having taken a bad beating during the early and middle rounds of the contest. But even then the promoters did not mind the conditions in which their boys boxed, and medical controls seem to have been observed in their breach. Earlier, on 10 December 1937, Boon damaged his hand knocking out Con Flynn in the third round. He was due to fight Llew Thomas at Bury St Edmunds three days later and using only his left he won the contest, again in three rounds.

Relations between Hulls and Solomons in one corner, and the Board in the other, had been tetchy for some time. Solomons had been written to, as had the seconds Nat Seller

---

[3] Boon had been boxing at the age of fifteen, a year before he was supposedly eligible to apply for a licence. He won a Lonsdale Belt three times before his twentieth birthday.

[4] East London *Advertiser*, 6 May 1937.

and Arthur Goodwin, about his unruly conduct in the corner at the Boon v Danahar match on 23 February 1939.[5] Then, in a fight promoted by Hulls, Boon won the Lonsdale Belt outright. Unfortunately there was no belt to present and Solomons went back to the ringside to protest, asking, 'Where's Boon's belt?' The cry was taken up by the crowd and Solomons was called before the Board to explain his conduct.

Separately, Hulls was also called, allegedly for refusing to allow a Board's inspector to act at the Stadium Club on 20 November 1939. He said this was only a joke. Solomons weighed in from the Southern Area Council, saying the council wanted to hear the complaint. This would undoubtedly have meant its dismissal, but the Board was not interested.

At the meeting with the Board in December 1939, Hulls resigned. In what was clearly a stage-managed affair, he asked if the press could be present. When he was told they could not, he handed in his licence. Later in the meeting Solomons, called to explain his conduct, also asked if, given the popular interest in the affair, the press could be present. When he was also refused, he handed in his licence.

For the next few months of the war Solomons ran unlicensed shows at the Devonshire Club. There was little other boxing and men were pleased to get work. Hulls began to promote similar events at the Stadium Club, Holborn. Now the Board was beginning to flex its muscles. Boxers were risking the wrath of the Board by appearing for Solomons and Hulls. Matters came to a head when Hulls contracted Boon, managed by Solomons, to box Kid Berg, this time at

[5] BBB of C Minutes of meeting held on 15 March 1939.

the Empress Hall. Bookings had reached £2300, when Boon telephoned to say he would not box. The Board had shown its claws and indicated to the champion that if he went through with the fight they would consider taking away his title. Worse, from Solomons' point of view, there were rumours that Boon was in need of protection from his manager.[6] Hulls promoted the rematched Berg with Eddie Ryan with great success.

By now the Board had stripped a number of boxers and trainers of their licences, and fined others for appearing on unlicensed shows. It was not something which appealed to boxing writers. Jack Hyams had been due to box an exhibition at a charity show at Watford against Eddie Phillips but the Board had stepped in. The *Daily Express*, whilst recognising that the Board had to fight the rebels, was annoyed that charity had lost out.[7] One by one the rebels were fined or suspended for short periods and reinstated. Then there was news that Sydney Hulls would be allowed to reapply for a licence. Would he stand firm with Solomons? No, he would not. He returned to the fold, leaving Solomons, Mike Milligan and referee Jack Hart as the only real remaining rebels.

By May 1940 Solomons had relinquished control of the Devonshire Club. The year before he had been fined £50 with 25 guineas costs for promoting public boxing there without a licence from the local council.[8] Now he was still in the wilderness, but he and Boon patched up their quarrel and Solomons continued as an unofficial manager for him, Harry 'Kid' Silver and Eddie Ryan. The club's building was destroyed in the Blitz.

---

[6] For Solomons' account of the affair see *Jack Solomons Tells All*.
[7] *Daily Express*, 22 March 1940.
[8] *The Times*, 18 April 1939.

Then, on 26 September 1942, the Board indicated that they would interview Solomons in the New Year if he cared to reapply for a manager's licence. It was on his reinstatement that he met the man who would later become his matchmaker – Sam Burns, whose father, Syd, had once boxed and who had himself managed Alf Danahar. At first it was Solomons who made the matches at the Albert Hall for John Muldoon. But when Muldoon retired from promoting, after the Board banned the Mills *v* Glen Moody contest, Jack Cappell took over and Solomons became his matchmaker at the Albert Hall.

Mills also found that his return match for London's heavyweight title was gone. As matchmaker, Solomons had planned a double bill at White Hart Lane: Jack London *v* Freddie Mills for the British heavyweight title, and Ronnie James *v* Eric Boon for the former's lightweight. Then, when the bombing started, his plans went awry. With Mills posted abroad, the top of the bill became Woodcock *v* London. Initially this was to be promoted by Jack Cappell, but when he withdrew Solomons did it himself. (Cappell pulled out because of his apparent reluctance to raise the £20,000 deposit required by Customs & Excise as a down payment against tax for the Woodcock fight.)

The rent of the Spurs ground was £450. London was paid £4000; Woodcock, who fought for Solomons without a written contract throughout almost all his career, was paid £1600. Eric Boon received £200 and substitute Henry Hull, who stopped him with such a body punch that Boon was unable to come out for the fifth, drew £65.

On 17 July 1945 Bruce Woodcock demonstrated the difference between class and mere ability by defeating London in six rounds. *Boxing News* had not been sure that he would manage it, but he did so with some ease. He won the first four rounds, was cut in the fifth and knocked London down in the sixth with a right to the chin. When he rose, Woodcock knocked him out with two more straight rights. Now London wanted a rematch. He never received one – in those days there was certainly no peace for the wicked, let alone defeated heavyweight champions. On 1 August London was outpointed by Jock Porter over ten rounds at the St Mirren FC ground before a crowd of 12,000. London promptly announced his retirement.

Solomons made a profit of £400 from the London fight and the promotion set him on his way to becoming Britain's Mr Boxing.

After the match with London, he promoted one extremely curious bout which matched Woodcock against Martin Thornton of County Galway. The contest was scheduled for ten rounds at the Theatre Royal, Dublin on 24 August 1945. Thornton had a good, if patchy, record: he had a knockout punch and had knocked out or stopped twenty of his opponents. But there were also a number of losses, mostly in England. In Ireland he had given any local who stepped in the ring with him a good beating. In 1944 Thornton had been ranked ninth in the world, but because of the war the rankings were perhaps not as well researched as might have been. Woodcock had already comprehensively beaten Thornton, who was supposedly then at his peak, in two rounds on 19 November 1943. No one, except the Irish, thought that two years later, with Woodcock very much on the up, the result would be any different. However, the Irish press, fuelled by Thornton, carried reports that, once their man had disposed of Woodcock, there was no reason why he should not do the same to Joe Louis.

The fight was a fiasco. Thornton, who normally began full

of fire, did not want to know, and spent the first two rounds trying to avoid punishment. In the third round, when he was bleeding from a cut eye, he put his tongue out at Woodcock and then asked the referee to stop the fight. Andy Smythe refused and Thornton's seconds promptly threw in the towel. The Eire Boxing Board of Control immediately suspended Thornton *sine die*. From then on he gave out a variety of versions of the story to any pressman willing to listen and foolish enough to put up money for the privilege. Initially he said he had been paid his £800 purse in advance, which he had then bet on Woodcock. Over the weeks, months and years the story changed and by February 1981 he was telling the newspapers that he had been paid £4000 to take a dive. He had been offered £2000 to take his chance and £4000 to throw the fight. Solomons had, he said, paid the money to him in the Ormond Hotel. He had invested £3000 of his ill-gotten gains and had picked up £8000 all told. As for the cut eye, he thought his corner might have nicked it.[9]

Solomons admitted that he had succumbed to the blackmail or the charm of Thornton, who apparently had 'the Gaelic gift for story-telling' and had paid him his share of the purse in advance. There is little doubt that the money had indeed gone straight to the bookmakers in the form of a bet on Woodcock, probably to win in three rounds.

Now Solomons was promoting at the Empress Hall at three-weekly intervals throughout the year. There were snack bars, and plans for a four-sided clock to enable the punters to see the seconds ticking down. Initially there was talk of a twelve-round non-title fight for Mills against Woodcock, to be staged, for tax reasons, in Dublin. Immediately, Ted

---

[9] Cormac MacConnell, 'I Threw the Big Fight for £4000', *Sunday Press*, 1 February 1981.

Broadribb received requests for over 250 tickets. But the idea
was heavily criticised and came to nothing.

Meanwhile, Mills was travelling back from India, happily
sparring with Al Robinson and the lightweight Tommy Shaw
en route. There were three days of bad weather before they
reached Liverpool, where there was a smallpox scare on other
boats and everyone had to be inoculated. The discharge camp
was at Heaton near Manchester, a short train- and lorry-ride
away from the docks. After three days at the camp in the
rain Mills had had enough. The men were allowed into
Manchester and then he made another of his spontaneous
decisions without thought for the consequences. He simply
took a train to London to see Broadribb.

Unsurprisingly, his manager was not pleased and Mills
was quickly back on the train north. When he arrived back,
he found that he need not have bothered with another
temporary desertion. Everyone had been given a week's leave
and of course his absence had been noticed. Again he was
fortunate. The commanding officer was not about to deal
harshly with one of Britain's sporting heroes, and instead
squared up to him and shadow boxed. 'After telling him
about my worries', Mills was duly sent on the week's leave.[10]

---

[10] Mills was much more fortunate in his military career than Private Louis Phal,
better known as Battling Siki, who later defeated Georges Carpentier for the
World light-heavyweight championship. Awarded the Croix de Guerre, he was
promoted to corporal and given leave, after he single-handedly captured nine
Germans and solved the problem of taking them back to camp by putting them
in a cellar and throwing in two hand grenades. He then failed to return to duty,
preferring wine and women. He was reduced to the rank of private and dishon-
ourably discharged in 1919. As for the fight itself, Siki had agreed to lose but
when Carpentier, who may not have known of the arrangement, hit him too
hard, he battered the unfortunate Frenchman to defeat. He lasted as world champion for a year and then, always prey to drink and women, went completely
wild. He was found shot in the back on a New York street.

One of these worries had been how he was going to survive on his £60 army gratuity and possibly some post-war credits. It is difficult to know where his money had gone. He had earned substantial sums from the McAvoy and Harvey fights and had been a serving airman during the war with his bed and board paid. Even allowing for tax and Broadribb's commission, he was by no means destitute. It seems to have been another manifestation of his inability to cope.

In fact, Mills need not have troubled himself over his potential earnings. Broadribb and Solomons already had plans for him to meet Gus Lesnevich. Broadribb had pencilled in a tour of America, culminating with the match against Lesnevich, but Solomons wanted the contest immediately in England. Mills would be receiving good money, even after expenses and tax at 48 per cent had reduced his take-home to around a shilling in the pound.

7

Freddie Mills Meets Gus Lesnevich and Bruce Woodcock

Mills' first contest after his demob was scheduled to be his non-title match over twelve rounds with Bruce Woodcock on 4 June. It was to top the bill of what would be the first of the Solomons' 'Eve of Derby' shows, which marked the informal end of the boxing season. If Mills won, as Broadribb anticipated, he would not be committed to any title defences by the Board and he could go to America with the kudos of a good win under his belt. Then, suddenly, Woodcock's manager Tom Hurst agreed terms for his man to go to America to meet Tami Mauriello at Madison Square Garden on 13 May. Technically, he was within his rights. The contract for the Mills fight said neither man was to box within twenty-one days of their contest. Nevertheless it was a considerable risk by Hurst. If Woodcock was injured, then the Mills fight would go out of the window. Broadribb retaliated and, with Solomons as the promoter, terms were agreed with Gus Lesnevich for the World light-heavyweight title on 14 May. Strictly speaking, this would be within the time limit, but Hurst was really in no position to argue. The BBB of C did not seem to mind either.

After Mills had knocked out Len Harvey, there had been claims that Freddie was now the light-heavyweight champion of the world. The argument went that John Henry Lewis had been deprived of his title by the New York Athletic Commission after he failed to defend it against Tiger Jack Fox. But this decision was not generally accepted, and there were suggestions that Lewis should box Len Harvey. These came to nothing when Lewis finally retired through eye trouble. The British Boxing Board of Control then named Harvey and Jock McAvoy to meet for their version of the title. Harvey beat McAvoy, and then Mills beat Harvey. *Quod erat demonstrandum*.

The American version of who held the title was rather more convincing. After their decision that stripped Lewis of his title, the New York Athletic Commission nominated Tiger Fox to meet Al Gainer. Fox won, but was then stopped by Melio Bettina in a second contest. In turn Bettina was beaten in nine rounds in 1939 by Billy Conn, who defended the title against Lesnevich before he stepped up to the heavyweight division, leaving the title vacant. The National Boxing Association then set up an elimination tournament. The winner, Anton Christoforides, was matched with Lesnevich, who in turn won on points. Lesnevich went on to defend the title twice against Tami Mauriello who then moved up to heavyweight.

So far, the classy Polish-American Lesnevich, whose

mother ran a restaurant in Cliffside, New Jersey, had had a
steady, if not spectacular, career, missing out on the really
big pay days. Described as a warrior more than a blaster, in
1933 he won the New York middleweight Golden Gloves
title. He turned professional the next year, winning twelve
and drawing one contest. In 1935 he won eight and drew
one. Now he was moving up in class and in 1936 he was
knocked out by Freddie Steele in Los Angeles. This was by
no means a disgrace, for Steele was recognised as the world
middleweight champion. Lesnevich was stopped in 1937 with
a cut eye inflicted by Young Corbett III. He then went undefeated until two fights with Conn. The first, on 17 November
1939, was over fifteen rounds at Madison Square Garden.
His contract had ensured that he was kept out of the ring
for five months prior to the contest but it made no difference because he was again defeated by Conn on 15 June
1940.

Lesnevich comfortably defeated Christoforides on 22 May
1941, but retained his World title in a disputed decision with
Mauriello, winning a return much more convincingly on 26
August 1941. In January 1942 he then lost a ten-round decision to the heavyweight, Bob Pastor. An article concluded,
'He is 31 next month and will not have much longer in which
to make a pile sufficient to retire on.'[1] Lesnevich's first post-
war fight was in Portland, where he knocked out the up-
and-coming Joe Kahut in the first round. The betting had
been on Kahut.

Mills weighed thirteen stone and had been back in England
for less than two months when he began training for the
contest. He was still unacclimatised following his posting

[1]   Blue-Bird's Eye, 'Gus Lesnevich World "Cruiser Ace"', *Boxing News*, 11 April
1942.

abroad and the debilitating dengue fever lingered. Exhibitions apart, he had only boxed six competitive rounds in fifteen months. It did not matter. Solomons wanted the match. The British public, deprived of international boxing for so long, wanted the match. The match there would be.

The heavyweight Nosher Powell recalls: 'Freddie came on the scene when there was nothing. Suddenly on the scene comes this young man – heart of a lion. He looked like a lion, had a punch if he had nothing else and a cast iron chin. He was what the people of the fight game were looking for. We'd been knocked around enough in the war and suddenly we'd got a Montgomery come up and this was Freddie.'[2]

It is easy to see why Broadribb wanted the second match. There was serious money to be made. Whether he had his charge's other interests at heart is more open to question. It was a pattern that would be repeated over the next four years. Nat Seller was asked to train Mills at Jack Solomons' newly opened gym in Windmill Street. Seller had been Dave McCleave's manager when he had outpointed Mills in 1938. He had fallen foul of the Board's purge following the Solomons fiasco, but had been given his licence back in 1942. Highly regarded, he was acknowledged as the man to get Mills back into shape. During training Mills, along with his friend Duggie Bygrave, lodged in Grosvenor Terrace, Camberwell Gate, with Broadribb's daughter, Chrissie, who was still married to Don McCorkindale. It was the start of what some saw as a grand romance.

Mills held a training session in public, something *Boxing News* thought was unnecessary and, as was the fashion, he also boxed a number of exhibitions. Things were going well

[2] Conversation with author.

when came the sad news that his father had died.
Understandably Mills wanted a postponement, but his
mother was adamant: 'No, our Fred, your dad would have
liked you to carry on.' Mills, of course, went down to
Bournemouth for the funeral and stayed a day more.[3]

Importantly, he, or Broadribb on his behalf, had elected
to take a percentage of the gate and it was with great interest
that he learned that the top-priced tickets were twenty
guineas and the capacity of the arena was 15,000.

Lesnevich trained at Brighton, in a gym over the Pelham
Arms in Russell Street, running on the stony beach. The
amateur heavyweight Dennis Slade, who later sparred with
Joe Baksi when he was training for his contest with Bruce
Woodcock, recalls watching Lesnevich: 'I saw him knock
down one after another of his partners. When he ran out of
them he'd just shadow box the rest of the round. He was
offering good money and he couldn't get anyone. I kept my
kit under my seat.'[4] Frank Butler, tipping Lesnevich in the
Daily Express, thought that the American would begin by
outscoring Mills but, noting the scar tissue around his eyes,
he was not sure how long he would last.[5]

Solomons insisted that Lesnevich travel from Brighton by
train rather than by car. The newspapers thought this odd,
since he had risked rather more by flying from New York.
Mills entered the ring not with the usual fanfare, but preceded
by a Flight Sergeant carrying the Union Jack. 'There'll always
be an England' played over the tannoy. In turn, Lesnevich
had the American flag carried before him and 'Stars and
Stripes For Ever' was played. The former Scottish welter-

[3]   Freddie Mills, *Twenty Years*, p. 132.
[4]   Conversation with author.
[5]   Frank Butler, 'Gus Will Settle Title Dispute', *Daily Express*, 14 May 1946.

weight Eugene Henderson, who had been the third man in a number of Mills' previous bouts, was the referee.

The second round was nearly the last. Mills was immediately hit on the jaw with a right and then a left. From then on he took a dreadful hammering and was knocked down for four counts – six, six, eight and nine. Butler wrote: 'When this [the third] round began there were many who anticipated it would be the end of the contest. But they had counted without knowledge of Freddie's remarkable capacity for taking and absorbing punishment. Mills came out of his corner in such a sprightly manner that one could hardly believe it was the same man who only a minute before scarcely knew the way to it.'[6]

It is an example of Mills' bravery that somehow he weathered the punishment. Eventually, as Butler had earlier predicted, Lesnevich's left eye began to go. By the tenth round Mills was on top. Broadribb thought he was ahead on points and now merely had to stay there. Instead Mills thought he saw an opening and went for it. Lesnevich hit him with a straight left and the tiring Mills went down. He was then knocked down again with another right to the jaw, and then a third time. With only four seconds of the round to go Henderson stopped the contest with Mills' head under the bottom rope. Later Solomons wrote, 'This was the most savage fight I have ever seen. In fact, sometimes I am doubtful about being remembered as the man who promoted it.'[7] Broadribb believed that Mills lost because he had got into a routine when fighting exhibitions against Al Robinson. In those he would demonstrate an overhand-right-left-hook combination. This was fine against someone of Robinson's calibre, but not inventive enough to rattle Lesnevich.

[6] Ibid., 15 May 1946.
[7] Jack Solomons, *Jack Solomons Tells All*, p. 82.

After the fight, Eugene Henderson came under fire for stopping the contest with so little time to go. The argument advanced by Frank Butler was that Mills would have been saved by the bell and that the badly cut Lesnevich might not have come out for the next round. Therefore Henderson had deprived Mills of the World title. It was all part of the ongoing controversy over what was seen as the interference of referees. Henderson handed in his licence and for some years never attended another boxing tournament. It was suggested that he too had been sickened by the beating Mills had taken. The truth was rather different. The month before the contest *Boxing News* had published an editorial:

We are becoming a bit perturbed at recent action taken by the third man in the ring. Several contests of late have been stopped by the referee when the count has reached three or four with a man on the canvas.

We should have thought that at least the referee might have waited until the full count before declaring the fight off. In many cases we are sure the fallen boxer would not have beaten the count.

Their argument was that a clean knockout looked better on the ring record of the winner. Why is this action being taken? Is it because the referee of today becomes over eager in his work or is it because he thinks those vital seconds are in the interest of the fallen man to aid his quicker recovery from punishment after the fight?

From the results we have seen we cannot concur with the latter idea as in many cases the men are not apparently hurt to the extent of being incapable of rising and aid is not necessary to resuscitate them.

When a man has been hit so hard that fears of serious injury are entertained we say by all means get quick aid into the ring but in cases where quick action is not necessary we feel that the referee's action is an injustice to the winner and a travesty of the sport.

Boxing has never been for the squeamish. In the same issue there was a short report: 'It is regrettable to note that Bert Veale, the Worcester welter, who collapsed on the way to the dressing room after his contest with Herbie Smith, died the next day at Gloucester Infirmary.'[8]

After the Mills–Lesnevich fight, *Boxing News* repeated its editorial, adding:

It will long be debated whether in this case the bell could have saved Mills and, in view of his previous recovery in the fight he could have recovered again and finished the 15 rounds. Also whether if Mills had been given the opportunity and had recovered whether Lesnevich would have been able to go through to the end in view of the state of his left eye and broken nose. These are problems none can answer. The fight is over and Lesnevich is the winner.[9]

Henderson's stoppage, which might have prevented the glory of a world title coming to England, did not please some members of the Boxing Board of Control, and he was summoned to explain his conduct under Regulation 17.1, which then dealt with misconduct and incompetence. The

[8] *Boxing News*, 17 April 1946.
[9] Ibid., 22 May 1946.

general opinion ranged against him was that Mills had been
in worse trouble in the second round and Henderson hadn't
stopped the bout then. There had only been four seconds
to go of the tenth. Should he not have had a mental clock
in his head and known that by rising Mills would save
himself? Henderson came down to London and recalled
the general atmosphere of friendliness, until he was asked
to admit he had made a mistake in stopping the contest
when Mills was on the canvas. He refused to do so, saying
that he had stopped the fight when Mills was trying to
rise.

It was then he advanced his theory of post-traumatic
automatism (PTA). When Henderson had fought for the
Scottish welterweight championship, in the twelfth round he
had received a blow, after which everything had been a
complete blank to him. Later he would say that he remembered coming up for the eleventh round, and then taking a
shower. Twice in the following fortnight he had collapsed.
He believed that he had suffered from PTA. His lower brain
had taken over from his higher brain, which was temporarily
paralysed, at which point 'man's baser instincts come into
operation'.

Henderson later wrote: 'He moves automatically, not
conscious of his rising from the floor or of his continuation
of the contest, and it is while he is in that state that he can
suffer irreparable damage. He keeps coming to his feet, and
a further blow may possibly damage the lower brain centre.
A cerebral haemorrhage may result – or the aftermath may
be a pitiful specimen who may never again be able to speak
coherently or walk or move with his usual grace.' If the man
was a boxer then he would go on fighting by instinct. He
might win the contest but he would take tremendous punish-

ment in doing so. He believed that Mills jumping to his feet four times in the second round showed he was approaching that state. A good referee, thought Henderson, would stop the contest long before then. Why, then, did he not do so? he asked rhetorically: 'The reason was because Mills was physically fresh, and with the wonderful resources of Nature, no one can tell how long that condition of unconsciousness may continue. Freddie had trained long and hard for the contest, and his body was quite able to absorb extreme punishment. As his physical condition was perfect, I felt I had to give him the chance. And how magnificently he accepted.'

Henderson's argument did not go down at all well with the stewards. Henderson had taken with him the findings of an eminent brain surgeon which supported his theory but, he says, the stewards refused to allow him to produce it. It was then he advanced another unpalatable argument, suggesting that if the stewards were unwilling to permit a referee to stop a contest as he had done, then the rules should be changed to allow him to do so.

Henderson returned to Edinburgh believing he would get a formal rebuke. He received something far stronger. It was a letter from C. F. Donmall, the general secretary, saying that the stewards had unanimously decided that before he was allowed to handle championship contests in the country he must demonstrate that he had benefited from his discussion with them.

Henderson promptly resigned. He had been a referee for sixteen years.[10]

Broadribb supported the referee: 'To this day I will say as

---

[10] Eugene Henderson, *Box On*, Ch. 1.

I did five minutes after the fight that had I been in Henderson's shoes I would have stopped the fight if Mills had beaten the count.' Mills had taken a dreadful beating, much of it to the body, and on the way home with Broadribb he began to vomit. It seems that people had given him tea, minerals and even champagne. By the end of the journey he was vomiting bile and Broadribb was seriously worried. But there was no question of a visit to hospital: 'Perhaps, however, it was just as well, for there is no more efficient safety-valve for concussion, and I am sure that for several days afterwards Freddy was severely concussed.'[11]

Mills himself wrote: 'Certainly for a week afterwards I found my speech blurred at odd times and every morning I used to have to be wakened up from a sleep which was more like a deep coma than anything else.'[12] Over the years Mills would be asked by many how he had managed to carry on. On one occasion he told journalist Peter Wilson, 'Well, it's automatic really. You don't know much after knockdowns like those first two.'[13]

Just how much training and rest should a boxer have between major contests? Giving evidence in the pre-war Farr injunction case, the Board's general secretary Charles Donmall told the court that a boxer needed four weeks training and three weeks rest between fights.[14] Not so for Mills, nor Woodcock for that matter. Certainly not when Solomons had a top of the bill to fill.

Meanwhile, the British heavyweight champion Bruce Woodcock had gone to New York to box the highly rated

[11] Ted Broadribb, *Fighting is My Life*, pp. 110–11.
[12] Freddie Mills, *Twenty Years*, p. 135.
[13] Peter Wilson, *More Ringside Seats*, p. 89.
[14] The Liverpool *Echo*, 13 July 1937.

Tami Mauriello. Woodcock who, unlike Mills, had been a good amateur, still retained the habits he had picked up before he had turned professional. Although he had knocked out his first nineteen opponents, his was a good, but not devastating punch and he tended to stand back when he had hurt his man. Worse, he was not a big heavyweight, going in the ring at around thirteen stone seven, and even worse, he had a tendency to cut. He was, none the less, thought to be a better prospect than Mills.[15] Despite the paper's earlier adulation of the Doncaster man, *Boxing News* now believed the proposed match with Mauriello was a big risk operation and that, 'If Woodcock failed British boxing credit would suffer a slump which it might not recover from for a generation.'[16]

His effort at Madison Square Garden ended in the fifth round, at which time he was thought to have been ahead on points. Mauriello was cut on the left eyebrow, and bleeding from the nose and mouth. There was a clash of heads and Woodcock stood swaying and looking dazed. Mauriello was not one to hang back and admire his work. He hit Woodcock with a crippling left hook, doubling him over and following with a right to the jaw. After the bout Woodcock required four stitches in his forehead. *Nil desperandum*. The trade paper thought there was honour and glory in defeat for both the British boxers.[17]

In those days there was no Board rule that a boxer who is stopped in a contest must not box again for twenty-eight days, providing a doctor's certificate before he does so. So *pace* Donmall's thoughts a decade earlier, with both Mills and

---

[15] Old Timer, 'Position of Our Big Boys Analysed', *Boxing News*, 23 January 1946.
[16] *Boxing News*, 13 March 1946.
[17] Ibid., 22 May 1946.

Woodcock stopped in their previous contests they were back in the ring together, with Mills matched once more to meet a heavier man over twelve rounds. Broadribb was keen to explain himself. Contracts had been signed before the Lesnevich match and Mills, as the crowd puller, was to receive £8000. This was £889 more than he was paid for the Lesnevich contest. Woodcock was to receive £4000, or 20 per cent of the profits – whichever was greater.

It was thought that if Woodcock could not beat Mills then the British heavyweight champion would be washed up on what was called Jacobs' Beach, so named after the American promoter. Heavyweights who could not beat light-heavyweights were more or less taken out and shot. The press almost unanimously favoured Woodcock, citing his fine left hand and superior punching. But there was no question who was the crowd's favourite. *Boxing News* devoted a double-page adulatory spread to pictures of Mills gardening to show how he had returned to training.[18]

A week before the fight, Mills suffered a shivering fit whilst training at Solomons' gymnasium. He was examined by the Board's doctor Philip Kaplin, who apparently was quite prepared to give Mills a medical certificate to postpone the fight. But Freddie wanted the contest to go on. It was, he said, nothing more than a recurrence of the dengue fever he had suffered in India, and in a couple of days he would be fit and well. 'He had his two days' rest, self-prescribed, and a lot of people closely connected were more than a little relieved when he said that he would be able to fight.'[19]

The contest, which ended with a points victory for

---

[18] Bert Callis, 'Freddie Mills in a Playful Mood', *Boxing News*, 29 May 1946.
[19] Jack Solomons, *Jack Solomons Tells All*. In March 1943, Mills had been scheduled to box Thornton in an exhibition in Brighton, but he took on a substitute.

Woodcock, was punishing and not one for the purists. 'Scrappy', thought the *Daily Express*. Neither man had displayed much skill in defence, and Woodcock had won convincingly and although Mills thought he hit harder than Lesnevich, the Doncaster man showed that, when it came to it, he hadn't all that much of a punch. Mills, however, showed once again, to his cost, great courage under a relentless battering.

After the contest, both men were given a rest. Mills was to go with Solomons and Broadribb to New York to watch the Joe Louis v Billy Conn fight. Mills was mobbed at Idlewild Airport and was pictured shaking hands with Anthony Eden. For a week he was taken around the city, appearing on the radio with James J. Braddock and Abe Simon, both of whom had been defeated by Louis. There were visits to Jack Dempsey's restaurant just off Broadway. There was a meeting with Rocky Graziano and a visit to a Jewish youth club, where Mills spoke with and heard Sugar Ray Robinson impersonate the Ink Spots. He stayed with Nat Fleischer, founder of *Ring* magazine, at his home on Long Beach and he met both Jimmy Durante and Frank Sinatra. Fleischer thought that Mills was the life and soul of the party.

After Louis knocked out Conn in the eighth round, Solomons went back to England to finalise details of a Brighton tournament for 13 August, on which Mills was to top the bill. Soon Mills was bored with his tour of Niagara Falls, Chicago and Los Angeles. His depression set in again. He told Broadribb he wanted to go home, and their holiday was cut short.

On 13 August he was matched with the Swede John Nilsson, regarded as one of the hardest-hitting heavyweights in Europe. On his debit side Nilsson had lost on points to

Fred Price, a relatively unknown Irishman. But he had also knocked out Mills' old friend Tom Reddington in ten rounds. It was a contest with a good deal of hype. Solomons received a cable from Sweden asking him to send sparring partners for Nilsson, who had, apparently, put one in hospital, a situation which had sent another scurrying from the training camp.

When it came to it, though, the Swede was no great opponent and Mills walked through his counter-punches knocking Nilsson down three times in the first round, before he tried to pull himself up on the ropes and failed. This was much more like Freddie and *Boxing News*, for one, was much happier. This was the true Mills: 'Now Mills has got the humidity of the East out of his blood we can look for much improved form and predict a brighter future for our Bournemouth lad.'[20]

Once again, the almost cloudless sky seemed to be Mills' limit. Solomons, however, could see no further than another shot at Lesnevich, and then possibly the giant American Joe Baksi. Neither manager nor promoter seemed concerned that Mills would be conceding height and considerable weight to the latter. Their worries were more fiscal than physical: in post-war Britain, Mills had simply earned too much too soon. If he fought another big purse contest he would be taking home two shillings in the pound. Broadribb told Solomons another match would have to wait until 1947. Meanwhile Solomons had yet another great idea: his opponent could be Joe Louis. The reasoning was that the undoubtedly heavy overheads in training for such a contest would reduce the tax burden. Another suggestion which, given that he had struggled against the limited Woodcock, might have made some, if not much more, sense for Mills, was to fight Tami Mauriello.

In the end, though, Broadribb agreed that Mills should box Baksi at Harringay, not in the New Year but on 5 November. It was what the Board would have called 'a criminal contest' a few years earlier. In his memoirs, Jack Solomons justifies things by saying that Freddie and Broadribb had said they would fight any American heavyweight, with the exception of Joe Louis. He had merely obliged them.

Mills' reward, lucky man, would be a share of the gate. By today's standards Baksi would not be regarded as a big man, but he was then. Ranked number ten in the world heavyweight division, he possessed a forty-eight-inch chest, stood six feet high and weighed over fifteen stone. He also had a formidable record, losing only four of sixty-eight contests. Recently he had stopped the useful Sandy McPherson and Henry Jones, the latter in five rounds. Apart from the money, it was difficult to see what was in it for Mills, who would be giving away two stone, other than another bad beating. Some of the press said as much. The *Sunday Express* wrote, 'Mills v Baksi Looks Like a Massacre'.

Over the years there have been a few light-heavyweights who have had sufficient talent and power to equal the heavyweights. Sam Langford, 'the Boston Tar Baby', who had a devastating punch, was one.[21] But it was not thought that

---

[21] Sam Langford's career lasted some twenty-one years. Standing five foot six inches tall and weighing ten stone ten, he fought Jack Johnson before he became heavyweight champion. In 1909 he gave away three stone in weight to Iron Hague. In his last contest, nearly blind, he was led to the ring in the Mexico City bullring where, fighting by instinct, he knocked out Jim Flynn. More recently, in 2003 Roy Jones, the former middleweight, beat the limited heavyweight champion John Ruiz.

Mills was another Langford. Curiously, the former flyweight champion Jimmy Wilde at first went against the general opinion, arguing Mills' toughness would see him through. Nothing was mentioned about safe and sound, though. Others who thought Mills had a chance included *Boxing News* and *The Times*, both of whom used the same argument. Mills was ranked third behind Lesnevich and Ezzard Charles in the cruiserweight division. Woodcock was ranked fifth and Baksi tenth in the heavyweights. In the curious self-justification which has afflicted boxing writers over the years, it was reasoned that Woodcock had given Mauriello a hard time and now Mauriello was going in with Joe Louis for the world title. Mills had stood up to all Woodcock could offer. Therefore Mills had a sporting chance. All this told *Boxing News* that it was a good match. 'His chances of success against Baksi cannot be so bad as some of the scribes would have us believe,' *The Times* said: 'Mills' qualities and defects are well known and are unlikely to alter very much at this stage in his career. The one thing certain is that Mills as usual will spare neither himself nor his opponent in attempting the necessary heave.'[22]

But after watching Baksi deal harshly with his sparring partners, Wilde changed his mind.

For Mills, it was off to Brighton again. Broadribb had him on a Guinness diet to try to bulk him up. As for dealing with the heavier man, Jules 'Mo' Kiki, the Brighton wrestler, was employed to shove Mills around so that he would get used to the bruising style of Baksi. Baksi trained just down the road at Billy Sinclair's gym.

Broadribb was quite happy with things: 'Freddie likes them big. He gave Jack London more than three stone and both Al Robinson and Jim Wilde were more than fifteen stone when Freddie fought them. Baksi's weight is not nearly so important as the press are making out. If Mills doesn't win then all I can say is I am slipping.'[23] It may have been quite correct that Mills had given chunks of weight away over the years, but London, Woodcock, Robinson, Shaw and Wilde, possibly even all of them rolled into one, were not Baksi.

It was terrible the way Broadribb and promoter Jack Solomons grossly over-matched Mills. They were wicked to do it. He was only really a big middleweight. Yet he fought heavyweights weighing over 220lbs. It was absolutely ridiculous, but Freddie was so brave he'd go in with anyone. Mind you, Freddie made some wonderful money, but as far as I'm concerned Broadribb was a very hard, very brutal man. He was a good manager as far as manoeuvring his fighters but he was ruthless.[24]

In the first round, Mills hit Baksi flush on the chin with a number of left hooks, but the punches made no impression on him whatsoever. Mills took the round, but it was his last. Baksi did not even take a step backwards. By the end of the second, Mills was cut about the eyes and was shipping punches to the body. Baksi moved forward and no amount of Mills counter-punches could stop him. In the third, Mills tried to force the pace, but was met with a series of short arm jabs. By the fifth, Mills was in distress and Baksi was dropping his hands, beckoning him to come on. At the end of the sixth, the cut and exhausted Mills, however, was in no

[23] Jack Birtley, *Freddie Mills*, p. 125.
[24] Ex-boxer Harry Legge, quoted in Nigel Collins, *Boxing Babylon*.

condition to do so. Broadribb, safely in the corner, was still egging Mills on and when the referee, C. T. Thomas, considered stopping the contest, Broadribb insisted that the cuts were not serious enough for him to do so. Later, Mills would say he might as well have been punching a small Alp. 'I'm turning this fight in thank you very much,' he told his corner.[25] Mills was taken to King's College Hospital, where his cuts were found to include one between the eyelashes of his right eye.

Frank Butler wrote in the *Daily Express*: 'The fight was a massacre and must not happen again. My advice to Mills is to take a long rest. He cannot go on taking such terrific beatings. One day his strength will give. He must now concentrate on the light-heavyweight class for last night he was out of his class.' The *Express* also had words for Solomons: 'Who staged last night's big fight? It contributed nothing to sport even for those who paid 10 guineas to sit at the ringside. After the first rounds it became quite clear that Mills was nothing but a chopping block.'[26]

The Times summed it up: 'Mills at least had done as well as anyone really was entitled to expect. Baksi was too big for him.'[27]

Boxing News changed its mind after the contest, admitting it had been wrong. Now it offered sensible words for Mills, Broadribb and Solomons: 'It would be folly to match him again with high ranking American heavyweights now there are really good American light heavyweights available.'[28]

And for Mills, there ended 1946.

[25] *Sunday Graphic*, 16 November 1958.
[26] 'The Slaughter of the British', *Daily Express*, 6 November 1946.
[27] *The Times*, 6 November 1946.
[28] *Boxing News*, 13 November 1946.

8

Freddie Mills Eats
the Wrong Food

1947 was a mixed year for Mills and a dreadful one for
Woodcock. First, Woodcock was matched against Joe Baksi.
The idea behind this was that if Woodcock beat the giant,
he would have erased the defeat by Mauriello. And, after
all, hadn't he handily beaten Mills, who had not even been
knocked out by Baksi? Then there was his eighth-round
knockout of Lesnevich in the September of the previous
year. According to Solomons, Woodcock fancied his chances
and wanted the fight after noting that Mills may have been
out on his feet, but he was not on the floor. In fact,
Woodcock had struggled to beat Stephane Olek on 17 March
1947. Later he would say his training had been interrupted
because of flu.[1] The Baksi bout was to be another gross
mismatch.

[1] Bruce Woodcock, *Two Fists and a Fortune*, p. 138.

The Polish-American again trained in Brighton at Billy Sinclair's gym. Dennis Slade remembers him:

> I came home on leave from the army and took my gear to Billy Sinclair's gym. I'd won the Southern Command lightweight championship and was now in the finals which were at the Royal Albert Hall. Billy called me over and said that Ray Arcel had been watching me and he thought I had a style similar to Woodcock. Could Baksi do a bit of sparring with me? What an imbecile. I said 'Yes'. I was given extra leave and since I was a PT instructor in the army, I used to lead him on runs through Hove Park.[2]

Baksi had taken 25 per cent of the gate for the Mills contest and ended with £5,699 9s 6d. On 15 April 1947 at Harringay he earned £12,736 2s for annihilating Woodcock. He had been told to start fast and he obeyed his instructions. In the first round it was effectively all over: three crushing punches, the first a left to the jaw, each flooring Woodcock before the fight was three minutes old. Woodcock swayed and reeled on legs of paper and at the end of the round was carried like a sack to the corner. He took counts of eight and nine in round two and was stopped in the seventh. His jaw had been broken and one punch had caused damage to his left eye, a condition from which he never fully recovered.

As far as Mills was concerned, there were to be no more matches with heavyweights. 'In future, my lad will only fight at his natural weight. No more overweight matches,' said the newly responsible and sensible Broadribb. This was all very

---

[2] Conversation with author.

well, but no light-heavyweight in Europe was really capable of giving Mills a decent match. The first to try was Willie Quentenmeyer in a contest at the Royal Albert Hall, announced as for the European title, something which overlooked the fact that Quentenmeyer had already been matched with the Belgian champion for that honour. These small difficulties matter little in boxing, and mattered even less fifty years ago.

Like Woodcock's for the Olek fight, Mills' training was hampered by an attack of flu. Later he would say that for days all it consisted of was walking. He wanted to pull out of the contest but Solomons and Broadribb persuaded him to go through with it, so Mills could expect little help from the doctors.

'Actually I was fit enough, apart from the flu,' Mills wrote later, 'but at the weigh-in, when we were being posed for the usual photographs, I had to cut it short to get back into my clothes.'[3]

Ray Clarke, who went on to become the Board's General-Secretary, remembers, 'In those days the Board's chief medical officer was Phil Kaplin and he was Solomons' man. If Solomons wanted it, he would OK it: "He's fit to fight".'[4] When it came to it, the flu caused Mills little difficulty. On 20 January 1947 the Dutchman was outclassed and knocked out in the second round.

The second contest of the year did, however, cause him rather more trouble. Mills believed the fight had sweated the last of the flu out of him and when some people came to talk to him the following day about starting a business, he was fit as a fiddle. The proposal was to open a Chinese restaurant at 143 Charing Cross Road, in which he was to be a partner

[3] Freddie Mills, *Twenty Years*, pp. 150–1.
[4] Conversation with author.

with the Northamptonshire businessmen George Ribey and Charles Luck. The manager was the actor Andy Ho, who may not have initially been a partner. The premises were in poor condition, and one of the men he employed to clean the place out was Alf Knight, whom Mills had known during the war. The former boxer Sid Green remembers Knight: 'He was the strongest man I've ever seen. He gave an exhibition of strength that impressed Freddie. Alf would do 1000 press-ups, 2000 squats. He would break a six-inch nail in seventeen seconds. After the war Alf met Freddie again and Freddie set him on to clear out the premises he and Andy Ho bought from a Greek. Rationing was in force and in return Freddie gave Alf some dinners. Alf says the worst thing was removing the chewing gum the Americans had stuck under the tables.'[5] Once renovated and opened, at the bottom of the stairs was a full-size cardboard cut-out of Mills in fighting stance.

The signs were that Mills was concentrating on the new venture more than boxing, because in his next fight with the Italian champion Enrico Bertola a month later, on 17 February, he received more than he bargained for. Bertola was after him from the opening bell and was countering Mills' swings and hooks with straight jabs to the face. By the fourth round the Italian, then well on top, trapped Mills in a corner and threw a barrage of punches. Mills took them and just before the bell, launched a counter-attack, hooking the Italian to the jaw and upper-cutting him. The count was stopped at six but the minute's rest was not sufficient. Bertola was knocked out in the next round. Mills later said, 'I kept hitting him on the chin and began to think someone had carved his head out of marble. My blows were making about as much

---

[5] Letter to author.

impression on him as a sorbo ball would have made on a cricket bat.'[6]

Meanwhile, Woodcock was recovering from the Baksi beating. All the sensible thoughts of Mills not taking on heavyweights went out of the window when Solomons had problems finding a suitable opponent for Stephane Olek, the French-born heavyweight. The logical stepping sequence for Mills was Olek, then the black American Lloyd Marshall, then a return with Gus Lesnevich, who was making noises that he would be happy to come to England again. This schedule went belly-up when Lesnevich decided that, after all, he wanted to defend his title in America. The Olek match was put on hold. Mills' next fight would be against Lloyd Marshall.

Broadribb, however, had other ideas. He had already been negotiating with the Transvaal Sporting Club, and now he matched Mills with the South African heavyweight Johnny Ralph.

In the spring, with Woodcock still recovering from his terrible beating, it was a question of who was going to top Solomons' Harringay Eve-of-Derby show. Mills really was the only candidate, so he would face Marshall in one of the 'Black v White' tournaments which were so popular before being banned by the Board of Control. Unfortunately, because Ralph had damaged his knuckles, Mills was touring the country in a *ménage à trois* with Broadribb's daughter Chrissie and her husband, Don McCorkindale. When Ralph's knuckles did not heal, an open-air match was made with Nick Wolmarans, another South African. Mills knocked him out in five rounds on 29 April. Solomons sent a telegram to Broadribb to bring Mills home.

---

[6]   Quoted in 'Death was the verdict for 11 fighters', *Empire News*, 30 September 1951. One of the eleven was Bertola, who moved up to the heavyweight division and died after a bout in America in 1949.

Mills was given the Marshall fight at two weeks notice. 'Negro battler for Mills' headlined *Boxing News*.[7] Three years earlier Marshall had been rated a place above Mills and only behind Lesnevich in the American-based National Boxing Association's cruiserweight ratings, but he was reckoned to have slipped. The boxers lunched together with Solomons at Mills' Chinese Restaurant and both worked out in the Windmill Street gym, although they never saw each other because the training sessions were two hours apart. Broadribb had, however, been warned that Marshall carried a variety of punches.

However, the boxing critic L. N. Bailey thought that Marshall was in for a beating. He accepted that the man had 'Plenty of experience, a sound knowledge of the game and is fast. Mills, however, is his equal in those things, and what is more, I believe he is tougher. Once Mills goes on, I think Marshall will crumble under his hard punching.'[8]

This time Mills was getting weight rather than conceding it. Marshall weighed in at eleven stone twelve; Mills was ten pounds heavier. The contest was fought in a heatwave and there is a cartoon of Mills and Marshall stripped to the waist with the caption, 'At least we're sensibly dressed.' From the start Mills looked ponderous. According to the Boxing Board's ring inspector, Mills looked pasty and slack. In fact, he was almost certainly in another bout of depression. In the first half minute he was hit by a punch he apparently never saw, although it seems to have been apparent to most of the ringsiders. 'The long, loping left', wrote Van den Bergh alliteratively, had Mills back against the ropes bemused, his gloves down and his legs almost unable to hold him. Fortunately, Marshall stood and admired his work. Mills partially recovered, planted his feet wide apart and came forward.

Matters did not, however, improve. He went to the canvas twice from punches that at best were light and at worst did not even land. Peter Wilson, writing in the *Sunday Pictorial*, thought the referee should have warned Mills over his conduct. He was knocked out in the fifth round resting on one knee. He had been cut over the eye and blood was dripping on to the canvas. The quick-tempered Broadribb was not at all pleased. Nor was the crowd, sections of which were yelling, 'Carve up' and 'Rubbish'. Broadribb was pounding the canvas, telling Mills he was 'Yellow'. Tony Van den Bergh writes that he even spat at his boxer.[9]

In the dressing room there were angry recriminations, with Broadribb claiming Mills had not been doing proper road-work and offering the contract to anyone who might care to take it over. The next day, however, wounds and pride had partially healed and it was a question of presenting a united front. The *Star* reported a more conciliatory Ted Broadribb as saying: 'Something went wrong with Freddie in the first minute and I have never seen him box so poorly as he did afterwards. I am going to advise him to take a month off and then train seriously for a spell.'[10]

Broadribb's complaint was that Mills had spent too much time in his Chinese restaurant. Now, ignoring the fact there was an English, in addition to the Chinese menu, there were suggestions that he had eaten the wrong food as well. In future he would eat Scottish steaks and Welsh dairy produce and drink English milk.

As for Marshall, he said he was quite prepared to stay in

---

9 Tony Van den Bergh, *Who Killed Freddie Mills?*, pp. 71–2.
10 *Star*, 3 June 1947.

England until Mills was ready for another bout. The defeat was put down to a damaged optic nerve.

The diary columnist in the *Star* had other thoughts. He noted that Bruce Woodcock had earlier suffered from a broken jaw, and went on: 'Why not say that our boxers are not good enough at present to meet overseas challengers? We need not be ashamed of the fact for we are suffering from the effects of the war. American boxers do not get these broken jaws and hurt optic nerves so frequently. They are toughened in a harder school and as Mills said to me, "Americans hit so much harder than our own boys."' As for a proposed rematch with Marshall: 'The manager of a winning boxer once said to me after the loser had asked for a return, "Why have Sunday's dinner again on Monday?"'[11]

Solomons had thought things had gone wrong well before the fight. Here was Mills in another depression signalled by his unenthusiastic attitude to training. Solomons claimed later that Mills went through it, 'like that plodding ploughman my schoolteacher used to tell me about. He also tended to be terse with his sparmates – not at all like the cheerful, wisecracking Freddie the whole of the fight world had come to love and admire.' And on the night of the contest?

> Where, I demanded of everybody within reach, was the usual bright blue dressing-gown adorned with a red and rampant lion on the back, and presented to Mills by admirers at a London pub? Why had Freddie discarded this mascot for a nondescript towel? What was he doing in a scruffy pair of trunks? Doesn't he know it's a crime to appear improperly dressed on a Solomons parade? What's it all about?

[11] Ibid., 4 June 1947.

Nobody answered me, but I soon found out. Freddie Mills no more had his mind on fighting Lloyd Marshall that night than mine is on climbing Nelson's Column right now. Let it go at that.[12]

In the blame merry-go-round, Broadribb then turned his attentions on Solomons: it was his fault for demanding Mills be brought back from South Africa. After the fight Mills and Broadribb, to use the latter's expression, were 'off the hooks': 'We just had one of those quarrels with each trying to blame the other for the defeat and although to this day we have never admitted it to each other, I think we both decided in our own minds that we would leave the fight game to someone else.'[13] In his autobiography, Mills said that he had had difficulty acclimatising after the trip to Johannesburg. He had, he said, been caught with a left swing just under the right eye and there had been a blinding flash. He had been unable to focus.

What I do know is that when my eyes came back into focus I found I was shaping up sideways to the air at an angle of about thirty degrees to Marshall.

The fight went on and still I was having vision trouble and just could not concentrate. I remember in the third round going down three times and all my swings seemed to be missing by a mile. When the end came in the fifth with me on my knees, for the first time I could accept defeat rather than carry on the fight. It was far and away my worst show.[14]

[12] Jack Solomons, *Jack Solomons Tells All*, p. 106.
[13] Ted Broadribb, *Fighting is My Life*, pp. 115–16.
[14] Freddie Mills, *Twenty Years*, p. 164.

Peter McInnes suggests that troubles had arisen between Mills and Broadribb over Freddie's burgeoning romance with Chrissie. Broadribb does not seem to have had any objection in principle to his daughter shifting her affections from one of his boxers to another, but he wanted this to be delayed until after Mills' ring career was over. In any event, on the weekend before the Marshall contest Mills broke training and went to see McInnes box in an amateur tournament at the Guildhall, Winchester. Once there he had broken training comprehensively and: 'Poor Fred, disturbed, agitated and besieged by the soft words of dignitaries and fraudulent friends, probably took more drink that night than he had ever consumed in his entire life. That I was given the decision after my bout made him even more celebratory. Anyway, returning to London next day he was hung over noticeably, a state which was not aided by walking slap into another rumpus with his manager.'[15] It was yet another example of the rushed and potentially disastrous decisions he made throughout his life.

If the public was going to pay good money to see Mills in action again, it had to be clearly explained why he had failed so badly and why he would succeed the next time. Certainly a troubled love life was not going to be a palatable explanation. One that was mooted was that he needed to train in the clean air of the British countryside away from the smoke of London. This line of thought had already been put into practice immediately after the fight, when he was packed off to Lincolnshire for rest and recuperation and where he might get the much-needed steak.

*   *   *

15 Peter McInnes, *Freddie My Friend*, p. 123.

And as for Randy Turpin on the undercard? It was the only time in which he appeared on a bill with Freddie Mills. He was matched against the experienced Mark Hart, but because Turpin was under nineteen, he was only allowed to box six three-minute rounds. Hart, a slow starter who often needed time to catch up, had wanted an eight-round contest, but agreed to the stipulation.[16]

Turpin convincingly outpointed Hart but under the rules of the time – a boxer under twenty-one could box for only thirty minutes – it was Hart who would go forward to challenge Vince Hawkins for the title. There was another brake on Turpin's progress, too: the colour bar against black boxers fighting for the British title.

All in all, it had been a good night for the black half of the bill. 'Kid' Tanner won a points decision over Dickie O'Sullivan. The Kid's younger brother, boxing as Jack Johnson, stopped Alby Hollister in two rounds. *Boxing News* thought that when he could control his right swing he would be really dangerous. Berry Wright knocked out Arthur Danahar in two rounds. The only one to blot his copybook was Jackie Turpin, who was knocked out in two rounds by Johnny Malloy. This was not really surprising. Jackie, along with brother Dick, had been in another 'Black v White' tournament four nights earlier, this time in Liverpool, when he had been retired after four rounds with Billy Kenrick.[17]

As for Solomons, he left for Cannes in the South of France. He stayed out of the way for three months, before ringing Broadribb to ask if he wanted another crack at the light-heavyweight title.

---

[16] Hart, who was then managed by Jack Hyams – Freddie Mills' old opponent – had won the ABA heavyweight title in 1944 and early in his professional career had boxed at that weight. He had already beaten Albert Finch.
[17] Dick Turpin won on a cut-eye decision against Billy Stevens in the third round.

9

Randolph Turpin Meets George Middleton

Randolph Turpin's professional career began in London on 17 September 1946, when he stopped Gordon Griffiths in the first round. John S. Sharp wrote, 'I predict a bright future for the young Negro from Leamington Spa. Randolph Turpin is the name for your reference book.' Peter Wilson was even more enthusiastic: 'The way Turpin leapt on Griffiths, like a bronze tiger devouring a tethered kid, battering him half-way through the ropes until the referee intervened in the first round, was enough to prove that a new middleweight menace had arrived.'[1]

Despite strong advice to the contrary, Turpin had decided to join his brothers under the George Middleton management umbrella. Under the Board's then rules, Jack Solomons as a promoter could not hold a manager's licence because there would be a clear conflict of interest. Initially, he had

[1] *The Ring*, December 1946; *Daily Express*, 18 September 1946.

tried to have Turpin sign with Nat Seller, Freddie Mills' old trainer, but that had come to nothing. There had also been suggestions that Turpin be given an education and elocution lessons under the aegis of another manager, but he had preferred the philosophy of 'Backstreets I am, backstreets I'll be.' There was yet another suggestion that he could have come under the tutelage of Larry Gains, the great black Canadian boxer. Gains had seen him as a young amateur and had told him to come back when he was eighteen and he would make Turpin a world champion. Another story is that Gains sent for Turpin when he was staying in the Seven Stars in Warwick with a view to signing him, but that Randy had signed with Middleton only a few hours previously.

Peter McInnes claims there was a secret written agreement between Solomons and Middleton, which gave Solomons control of the hottest British prospect since Freddie Mills. In return Middleton moved into the ranks of major manager, something which he should have been able to use to the advantage of the rest of his stable. Turpin, as the protégé of a top promoter, had immediate access to the major boxing venues, and he did not have to leave the Warwick area. As for Solomons, he thought that George Middleton was 'one of the most reasonable men in the world to do business with'.[2] In fact Middleton was wholly Jack Solomons' man. Danny McAlinden, the British heavyweight champion and the last Solomons–Middleton protégé, recalls his old manager: 'George Middleton wasn't an ordinary working man. He bought and sold; he lived on his wits. He'd say to me, "Go with an attitude. I needs the coin." If Jack Solomons said, "Jump", George would ask "How high?"'[3]

[2] Jack Solomons, *Jack Solomons Tells All*, p. 148.
[3] Conversation with author.

For his first contest, Turpin had been originally matched with another former ABA champion, Jimmy Hockley, who had won titles before him. This would have been a dangerous and indeed pointless match. One of two bright prospects was, in all probability, going to lose, and thus suffer an immediate career setback. Turpin, it seems, did not know his new opponent's name until the weigh-in. It was a pattern that would be repeated throughout his later wrestling career.

But whilst he was making his way up the rankings, his brother Dick was very much at the top. Dick Turpin's first contest after the war, when he was not fully back in training, was a loss to Johnny Boyd over eight rounds in Birmingham. He then lost two subsequent contests and in January 1947 he was knocked out by George Howard. After that, however, it was onwards and upwards. But he could only go so far because of one of the least attractive aspects of the sport at the time: the colour bar. Black fighters could not box for the highly prized British titles. This had come about as something of a reprisal, after Jack Johnson had cut a swath through the white champions and contenders and, rather more importantly at the time, through a swath of white women. The colour bar produced considerable anomalies. Back in the 1930s Cuthbert Taylor, who had won the ABA flyweight title in 1928, was not allowed to box for the Welsh professional title. On the other hand in 1934 two white South Africans, George Cook and Don McCorkindale, were matched in an eliminator for the British heavyweight title.

The colour bar had long been a bone of contention and the Board of Control attempted to justify the ban when the General Secretary of the Board, Charles Donmall, told the *News Chronicle* that a departure from the colour bar was neither desirable nor necessary:

It is only right that a small country such as ours should have championships restricted to boxers of white parents. Otherwise we might be faced with a situation where all our British titles are held by Coloured Empire champions. The Board has done much for the Empire boxers of colour. We have a very high regard for them as men and boxers. They are not penalised by this rule. They have the British Empire championship open to them and the Empire titles have always been regarded by the Board as infinitely more important than the purely domestic British championship.[4]

The fear was that black fighters would soon take the majority of titles from white boxers and it would not be good for the game. The other reason was purely financial. In those days Solomons was never going to fill the White City with an all-black main event, something which was proved when some years later he matched Archie Moore and Yolande Pompey. At the time, a racist saying had been coined: 'Two Blacks don't make a Fight'. In other words, they didn't put bottoms on seats which is, after all, what a boxing match is ultimately about. Twenty years later the trainer George Francis wrote:

In those days black fighters didn't draw any support. They were unknown. They didn't put bums on seats and because boxing is a business as well as a sport, promoters weren't interested in giving ring-space to boxers who, as they put it, brought only their bag with them when they came to fight. It wasn't prejudice against them being

[4] *News Chronicle*, 23 January 1947.

placed; it was that they were unknown, outsiders, simple as that.

And even if black fighters did get taken up and put in a show they tended to get overmatched – an easy win for the white guy and no rating for them. Getting into the ratings was crucial: if they weren't rated, the public got no chance to change their mind about them. They continued as outsiders, no-hopers in the opinion of most people.[5]

In that period, black boxers could expect no favours against local boys. One of the most controversial contests was that of Al Phillips, 'The Aldgate Tiger', against Cliff Anderson, for the Empire featherweight title at the Albert Hall on 18 March 1947. After Anderson had knocked Phillips down three times, he found himself on the wrong end of a points decision by referee Peter Muir, which was greeted with an uproar lasting until the second round of the following contest. It was generally regarded as the worst decision by a British referee for many years. John Macadam summed up the general feeling: 'Anderson clearly stamped himself as the best featherweight in the British Empire. He lost the Empire title by the decision of the referee and he is debarred from fighting for the British title by his colour.'[6] One lifelong follower of boxing, George Ingram, wrote to *Boxing News* saying he wished to put up £20 towards a trophy for Anderson, and the paper organised a collection with subscription cards. Donations came to over £200, including

---

[5] G. Francis and G. Fife, *Trainer of Champions*, p. 127. Francis was indeed a trainer of champions, working with John Conteh, Frank Bruno, Cornelius Boza-Edwards, Bunny Sterling and many others. Suffering from cancer, he committed suicide in January 2002.

[6] *Boxing News*, 26 March 1947.

five guineas from the comedian Will Hay. Anderson was presented with a belt at a luncheon. The Board defended their referee but a rematch took place. Sadly, Anderson, who had knocked Phillips down four times, was unluckily disqualified for a kidney punch, described by *Boxing News* as: 'Perfectly delivered and aimed at the body just above the belt. But before it reached its objective Phillips had taken a half turn and when the blow finally landed it connected with the kidneys.' Anderson was distraught. In tears he lay down by Phillips' side.[7]

There had been much less trouble for young Randy Turpin on the original Phillips *v* Anderson bill. In his seventh contest he knocked out Bert Hyland in the first round. Before then, on 9 November 1946, in his second contest, he had outpointed Des Jones over six rounds in London, and just before the year ended, he defeated Bill Blything in Birmingham. It took him ninety-eight seconds, during which time Blything was on the canvas for two counts of eight. When he was finally knocked out, he fractured his collarbone in the fall and was taken to hospital.

By now there was a team assembled around Turpin and the Nelson Gym in Warwick. The gym itself, which was damp and draughty, was on the first floor of a glue factory and it stank from the pigskins which were being turned into gelatine to make lozenges. It was run by Arthur Batty who had, for the era, unorthodox ideas. Batty's theories ran contrary to the prevailing belief that boxers should be light, loose and flexible, and that the muscle-building exercises

---

[7] Although Anderson boxed in elimination contests, he never again fought for a title. In fact, Phillips was lucky that year. He beat Ray Famechon for the European title, again on a disqualification, after being on the floor a number of times. (*Boxing News*, 2 April, 4 June, 1 and 8 July 1947.)

for wrestlers and weightlifters were harmful to them. Turpin, in his early days an assiduous trainer, adopted Batty's routines wholeheartedly.[8] Mick Gavin, who had boxed professionally, was initially Randolph's chief trainer and also in the gym was Frank Algar, Randolph's friend from his National Service days, who had run a naval boxing team. He would spend his leaves with the Turpins, and when Dick was preparing for his first British title defence, he overstayed his leave. He was rounded up after his name as a cornerman was announced on a radio broadcast of the contest. He would play a very significant part in Randolph's career in and out of the ring. For a time Dick Turpin took over as chief trainer, relegating Mick Gavin.

Later in June 1948 they were joined by Bill Hyam, a travelling tobacco salesman who was allowed time off from his day job and thereafter was with Turpin for many years. He had been an army boxer who had fought professionally under an assumed name whilst serving with the Lincolnshire Regiment and had sparred with Jim Driscoll. He was also a qualified masseur.

At the beginning of January 1947, many people thought that Turpin was being stretched against the experienced Jimmy Davis from Bethnal Green, one of the undercard bouts on the bill in which Dick Turpin was knocked out in the seventh round of eight by George Howard. But with young Randolph, it was a totally different story. He knocked out Davis in the fourth round of six. Davis had already taken three counts of nine and an earlier count of three in the second. 'Turpin's was a performance of which he can feel proud,' said *Boxing News*.[9]

---

[8] Batty died on 1 July 1989 at the age of seventy-six.
[9] *Boxing News*, 22 January 1947.

Later that month, he knocked out Dai James in three rounds. James had taken a count of eight in the second round and two counts of five. The next day, Turpin married Mary Theresa Stack – whose brother Michael had been the Midland Boys' Club Champion the previous year – at St Peter's Roman Catholic Church in Leamington. Their honeymoon was spent in Portsmouth after which Mary moved in with his mother at Wathen Road.

Less than a month later, Randolph was part of the undercard at the Seymour Hall when Jack London, out of retirement, knocked out the Dutch champion Jan Kleur in one round. It was a short if exciting night for the fans. Turpin met Johnny Best, who took counts of three, eight and nine before the referee stopped the contest in the first round. After that Bert Saunders was beaten on points in London; Ron Cooper was stopped in four in Oxford; and Jury VII, the youngest of seven Algerian boxing brothers, was defeated on points in London.

So it went on until the Eve of Derby show, at which Marshall battered Mills and Turpin secured his easy points victory. Twenty days later, on 23 June, Leon Fouguet was knocked out in the first round in Coventry.

On 9 September 1947, Turpin fought Jimmy Ingle, the elder brother of the celebrated trainer Brendan. Later Ingle wrote that he was paid £200 and had been training properly; he was up at 6 a.m. for ten miles' roadwork and, following a rub-down, returned to bed for two hours. Later he would spar with Mick McKeown and Willie Duggan, two Irish amateur champions. As for the fight:

No less than 10,000 people packed the Butts Stadium, Coventry, that night. Virtually all were, of course, Turpin

fans. The reception he received when introduced from
the ring lasted at least a minute – the crowd standing,
clapping and cheering. Randolph was their hero and
deservedly so. The fight lasted three rounds. Afterwards
I could recall only the first minute. A right-hand punch
exploded on my chin and for the remainder of the bout
I boxed only from instinct. Later David Stewart told me
I was down for three counts of nine in every round and
that the referee had stopped it at the end of round
three.[10]

On 13 October 1947, Turpin's first child, Randolph Jnr, was
born. At the same time came the first blot of the year, although
it was a minor one: Turpin drew in a rematch over eight
rounds with Mark Hart.

At the beginning of 1948 Freddie Price lasted less than a
round in Coventry, and Gerry McCready did no better the
next month in London. Professionally, everything seemed to
be going well. Turpin was about to be discharged from the
Navy and was to face a very useful man indeed, Vince
Hawkins, on 16 March. Emotionally, however, things were
not so happy. Within eighteen months, his marriage was effectively over. Assuming – and this is a large assumption – that
Frank Algar is a reliable witness, the marriage was happy
until after the birth of Randolph Jnr. It was then things began
to go awry. After Turpin was demobilised in March 1948 the
marriage deteriorated further.

Mary Turpin first left her husband that month, but after
the Vince Hawkins fight he traced her to 146 Harrow Road,
Paddington, and the pair were temporarily reconciled.

[10] Jimmy Ingle, *The Jimmy Ingle Story*, p. 84. He was later killed working on the
pads.

As for the contest, Turpin outpointed Hawkins well enough, but he had seemed to look uncomfortable against Hawkins' body punches. It was explained that he was not hurt at all but had been twisting his body to ride the punches. Frank Butler, for one, accepted the explanation.[11] *Boxing News* was well pleased with Turpin, saying that he and two other young boxers on the same bill would uphold the prestige of British boxing. The others were Eddie Thomas and Frank Ronan, Woodcock's sparring partner. The paper was not, however, happy with the range of skills shown by Turpin, though it admired: 'the pluck of the coloured boy who was often in trouble through the heavy punches in the early rounds but his courageous outlook as the fight wore on is something which one will not easily forget.'[12]

The year before, there had been a suggestion that Turpin was going to the United States to gain more experience, but this had been put off as he had to have a minor operation on his right hand. Frank Butler christened Turpin's short left hook the 'Alakasam'. Devised by brother Dick and possibly George Middleton, it was designed to compensate for the swelling of the knuckles. In training, his right hand was strapped behind his back and he punched with his left only.

Then, in early April 1948, came the announcement that the colour bar had been rescinded and all British subjects born and normally resident and domiciled in the United Kingdom would be allowed to contest British titles. Dick Turpin could now fight for the middleweight title. Unfortunately, it was Hawkins' title which would be at stake

[11] Frank Butler, *Randolph Turpin . . . Sugar Ray Robinson: their story in pictures.*
[12] *Boxing News*, 24 March 1948.

so the prize was rather devalued because of his defeat at the hands of Dick's little brother.

By now the Turpin–Stack marriage was undergoing a period of reconciliation. None the less, it was still rapidly descending into a match itself, and was clearly causing Randolph trouble in his training. On 26 April he lost to Albert Finch. On paper, there was no great disgrace in this. Finch had only lost four times in his thirty-two-fight career, but afterwards Middleton said: 'Randolph would have walked out of the Albert Hall that night without having climbed into the ring, if we had let him. He has never been like that before and, I hope, never will be again.'[13] He would be – many times.

By August, Frank Algar would tell a court that he had noticed Turpin was tired when he came in for training, as if he hadn't had enough sleep. Things improved for the Turpin brothers a month later when, on 10 May, Dick Turpin knocked out Bos Murphy of New Zealand with five seconds of the first round to go, to win the Commonwealth title. He followed this, as expected, on 28 June before a crowd of 40,000, by comprehensively defeating Vince Hawkins in pouring rain at Villa Park to become the first coloured boxer of the modern era to hold a British title. Also on the bill were Jackie, who beat Ben Duffy, and Randolph, who beat Alby Hollister on points. In a furious first round both men were knocked down, but then Turpin took control, despite his hand going in the third.

Afterwards, Dick told reporters that he would endeavour to hold on to the title until Randy was old enough, but he did not say whether he would accept Licker as a challenger.[14]

13 Jack Birtley, *The Tragedy of Randolph Turpin*, p. 29.
14 *Boxing News*, 12 May 1948.

In fact, they had promised their mother they would not box each other competitively. Diplomatically, the brothers wrote a letter thanking the Mayors of Leamington and Warwick, as well as all 'Warwickians' and 'Leamingtonians', for their support. In the years that followed, that support would fade to less than nothing.

Turpin was, however, still having the serious domestic problems which would dog his professional career and, indeed, the rest of his life. Mary left him again in June after a row between her mother and Turpin, and took a job at the Marlborough Hotel in Leamington. They were back together on 12 July. It did not last, and on 9 August 1948 a summons was heard in the Warwick Magistrates' Court alleging that Randolph had beaten her, causing her actual bodily harm. Mary Turpin told the court that on 24 July they had been together at a fair in Leamington and she had caught the 9.35 p.m. train back to Warwick. She had waited up for him, worrying, but he had not returned until 5.30 a.m. and when she asked where he had been, he had hit her, taking a broomstick handle and beating her until it broke. She claimed that when she told him she was going to have a baby and did not want him to hit her he replied, 'I'll soon fix that', and kicked her in the stomach. She ended with bruises to her back and groin. She had seen the doctor and stayed in the house until young Randolph, who had been ill, was better. Then she fled in a taxi. She left behind a note: 'Dear Randolph, I am leaving you with the baby because you can look after it better than I can. I prefer being out at work and having evenings free. I can't be at work and looking after the baby at the same time.'

Mary told the court that Randolph had made her write the letter and other similar ones at knifepoint. He claimed that she was an hysteric accusing him of going out with other women, throwing herself downstairs and pulling her hair out. Once, his brother Jackie had been obliged to take a knife away from her. Mary had been goading him into hitting her and he admitted giving her a slap when she became hysterical.

But she denied accusing him of having affairs. It might have been better for her case if she had admitted it, because a letter was produced, allegedly from a girl Pam. It began, 'My own darling Randy', and continued, 'Just remember I love you and I will prove how much when I see you again. It was signed, 'Your ever loving Pam'. Turpin admitted knowing the girl, claiming she was deaf and dumb. He denied having seen the letter and his solicitor ingeniously suggested it might be a forgery.

The faithful Frank Algar was called to give evidence for Turpin. He told the court, 'He is a very quiet lad and very placid.' Turpin's solicitor then produced a good piece of magistrates' court advocacy, telling the justices, 'A man who earns his living by hitting other people has more control of his force than other people.'

Faced with diametrically opposing evidence, the Bench took the line of least resistance and dismissed the summons. Mary Turpin's claim for maintenance was adjourned *sine die*.[15]

Overall, Turpin had done well in his two court cases. Others who lived in Wathen Road and nearby speak of Mary having a hard time. Bill Mills recalls seeing Turpin chase her across fields at the back of the houses and then watching him escape into the grounds of Warwick Hospital. Mary was pregnant at the time.[16]

[15] Warwick and Warwickshire *District Advertiser*, 13 and 20 August 1948. Turpin later gave his account of the fracas in the *Sunday Pictorial*, 22 April 1962.
[16] Conversation with author.

Back in the ring, Turpin was still distracted by the problems of his marriage when, on 21 September, he lost to the Frenchman Jean Stock, retiring in five rounds after being on the floor four times in the fifth. He was still on the canvas when the round ended and signalled he did not wish to continue. This was a bad defeat and Turpin did not fight again for the rest of the year. *Boxing News* were, 'very much afraid that Randolph Turpin is not going to fulfil all the promise shown in his earlier professional bouts'.[17]

Turpin resumed boxing in February 1949. It was a year of steady, if unspectacular, progress. Only Doug Miller went the eight-round distance with him. The referee stopped the contests against Cyrille Delannoit and Roy Wouters. William Poli was disqualified; Jackie Jones, Mickey Laurent, Jean Wanes and Pete Mead all retired. For his pains, Mead, from Arkansas, had had his ribs broken. That November contest was Turpin's last of the year. He was now earning good money: his purse was nearly £350 from the Delannoit match, and £600 from the Mead contest.

Randolph's series of unbroken victories continued throughout 1950, but this was also the year brother Dick retired. The latter's career came to an end after his third meeting with Albert Finch. It was clear that whilst he was top class, he was not in the very top class, and the difference was showing. He beat Finch readily enough the first time they met, but then in September 1949 he lost in two minutes thirty seconds of the first round to the very talented Australian, Dave Sands. Later in his career, Dick Turpin was knocked out by the Frenchman Marcel Cerdan, who would go on to win the world title. He also had a draw and a loss to Tiberio Mitri.

---

[17] *Boxing News*, 26 September 1948.

It was after that he lost to Albert Finch at Nottingham on 24 July. Dick suffered a cut eye and Finch claimed the win. It was the elder Turpin's fourth defeat against top-class opposition in ten months. Two of these defeats were to Finch. Realising that he would never quite make the very highest grade, and knowing just how much better his younger brother was, Dick retired. The trade paper was pleased that he had called it a day:

> We believe Turpin has been wise. He is not yet 30, but he has had a long innings having been fighting professionally since 1937. He is still one of the cleverest defensive boxers in the country but his lack of aggression in some recent bouts has been disappointing.
>
> Now it is up to brother Randolph to hit the headlines – and as he punches his way to European honours we hope and expect that Dick will be behind him to pass on the guidance and information that he is well qualified to give after his long, meritorious career.[18]

As for Randolph, the year had begun on the undercard when Roberto Proietti retained his European lightweight title in a disappointing bout against Billy Thompson. Randolph boxed Gilbert Stock, the brother of Jean, who had ended Turpin's contests for the previous year. Gilbert was not in the same class as his brother and Turpin won comfortably, taking every round except the sixth against the Frenchman, whose eye was badly cut.

The night before, Jack Solomons had been in Paris at the Palais des Sports to see Robert Villemain outpoint Jean

[18] Ibid., 12 July 1950.

Stock in a gruelling contest. Solomons had hoped to sign one of them to meet Randolph but Villemain wanted to get back to America to finalise details for a contest with Jake La Motta, and Jean Stock simply wanted a rest. Turpin's win came a week after Freddie Mills' defeat by Joey Maxim, and now George Middleton made noises about Turpin moving up to light-heavyweight if Mills stayed in retirement. At least he and Solomons had the sense not to match him with Maxim or indeed, if he had decided to box again, with Mills.

So, instead of a Frenchman, it was off to south London. Turpin might still be down the card, but he was now a name with the public – an exciting boxer with a punch, who could pull in huge crowds. He drew an audience of 4000 when he appeared with his brothers on 6 March 1950 at the Davis Theatre, Croydon and beat Richard Armah. The promoter Bill Goodwin recalls that the police had to clear away hundreds who could not get into the theatre.[19] It was not, however, a good contest. *Boxing News* thought, 'something was missing from Young Randolph's work'. He had hurt Armah with a right but had then been 'indisposed' to use it again. The crowd was slow handclapping by the time Armah retired in the sixth with a cut eye. There was also a small price to pay for the win and it became clear why Randolph was sparring with the right. His proposed bout with the American Baby Day had to be called off because Randolph had injured the knuckles on this hand.

But attracting such crowds meant money, and Randolph was now able to buy himself a house. His friend Mosh

[19] Bill Goodwin, 'Reminiscences', *The Southern Ex-Boxer*, Spring 2003.

Mancini was getting married, with Dick as the best man and Randy organising an arch of boxing gloves. Later Mosh and his new wife Maria went to live with Randolph: 'When we were married boxing didn't bring in much money and we lived in one room at Randolph's,' Maria recalls. 'That was a happy house. 68 Answorth Road that was. We split the cooking and we'd buy the food in turn.

'In the house was Dick and his wife, Randy and his girl and me and Mosh. The kitchen was known as the galley, and Randy liked to be called "the Master" and we all took it in turns to cook. It was like a big family. Then his sister Kath came to live there and Beatrice asked us to take a room with her at 19 Wathen Road. Then Kathy moved out and Randolph asked us back.

'Then, when Randolph earned good money he bought a house at Bridge Close on Bingham Road. He had a bedroom, a studio, a dining room and lounge. Randolph's sparring partner, Eddie Phillips stayed with us. He was a very nice man.'[20]

Over the months, Betty and Jackie Turpin also came to Bridge Close, a mock Tudor house which had once belonged to the local vicar, as did Dick and his wife and a whole host of others. Turpin was still married to Mary, but they had been separated since the 1948 court case and over the years there were, of course, other girls as well. Maria Mancini remembers when they lived at Bridge Close that one woman turned up and said she'd be prepared to sleep in the garage. Randolph gave her his bedroom and he slept in the studio:

Before Gwen [his second wife], he had the most wonderful girlfriend who'd been in the air force. They

---

[20] Conversation with author.

courted for many years. When he started going to Wales
she got jealous and said that unless they got married she
wasn't going on. One day she left the record 'Some
Enchanted Evening' on his bed and left. He never heard
of her again.

The policeman's wife came to Bridge Close. She had
to sleep upstairs with Joan because there was no other
room. You'd be surprised how many came to Bridge Close
and wanted to live there. There were quite a few nurses,
people claimed poverty, they were hard up and wanted
to be married, they'd lost something. They all got something. He had a good heart. He'd help anybody, particularly women.

Turpin liked a joke. One afternoon, George Middleton was
there having tea when Randolph put salt in Maria Mancini's
cup: 'I spat it out straight over his shirt and Randy laughed
so much he fell backwards off his chair. Middleton said, "No
man can knock you out but here's a woman who can knock
you down."'

Generally, Turpin's sense of humour was infantile. One
boxer hired to spar with Dick Turpin recalls that Randolph
enjoyed looking at the penises of others in the gym and
making disparaging remarks about their size. The British
light-heavyweight contender Stan Cullis remembers: 'He was
always on about dicks and cocks. That was the limit of his
humour. He was a physique specialist and he was narcis-
sistic. He'd make the muscle come up in his calf or biceps
and say, "Have you got a muscle like that?"'[21]

In those happier days Turpin was training well and, most

[21] Ibid.

importantly, doing his roadwork. He, Jackie and Mancini went to the gym Monday, Wednesday and Friday nights and Sunday mornings. Randolph had a radiogram and a record of bandleader Billy Cotton calling out, 'Wakey, waaakey.' He'd put it on every Monday to Friday at 6 a.m. and the men would do four miles' roadwork. Then it was home for breakfast cooked by Maria.

But idylls seldom last. Trainer Bill Hyam had told Turpin about Gwyrch Castle and the joys of the north-west coast. It sounded like a great improvement on the glue factory. Turpin went there to train, using the castle as his headquarters. Maria Mancini remembers: 'Then Joan came; Randolph started going to Wales and I began to pay £1 a week rent. When I told Joan I was expecting my second child, she must have said something to Randolph, because he wrote from Wales to say we'd better look for another place.'

She and Mosh lived for a time with Turpin's mother and then: 'I told George Middleton and he said, "Don't worry Maria. I'll buy a little house and you can look after my father." I was so excited. It had no bath, a tiny kitchen and an outside toilet, but it was the first place we had.' Meanwhile, Randolph's sister Joan had moved into Bridge Close. 'Randy would say to Joan that she was to tell him when he was losing it,' remembers Maria. 'He said she'd got to watch out for it, but she never did. Randolph was very, very generous to her. They expected it. They thought it was coming for ever. In turn he thought he'd be looked after. Then, when he got to the top, there was always people coming. More and more people began to see a meal ticket in him.'

On 24 April 1950 Randolph outpointed Gustave Degouve in Nottingham on the night Dick lost his title to Albert Finch. There followed a knockout win over Congolese Eli Elandon in the second round, after which Turpin was matched with Finch for the British title. However, Turpin had disposed of the Congolese man with such ease that it was difficult to assess either his stamina or how the right hand would hold up against the champion. He also complained of chest pains and had an X-ray, which showed nothing out of order.

Randolph and Finch met on 17 October. Revenge for Dick was all the sweeter when Finch was knocked out in the fifth round at Harringay. Finch, thought by some to have had weight troubles, simply could not withstand the power of Turpin's body shots, which admittedly were sometimes only marginally legal. For some, this was a new and very much improved Turpin: 'Finch was overwhelmed by the cyclonic punching of Randolph, who demonstrated qualities seldom associated with this fighter. He was the essence of calmness; he boxed superbly and timed his winning blow with telling effect.'[22]

Some spectators thought in this form and mood Turpin might even have accounted for Don Cockell, who knocked out Mark Hart to win the light-heavyweight title on the same bill. It was a night for more 'bronzed tiger' reporting – Peter Wilson wrote of: 'Turpin, shaven headed, his sleek brown body gleaming, his black gloved fists weaving a deadly pattern of destruction through the smoke scrawl over the ring, looked like some copper-coloured Warrior of the frontier days.'[23]

At the end of the year Turpin was matched with the experienced American Tommy Yaroz, who was disqualified for persistent holding. He had given Turpin trouble for the first five rounds but, when the end came in the eighth, with the American hanging on for dear life, Turpin was well on top.

[22] *Weekly Sporting Review*, 21 October 1950.
[23] *Daily Express*, 25 October 1950.

The win was regarded in some quarters as Randolph's best effort of the year.

By now, however, he was suffering from the same problem that had hampered Mills. The press, if not the public, was wearying of watching him bowl over indifferent foreign opposition. So now there were suggestions that he should meet Alex Buxton, one of three brothers from Watford, in an overweight match which, if Turpin lost, would be followed by one for his title. In reality there were simply no domestic fighters in his league and it was not a contest which had much appeal.

10

Freddie Mills Triumphant

What had Gus Lesnevich been doing with his title all this time? Well, for a start, he had two contests with Billy Fox, a boxer in the hands of gangsters. Lesnevich had first dealt with him in ten one-sided rounds, but after Jake La Motta – another in the hands of the Mob – had thrown an eliminator with Fox, there was a rematch for the title. On 5 March 1948, at Madison Square Garden, Lesnevich knocked Fox out in the first round. Fox simply had no defence to Lesnevich's right-handers and did not score a clean shot in the 118 seconds the bout lasted.

On the back of this slightly dubious pedigree, Lesnevich was now being touted as a future heavyweight contender. If he were to beat Mills decisively, as people expected, he would be matched to meet Louis at Yankee Stadium on 22 September. Officially Louis had retired, but apparently he would come out again to meet Lesnevich.

As for Lesnevich, did this venture into the heavies mean

he was having trouble making the weight at light-heavy? The answer was a definite yes. He had been to the scales five times before making the weight in the second Billy Fox fight.

Meanwhile, by June 1948, the rehabilitation of Freddie Mills was complete. First, he had knocked out Pol Goffaux in four rounds, flooring him five times, to win the European light-heavyweight title. Then he had finally seen off Stephane Olek, who had earlier made Woodcock look so poor, on points. Mills had been comfortably ahead after six rounds, but then had taken matters a trifle easily. At the beginning of 1948 he had been in with Paco Bueno, who put up little opposition in a successful two-round defence of his European title. Then it was back with the big boys and Ken Shaw, in a final eliminator for Woodcock's titles. Shaw suffered a split lip in the first three minutes, which Mills drew to the attention of the referee. Shaw's seconds retired him at the end of the round. Now the way was clear for Mills' and Broadribb's first target – Gus Lesnevich.

Although the betting for the rematch was 4–1 on Lesnevich and the real money going down was on how long Mills would last, *Boxing News*, for one, thought Mills had a chance. The longer the bout went, the better it would be for Mills: 'Undoubtedly the champion will find it hard to make the weight and he has padded the roads for long spells to achieve his purpose,' they commented. The worry was the Marshall fiasco: 'He has the ability and if he can combine this with full confidence and heart he should leave the White City to the cheers that applaud him as "the winner and new champion".'[1]

Lesnevich did indeed have weight trouble. He took off

---

[1] 'Freddie Mills can do it', *Boxing News*, 21 July 1948.

eleven pounds during training, and one and a half hours before the weigh-in he was sweating it out in Hyde Park, taking off the final one and a quarter pounds.

In fact, the bout was not all that dramatic, and in the tenth round both boxers were told by the referee to up their work rate. Mills responded immediately, knocking Lesnevich down for counts of eight and nine. The next four rounds were even. Old newsreel film of Mills show him tearing into opponents, swinging wildly and even using a windmill punch. But, if he put his mind to it, he could actually box, and he did, keeping Lesnevich on the end of a left jab for most of the fifteenth to win the title.

Later, Mills would say that this was the first time he had trained wisely, not tearing into his sparring partners. On the night before the fight he had been up Box Hill at midnight and at 1 a.m. he had been drinking cocoa. He was, he said, completely relaxed.[2]

Now came the honours. In Bournemouth on 5 October, some five hundred people were in the Grand Town Hall to see Mayor J. W. Moore present Mills with an illuminated copy of a resolution, congratulating him on winning the World light-heavyweight title. Before the presentation, there had been a luncheon in a room decorated in Mills' ring colours of black and red, at which the dessert had been a large book made from toffee and cake, inscribed, 'Achievement F. P. Mills'. Afterwards, the Mayor was in teeth-clenching mayoral form: 'It has been my pleasure to have his mother with me today. She is a very charming lady. We have had other members of his family and are pleased to have had that opportunity. You can take it from me that they are a grand example

[2] *Sunday Graphic*, 2 November 1958.

of English family life [Applause] . . . Here is an example of what an English boy can do by determination and hard work.'

Mills was suitably embarrassed: 'This is an outstanding day of my career. I am a very, very nervous man. I had a lot of big words planned but it would not be from the heart and I will forget about them anyway. I am very proud to come to Bournemouth for this presentation. If Bournemouth is proud of me, then I too am proud of the people of Bournemouth.'[3]

There had been plans for a bigger reception to be held in the Pavilion, but Mills had been ill and then had opted for the smaller one, unless arrangements had been made for a charity to benefit. Clearly this did not appeal to the council.

For the moment there were the triumphs, exhibitions, fêtes and presentations. There were also visits to Harley Street. Mills was now suffering dizzy spells, as well as increasingly painful headaches. The diagnosis from the examinations was that he was suffering from problems with his vertebrae and there was a displacement at the base of his skull. The lucrative third match with Lesnevich pencilled in for the September was postponed. In fact *Boxing News* had doubted it would ever take place. The crowd in the cheaper seats had certainly not seen a good contest in July and the paper thought that Solomons would have to put together a strong undercard if he was going to pull in the punters.

After three weeks, Mills claimed his health problems had cleared. But during the period Broadribb had been obliged to deny to the press that there was any suggestion of retirement. The British Boxing Board of Control advised a complete lay-off for two months. *Boxing News* reported, 'Freddie is

---

[3] Bournemouth *Echo*, 6 October 1948.

progressing fast under the treatment he is receiving for his dizzy spells.'[4] The postponed match with Johnny Ralph at Johannesburg's White City Sporting Club was back on the cards.

Whereas Randolph Turpin's sex life had been in the public eye from an early age, Mills was simply another good boxer quietly making his way to the top. There are no stories of his early romances: he simply lived at home and in the booths – women did not seem to enter into his lifestyle. Then, somewhere after 1942, Chrissie, the blonde daughter of Teddy Broadribb and the wife of Don McCorkindale, became his lover. Initially, Mills had lodgings at her home in South London. She moved in with Freddie on 26 June 1947, and divorced her husband in August 1948.

Earlier in the year McCorkindale had brought a petition in Johannesburg for the restitution of conjugal rights and malicious desertion, but it was something of a collusive affair. After all, the previous year they had all toured South Africa together. Christine announced that, once free, she would marry Mills.[5] The wedding took place at the Methodist Church, Half Moon Lane, Herne Hill on 30 September 1948, in what was intended as a quiet affair and was deliberately kept from the press – who had already found out about it.

Once the party were in the church, Broadribb noticed a reporter from the nationals outside. Although they avoided him and a photographer on their way home by using Freddie's smaller car rather than Broadribb's big Austin, the game was up. It was thought unfair that any one paper should have a scoop, and the missing reporters were telephoned and invited to Denmark Hill. There was dinner at Simpson's in the Strand and a visit to the theatre to see the farce *The Happiest Days of Our Lives*. The day was made complete with the announcement that Mills had been made a freeman of the City of London. There was no honeymoon. The wedding was kept from Freddie's mother, who learned the news from a Bournemouth reporter. Chrissie was seven years older than the twenty-nine-year-old Mills, who called her Mummy.

So, with the vertebrae problem supposedly cured, it was back to training, the heavyweights and the triumph of hope over experience. The bout was to be against the South African champion Johnny Ralph, and it was to be another eliminator for the British Empire heavyweight title. The venue was to be Johannesburg. Ralph was a man in whom the South Africans had a good deal of belief. Mills would again be giving away pounds in weight.

Three weeks after the wedding, Broadribb and Mills flew to South Africa. With them in the party was Johnny Williams, the Midlands cruiserweight, who was also managed by Broadribb and was to be Mills' chief sparring partner. As is often the case he would also appear on the bill, boxing Fred Vorster. Broadribb had met Johnny Williams while training Mills for the Marshall fight. Williams was tall and lean, weighed eleven stone three pounds, and history was given another chance to repeat itself. He sparred with Mills, who nearly broke his ribs, but he wanted to go back in the ring with him the next day. Now, with Mills' career not exactly on better than hold, Broadribb started to build the new light heavy up into a real money-earning heavy.

This was not a happy experience for Williams. Just as Farr and so many others had done, he fell out with the often vicious-tongued Broadribb. They had had a set-to previously,

when Williams had fought Don Cockell. The boxer telephoned Broadribb to say that his doctor had told him to pull
out of the fight because he had arthritis in his knuckle joints.
Broadribb had apparently said, 'So you want to cry off? What
does the doctor know about fighting?' and had slammed
down the telephone. Williams went through with the contest
and was outpointed over eight rounds. Now the idea was
that Williams would be left behind in South Africa to build
Mills up into a true heavyweight.

After a few days in the country, Williams developed a
heavy cold. Standing by was the faithful Don McCorkindale,
who was staying with the party at the Langham Hotel helping
with the training. This continuing close relationship between
Christine's ex and current husband led to speculation that
Don, rather than Chrissie, was the object of Freddie's affections.[6] McCorkindale found some penicillin tablets for
Williams, who developed a reaction to them. The pair were
apparently sharing a room – something which perhaps tends
to undercut the McCorkindale–Mills claim – and the night
before the contest Williams woke his roommate to say that
he couldn't sleep and that he was itching all over. By the
morning of 6 November his eyes were swollen and his skin
reddened. Broadribb was informed and took matters in his
own hands, telling Williams to bathe his eyes and keep out
of the way. He would arrange that the boxer did not need
to attend the weigh-in. Williams went through with the
contest, winning on points over eight rounds. Immediately
afterwards he was diagnosed as suffering from penicillin
poisoning and was sent to hospital, where he remained for
nearly a week.[7]

[6] Tony Van den Bergh, *Who Killed Freddie Mills?*, p. 68.
[7] Jack Birtley, *Freddie Mills*, pp. 145–6.

Mills' time in South Africa was happier. He spent some of his time there presenting an act in cinemas. It was a tried-and-tested routine for champions: he would shadow box, answer questions and, in his case, sing 'When Irish Eyes are Smiling'.

As far as the fight itself was concerned, the Rand *Daily Mail* thought Ralph might win if he could avoid an early big punch. But on this occasion hope and talent did prevail over weight. The relatively inexperienced Ralph was not in the top class, and on a cold, blustery night, Mills knocked him out in eight rounds before a crowd of 24,000 at Johannesburg's Wembley Stadium. Ralph took five counts in the sixth round alone. Yet again Mills displayed the sportsmanship he had shown against Shaw. This time, when Ralph had slipped he helped him up and back to his corner to have the soles of his boots resined. Ralph's management, however, was not so impressed by Mills' behaviour. They claimed their man had been finally felled by a rabbit punch.

With one notable exception, after the contest the boxing correspondents were ecstatic. The dissenter amongst their ranks was Peter Wilson, who regarded the fight as a mismatch and pointed out that, apart from the second match with Lesnevich who was, it was generally accepted, on the decline, the post-war light-heavyweight opponents Mills had defeated hadn't been up to much. And nor had some of the heavyweights.

After the contest there was a disagreeable incident. Mills had been invited to repeat his stage act in Cape Town, and he flew there from Johannesburg. His friend Denis Compton was playing for the MCC against Cape Province and invited Mills, Broadribb, McCorkindale and two locals to the England dressing room. The way was barred by a gatekeeper, who told the party they could not come in. Later Walter Mars, the president of the Western Province Club, said: 'I have no objection to professional boxers as a class. But I had only to take one look at Mills and his party to realise they were not the type we desire to mix with our members.' Mills later met with Mars, who offered what was described by Peter Wilson as a 'half apology'. The writer added: 'When a man in Mr Mars' position makes a remark as revoltingly snobbish as that, he does the grossest possible disservice to cricket in particular, sport in general and his country specifically. Mills is not only a world champion but the first gentleman of the ring and about the finest sporting ambassador we've sent from England for years.'

The Rand *Daily Mail* treated it all rather lightly. Mills and his friends would have had to pass through the Members' Bar on the way to the England dressing room, and as they were not accompanied by a member they were not allowed. It was as simple as that. In fact it occurred a second time when the party was obliged to have tea on the boundary.[8]

The incident did nothing but good for Mills' act. He played to packed houses and Johnny Williams, now out of hospital, joined him. When Mills returned to England he found he had been voted Sportsman of the Year by the *Sporting World* readers and was runner-up to Denis Compton in the *Sporting Record*'s similar poll.

And what had happened to Bruce Woodcock after Baksi had broken his jaw? There had been a suggestion – denied – that he was retiring. Now the Board indicated he would have to defend his heavyweight title against Mills. Although Woodcock had kept his hand in with a series of exhibitions,

[8] Rand *Daily Mail*, 6, 8 and 9 November 1948.

there would have to be a warm-up, probably against an American.

That American was Lee Oma, a man with a slightly dodgy reputation. His real name was Frank C. Zjewski and he had taken his *nom de ring* from the lorries of the Omaha Truck Company. Back in 1943, he had been suspended after being knocked out by Panther Williams in the first round of their contest. On the plus side, he had beaten Mauriello, Baksi and Lesnevich and had only narrowly lost to Jersey Joe Walcott. Regarded as an experienced and able man, but one who didn't carry a punch, he was thought by now to be well on his way down. He seemed ideal as the man to rehabilitate Woodcock, particularly as some of his evenings were spent in Murray's Club, an underground night spot off Beak Street, the haunt of louche businessmen and hostesses – those siren temptresses whose aim was to divide a man from his wallet. In later years both Christine Keeler and Mandy Rice-Davies would work there early in their respective careers.

Woodcock fought Oma on 21 September 1948. For several rounds, neither man threw a punch, with Oma feinting and Woodcock flinching. Oma was now running out of what energy he had ever had. Woodcock hit him on the shoulder and Oma was counted out. Solomons was not pleased, nevertheless, when he went into the dressing room to find Oma with blood coming from his ear. It was thought there had been damage to a mastoid. Solomons took him to Charing Cross Hospital and, he recalled, the ear was still bleeding when Oma was returned to New York.

Tony Van den Bergh, the Board's ringside inspector, remembered things rather differently. He wrote that he saw no blood coming from Oma's ear: 'As we closed the dressing room door, Oma did a back-flip in the air and said, "Back to Murray's Club tonight, eh?"[9]

The newspapers thought the whole thing stank. 'Oma-aroma', wrote Peter Wilson. One completely unsubstantiated rumour was that Oma had been paid £5000 to throw the fight in the fourth round. There would clearly have to be another warm-up. There was no real hurry. There was no indoor arena which could seat even half the number of the White City, and the Mills–Woodcock fight was always slated for the June show the next year.

Boxing News, for one, was not keen on Woodcock's next opponent, in a contest which matched him with Lee Savold in December. They could not understand why Tom Hurst, Woodcock's manager, had accepted the match. Savold's qualities and capabilities had to be taken on trust. The writer thought that the Doncaster man should be boxing some home-grown talent, but that rather begged the question, who? As with Mills in the light-heavy department, there really wasn't anyone who could realistically expect to give Woodcock anything much more than a gym workout. Savold had been around for some years. He had a decision over Baksi, followed by two losses back in 1944. In 1942 he had lost to Tami Mauriello. More recently, his record had been a good one, with a number of knockouts, although over whom was the question. He had twice lost to the unheralded Phil Muscato.

And he lost to Woodcock that December. He had already been warned about a low punch, and when he knocked Woodcock down again with a patently low blow, he was disqualified. It had not, however, been quite the way people

[9]   Jack Solomons, *Jack Solomons Tells All*, p. 137; Tony Van den Bergh, *Who Killed Freddie Mills?*, p. 70.

expected the match to go. Initially *Boxing News* liked Woodcock, championing his style over the swings of the rough and ready Mills, but in recent years its writers had generally become highly critical of him. There were certainly no medals for him after the Savold contest. The paper thought that Savold looked the likely winner. Woodcock may have been ahead on points, but the American was ominously walking through his left-hand punches. It was probable that Woodcock would have been beaten inside the distance. 'We regret to say it but he appears to have gone a long way back,' reported the paper.[10]

Boxing News thought that if Mills kept his form, he should be a firm favourite against Woodcock. However, Johnny Ralph was one thing, but Woodcock was another. Unless Woodcock had deteriorated very badly, there was never any clear reason why Mills should beat him if there was a rematch. Mills was once again going to have to give away weight in lumps. Nevertheless it was a big pay night for everyone concerned, and it would go ahead.

In the meantime, Woodcock went to South Africa and defeated Johnny Ralph. After his own fight with Ralph, Mills had suggested that Woodcock come to England and learn from the old pros, such as Reddington and Robinson. The reasoning was that he would not be damaged by them, but if he went to America he might well be badly hurt. The man's handlers would have nothing of it, pointing out that Ralph had already beaten Ken Shaw. They wanted people to come to him, and Woodcock duly obliged.

Mills was back in South Africa and had intended to watch the Woodcock fight, but Chrissie was taken ill and had to go

[10] *Boxing News*, 15 December 1948.

into hospital in Cape Town, where she underwent an operation to remove her appendix. Mills listened to the match on
the radio and cannot have been overly encouraged by what he
heard. On 26 March Woodcock took only three rounds to
knock out the South African, where Mills had taken eight.

Still, Mills thought that he had the beating of Woodcock:
'It's just something I'm superstitious about . . . I'm making
it my banker for a very good reason.' His reasoning was that
this was going to be in the open air. Mills had lost to both
Lesnevich and Woodcock indoors at Harringay. He had beaten
Lesnevich outdoors at the White City. He would, therefore,
beat Woodcock. He reckoned that as Woodcock would be
defending his three titles, the Doncaster man would have a
heavy psychological load to bear. If Mills lost, he would still
have his light-heavyweight title.[11]

His sparring partners in Surrey were Johnny Williams, Alf
Robinson and Ken Shaw, to whom Mills had behaved so
gallantly when they met. Helping out was Scamp the dog,
who joined all the training runs. Mills was immensely
popular; people slowed their cars to help pace him, and
cyclists pedalled beside him.

The second contest against Woodcock took place before
a crowd of 46,000. As was proper for someone writing in
the same newspaper as Mills, Jimmy Wilde refused to tip
Woodcock as the winner. At the weigh-in Mills, whose share
of the purse was £15,000, was found to be conceding twenty
pounds in weight, but it did not appear to faze him. He and
his trainer Nat Seller joined together to sing, 'There's No
Business Like Fight Business', a parody of the song from the
hit musical *Annie Get Your Gun*. Mills' ironic version was:

[11] *Empire News*, 27 March 1949.

> There's no bizness like the fight bizness
> They smile when they're hit low
> All the managers are such schemers
> Twenty-five per cent is all they know
> Managers go on for blinkin' ever
> But where, oh where, do fighters go?

During the bout itself, once again Mills absorbed tremendous punishment from the cleaner punching, hard-hitting and heavier Woodcock. He was counted out on the canvas holding his left ear in the fourteenth round. He had been so dreadfully beaten that over the next twenty-four hours there were rumours, both in England and abroad, that he had actually died. He was not dead, but he had certainly gone off his food. A number of Woodcock's blows had landed on Mills' neck and he was unable to eat more than bread and milk for two days.[12]

Wilde was disappointed. He thought that if Mills had used his straight left, he would have won. For his part Mills said he believed Woodcock could kick Savold in any rematch.[13]

Afterwards, Mills' headaches and dizzy spells increased. He could be seen sitting in a corner, away from the rest of the company, pressing his fingers into his eyes 'and grimacing with the excruciating pain'.[14] There was, however, no thought of retirement by his manager or promoter. As the rest of the year passed, Broadribb and Solomons began to concentrate on a lucrative defence of Mills' light-heavyweight world title against Joey Maxim.

---

[12] Freddie Mills, 'My Greatest Fights', *Sunday Graphic*, 30 November 1958. The pair actually boxed an exhibition at Harringay on 4 December 1951. *Boxing News* thought that Woodcock looked in better condition but, as usual, Mills took it out of himself and knew about it at the end.

[13] *Empire News*, 5 June 1949.

[14] Jack Birtley, *Freddie Mills*, p. 151.

11

Freddie Mills Meets
a Machine-Gun

Mills' first defence of his light-heavyweight title was against Giuseppe Antonio Berardinelli, whose manager, 'Doc' Jack Kearns, renamed him Joey Maxim, after likening his left jabs to the shots from a machine-gun. Maxim took up boxing at the age of twelve and turned professional in 1941, winning ten of his first eleven contests. Then came a slight hiccup. In July 1942 he beat Curtis Sheppard, 'The Hatchet Man', on points over ten rounds, but then was knocked out in one round by him in March the following year. Sheppard had bounded from his corner at the bell and had knocked him down almost before Maxim was off his stool. Later that month Maxim gained his revenge with another ten-round points win but now, on no more evidence, his chin was seen as suspect. He then beat the Swede Olle Tandberg over ten rounds at Madison Square Garden. Tandberg had beaten Woodcock in

Manchester when the British champion had temporarily lost his appetite for training and he had caused something of a sensation by outpointing Joe Baksi in Stockholm. (Though, at the time Baksi had been visiting the European fleshpots.) Maxim quickly exposed Tandberg's limitations. Then he beat Jersey Joe Walcott in Camden, New Jersey, but lost their next two meetings, both on points and both narrowly. Most recently, he had outscored and outsmarted the ageing Gus Lesnevich to win the United States' light-heavyweight title.

Maxim was regarded as being fast, clever and elusive, and with an educated left hand. But he was the reverse of Mills – a boxer rather than a brawler. He had a long scar over his right eye, which was thought to make him susceptible to a left hook. Nor was he thought to be keen on taking body punches. There was certainly no consensus of opinion that Mills would beat Maxim, although *Boxing News* rather thought that he should. Mills might hold on to his title by outfighting Maxim, but if the bout lasted the full fifteen rounds he might find himself outscored. The warning was clearly written. If Mills were to lose, he would find himself out of the hunt for any future world title bouts. Tom Phillips of the *Daily Mirror* thought it would be a tough fight, with youth and speed favouring Maxim, who would probably win on points. The great Ted 'Kid' Lewis thought, 'Joey's very good, too good for Freddie. I'm certain he'll stop him inside the distance.' Appropriately, Broadribb thought Mills was better than when he beat Lesnevich. Ominously, Phillips asked Tom Hurst, Woodcock's manager, how long a fighter thought he was on top of the world. Hurst replied, 'Right until the moment he retires from the ring for the last time.'[1]

---

[1] Tom Phillips, 'A tough fight', *Daily Mirror*, 24 January 1950.

The Times opted for a mixture of praise and doubt: 'Every boxer has his ups and downs but it takes a Mills to accept the punishment handed out to him over the years and yet never, even in apparently conclusive defeat, to lose either his popularity or confident readiness for "another go".' The boxing correspondent thought that Mills' prospects were not so good as the first time he fought Lesnevich, reflecting it was dangerous that: 'Mills had been unable to lay an effective glove on the jaw or body of Bruce Woodcock, a one-paced boxer always liable to be thrown out of a stride and made to flounder.'[2]

Before all this, however, there were protracted negotiations to organise the fight. Broadribb knew that Mills was coming to the end of his career and that one more payday was needed. But the level of his taxation was an issue. If Mills fought again in 1949 he would receive shillings in the pound for his efforts. Meanwhile, the Americans were displeased that he had held the title for over a year without defending it: there were a number of challengers queuing up and no promotion means no money for anyone. Broadribb tried to arrange a flexible payment over five years if Mills defended, but the Inland Revenue did not regard this as acceptable. He then tried to sell Mills' contract to an American promoter. The best offer he received was £1250. Then the National Boxing Association passed a resolution that Mills should be stripped if he did not defend within ninety days. In the nick of time, Solomons arranged an Earl's Court promotion, for 24 January 1950.

Maxim trained at Jack Solomons' gym in Great Windmill Street, but some said it had not been hard training. Doc

Kearns, who had always been known to bring 'a good 'un' when he came to England said, perhaps with a bit of games-manship, that his man had been ready to fight the moment he stepped off the boat.

Then came an unusual incident. Mills sacked the long-serving Nat Seller and decided to train himself, helped by his friend and masseur Frank Duffet. This was a surprise to everyone, and he soon changed his mind and reinstated Seller. After that slight hitch, Mills was reportedly training well in the country air at the Barley Mow, Betchworth, near Box Hill in Surrey, 'wading into his sparring partners with characteristic gusto and going through his training routine with joviality and zest'.[3] Percy Burnham, the licensee, cleared out his public bar and erected a ring and some scaffolding to take a heavy punchbag and ball. Mills did his roadwork on the cricket pitch opposite and the days passed.

All was not, however, as well as it seemed. The heavy-weight Nosher Powell, although then still an amateur, was a sparring partner for Maxim: 'As far as I understood, Maxim was a non-puncher, but he hit me on the chin a couple of times and it hurt. I thought there was a con going on so I said to Nat Seller, Freddie's trainer, "Who says this guy can't punch?" But Seller was confident. He said Freddie would go right through him.'[4]

In the fight itself, in the first three rounds Mills caught Maxim with left hooks, and in the third round gave him no rest. For a time it looked as though all the British hopes would be realised, but then in the fourth Maxim started to use his left jab. At the beginning of the fifth, Mills launched another attack and, for a moment, it seemed Maxim might be battered down. But suddenly he hooked Mills, who was left on the ropes for longer than he should have been. 'An unsuitable breather,' said *The Times* euphemistically. The sixth was even, but in the seventh, although Maxim took some hard body punches, he was outscoring Mills, who was now missing with his right hand and was being punished for the misses. Maxim had suffered a cut under the left eye in the early rounds but, although it bled throughout the fight, it was no real trouble.

But there was trouble in the eighth and ninth for Mills, when Maxim opened up considerably. By the end of the ninth he was jolting Mills with short-arm punches to the jaw and now he was ahead on points. Throughout the fight he had only been in serious trouble on a couple of occasions, but he had never lost his composure or his speed. Mills, however, was losing teeth, which were being pulled out by Seller with his fingers in the interval between the sixth and seventh rounds, and again later, when a tooth became imbedded in the gum.

The end came in the tenth. Mills sank down thoroughly exhausted and although he made a tremendous effort to get up, he could not summon the spirit or the strength to do so. He collapsed and, in a half-kneeling position propped up by his arms, he was counted out.[5]

'He was too tired and dazed to get up,' said *The Times*.[6] *Boxing News* thought the result was a surprise to the majority, but not to ringsiders. Maxim had only been seriously troubled once or twice, and each time he had recovered quickly and had not lost his speed. The *Weekly Sporting Review* wondered: 'Why didn't Freddie Mills box? Why did he adopt

[5] *Boxing News*, 1 February 1950.
[6] *The Times*, 25 January 1950.

an obvious all-in policy of sheer aggressiveness. Why did he swing so wildly? Why did he concentrate on sheer brawn in an attempt to wear his rival down? Against Gus Lesnevich, from whom he took the world title in 1948, Freddie revealed exceptional boxing qualities. He won the championship by boxing for it; he lost the title by fighting for it.'[7]

Ring thought that only in the first two rounds was Freddie dangerous. 'It was a case of a clever boxer outwitting a fighter in every department except courage.' *Ring* accepted there was always the danger of one big swing landing, but as the bout progressed the chance became more and more remote. Never again could it be said that Maxim's punches couldn't dent an egg.[8]

After the fight, Maxim was presented with a British Boxing Board of Control trophy 'emblematic of the world's title'. The paper commented wryly that Mills had waited eighteen months to be presented with his.

Mills himself thought that he had nearly had Maxim in each of the first two rounds, but he had been badly caught in the third, possibly through over-confidence. From then on he had fought half in a daze and knew he was taking some hard punishment. He could not remember the last three rounds at all.

After the bout he was sick in the dressing room. He had already been sick before the fight, and he told reporter Peter Wilson he had never been the same after the first Lesnevich fight. Mills also told the press, 'Since my first Lesnevich fight a punch on a certain spot on my chin seems to give me mental paralysis.'[9]

[7] *Weekly Sporting Review Annual Edition*, 1951.
[8] *Ring*, April 1950.
[9] *Daily Mirror*, 28 January 1950.

It is traditional that after a major contest the winner visits the loser in his dressing room. When Maxim arrived, Mills told him he had lost three teeth. Maxim assured him his own front bridge work had been cracked. It would be a race to the dentist's chair, he said courteously, if mendaciously.

Back home Mills stayed up talking with his friends. He said he had never been as thirsty after a fight, and he was probably seriously dehydrated. He drank half a dozen glasses of beer and half a dozen cups of tea. At 3 a.m. he went to bed.

But, before the visit to the dentist, Mills' future was discussed at the breakfast table. Broadribb told him that he was no longer prepared to manage him, saying that if Mills wanted to continue, he would release him from his contract. He added: 'Freddie, I think you should call it a day. When Nature begins to give out on you there is nothing you can do about it.'[10]

But Mills recalled a different version of events. He remembers talking things over with Broadribb for a couple of days and then, one morning when his breakfast was brought up to his bed, reading in the papers an announcement of his retirement. He went round to see Broadribb, who lived a couple of streets away, to tell him that in fact he wanted a return with Maxim, but his father-in-law 'smiled gently at me so I said, "Well, it's in the papers now, so it's perhaps just as well".'[11] Broadribb had already told journalists, 'What is the use and why kid ourselves? Freddie could make a ton of money by fighting Maxim for the title again but he would have no chance of winning.' Some weeks later Mills himself went to see Solomons to ask for a return. The promoter replied, 'You're retired now Freddie, leave it that way.'[12]

[10] Ted Broadribb, *Fighting is My Life*, p. 122.
[11] Freddie Mills, *Twenty Years*, p. 201.
[12] *News of the World*, 20 January 1950; *Sunday Graphic*, 26 October 1958.

Shortly after the contest, both Mills and Maxim appeared at a charity event for the British Professional Boxers' Association at the old Saville Theatre, with Mills singing his 'No Business like Fight Business'. There had been talk of Maxim remaining in Europe to undertake a series of bouts, but three days after the contest, Mills was at Waterloo Station to see his rival take the train to Southampton. Whilst at the station Mills was seen by Sir Winston Churchill, who spoke to him, patting him on the shoulder and shaking his hand.

Don Cockell was now promoted as Mills' light-heavyweight successor, and the British Boxing Board of Control was, for the umpteenth time, facing the wrath of its members. The cause on this occasion was the sudden disappearance of the long-serving General Secretary, Charles Donmall, and the arrival of his replacement. The chairman, the old Etonian J. Onslow Fane, was at his suavest and most masterly at the special general meeting. The stewards did not have to give explanations to anybody about these events, and they certainly were not going to do so. The ship was perfectly seaworthy, said Fane: 'You can rely on us not picking a fool or a knave or anybody likely to be distasteful to you gentlemen or those you represent.'[13] The man picked was certainly neither a fool nor a knave. He was the former referee E. J. 'Teddy' Waltham.[14]

As for the reason for Donmall's disappearance, he had been sacked; it was that simple. He had fallen out with Jack Solomons – 'Mr Maul' himself – who had led a delegation

[13] *Boxing News*, 11 January 1950; 11 February 1950.
[14] Waltham was only the second of five general secretaries to the Board. He was succeeded by Ray Clarke, on whose retirement John Morris was appointed. On his retirement Simon Block, the current incumbent, filled the vacancy.

of licence holders at a private meeting with Fane. Donmall had been with the Board from before its reconstitution in 1929, initially working *pro bono*, and asking only £1 for rent, heating and lighting and the use of a secretary, who would be paid out of the £1. Over the years, as the Board had grown in size and wealth, things had been put on a more formal basis. Then one meeting Donmall was there, and the next he had gone and there was an acting Secretary in his place.

Ray Clarke, who had joined the Board in 1946, recalls the infighting over the appointment:

Solomons and his friends ganged up on Donmall, who was a bit of a dictator. A good Secretary, tough, but he got on to people the wrong way. He was a bit of a bully. Eventually Solomons told Onslow Fane that if the Board didn't get rid of Donmall there would be a vote of no confidence at the next AGM. Charlie was told, 'You're out,' and he went.

A sports writer was given the job, at least verbally, but then at the last minute Jack Solomons proposed that Teddy Waltham, the Star referee, would fit the bill. Teddy was interviewed and took the job. He came round the offices and was surprised to see me. He asked what I thought and I said he shouldn't take it. Solomons had suggested that I take the job temporarily and see how I got on but I refused. If I'd done what Solomons told me I'd have been the General Secretary twenty years earlier. Waltham was the General Secretary from 1950 to 1972.[15]

---

[15] Conversation with author.

As far as boxing was concerned, Donmall was now effectively a non-person. There is no tribute to him in the Board's minutes, certainly no gold watch. The only note about him after his sacking is that he received £1200 in lieu of a year's notice. And some even wondered what he had done to deserve a pay-off.[16]

So who was Waltham? There was no doubt he knew the game. He had boxed himself and had also been the referee who had raised Mills' hand after the second Lesnevich contest.

'Waltham would never have got the job if he hadn't been a bit pally with Solomons. He was a good secretary in many ways. He'd been in charge of the RAF boxing team and so he held a commission. He could meet people and chat. Waltham and I worked at the North Met Power Company in Southgate before and after the war,' remembers Ray Clarke. 'He was in the wages department. Our office was known as the sweet shop. People came in to buy bars of chocolate before the war. I used to play tennis and cricket with him.'[17] It was Waltham who dealt with the sometimes recalcitrant Randolph Turpin throughout most of the latter's career.

As for Woodcock, he did not last the year. He was rematched with Savold in a final eliminator for the vacant world title, or the world title itself, if you believed the British Boxing Board of Control. It ought to have been the latter, but the now financially pressed Joe Louis had come out of retirement and was still the undefeated champion. Louis had nominated Ezzard Charles to meet him, rather than Savold.

Woodcock was originally scheduled to meet Savold for the second time in September 1949. Ever the showman, Leslie

---

[16] 'The Mighty Donmall Goes', *Weekly Sporting Review Annual Edition*, 1951.
[17] Conversation with author.

T. Salts, who would become Turpin's *soi-disant* business manager and nemesis, had two rings erected at his Gwyrch Castle near Llandudno. The first was outdoors, so that Woodcock could acclimatise himself to boxing in the open air, and the second indoors, a precaution against bad weather. Salts had bought the castle in 1948 and it is likely, but has never been fully established, that in his heyday Turpin took some share in it.

A month before the contest, Woodcock was driving to the training camp when he went to sleep at the wheel of his lorry and went down a steep bank. Woodcock had been doing exhibitions up and down the country with Matty Hardy and his regular sparring partner Ted Greenslade: he saw these not only as a way to earn money but also of getting really useful workouts in the ring. He had done shows in Bournemouth and Carlisle and had driven back to Doncaster after each of them. He was now due to go to north Wales to finish off his training. He had not gone more than a couple of miles when he crashed. Greenslade was uninjured, but Woodcock was told to take several days in bed. The fight was postponed, first until the spring and then until 6 June at the White City. Meanwhile, he was stripped of his European title.

Now the sniping began. He had been beaten by Mauriello and Baksi; Oma had been a phoney fight and he'd been lucky to beat Savold; he was afraid of Savold. Poor Woodcock was bedevilled throughout his life by tawdry and unsubstantiated allegations. There had been the Thornton episode, and before the contest with Jack London there were stories circulating that he was to be 5-2 on for the title and London would knock him out in the eighth.

Of the upcoming Savold contest Frank Butler wrote: 'Bruce

Woodcock faces two opponents – Lee Savold and Bruce Woodcock. He must first win the psychological battle of Bruce v Bruce to have any chance of success. As I can't hope to read Woodcock's mind, I must stand by class and pick Savold to win decisively.'[18]

He was right. Savold defeated Woodcock: the Doncaster man was stopped in the fourth round with a badly cut eye. Woodcock claimed that it was an accidental blow from Savold's elbow.

Things moved forward. On 27 September 1950 Ezzard Charles comprehensively defeated Louis at Yankee Stadium. Meanwhile Jack Gardner, the up-and-coming Leicester guardsman who had beaten Broadribb's protégé Johnny Williams in an eliminating contest, was now matched with Woodcock for the British title. Woodcock was regarded as too able, with too big a punch for the younger man. Amazingly, there was still talk of Woodcock being given a chance with Charles when, rather than if, he beat Gardner. He did not. On 14 November 1950 Woodcock, giving away five years in age, a stone in weight, and six inches in reach, was beaten by a British opponent for the first time in eight years, when Gardner stopped him on another cut-eye decision in ten rounds.

On the same bill Johnny Williams, still under the Broadribb management, won what was described as a 'David and Goliath contest' against the fifteen stone eight pounds Nisse Andersson.

Woodcock, who had been badly beaten, called it a day. Jack Solomons told him there were plenty of good fights left in him; the promoter's idea was that he should go in with

[18] *News of the World*, 4 June 1950.

Savold for a third time. But Woodcock had effectively been a one-eyed fighter since the beating by Baksi, something which had escaped the doctors. Now Gardner had shut his other one. He had had thirty-eight professional fights, and he retired a relatively wealthy man, according to his memoirs. He wanted, he said, to buy a smallholding – not to work it, but as a place for his children to keep animals.

So now Gardner became the new 'Great White Hope', the next in the line of pie-in-the-sky dreams. Already, however, there were worries he would be overmatched and rushed along: 'We don't want another Woodcock story – the sacrifice of splendid material on the altar of impatience. We know a great deal depends on Jack himself, but the heaviest responsibility lies with John Simpson [his manager] and Jack Solomons and we shall hold them to it.'[19]

Boxing News could have substituted 'Mills' for 'Woodcock', and 'Broadribb' for 'Simpson'.

[19] *Boxing News*, 14 March 1951.

12

Randolph Turpin Tastes Sugar

1951 started well for Turpin, and for nine months continued well for him. In the January he won the *Boxing News* readers' poll as the fighter who had done most for British boxing in 1950, polling over 2000 votes more than his nearest rival, Jack Gardner.

Throughout the first few months, the trade paper was cagey about Turpin's opponents. It was thought the Spaniard Eduardo Lopez might, in good journalese, 'cast a blight on Turpin's progress'. The Spanish Boxing Commission had refused to allow Anton Soldevilla to box Turpin, and Lopez, who had beaten Soldevilla, was thought to be a boxer to be reckoned with. On 22 January it was, as *Boxing News* reported, the Spaniard who was blighted. Turpin took fifty-eight seconds, including the count, to dispose of him. Turpin went straight home. He was, he said, suffering the aftermath of flu and had been in bed the previous weekend.

The former flyweight champion, Jimmy Wilde, whilst supportive of Turpin, was not blind to reality. Deploring the European champions from Europe who turned up and were dispatched in minutes, he accepted that an accident could happen and a boxer get caught cold but, 'A champion shouldn't be k.o.'d in the first round. He is supposed to have a fighting brain and instinct.'[1]

Then it was the turn of the rugged Dutchman, Luc van Dam. Wilde thought that Turpin was not at his best against 'a man who refuses to play by offering a vital part to hit'. Van Dam would be a test, thought the trade paper. He wasn't. On 27 February Turpin, pre-dating current fashion with his head shaved at the sides and back, knocked him out in forty-eight seconds. Manager and trainer Dennie Mancini, who saw the contest, thought that this was perhaps the best Turpin ever boxed.

There followed a two-round knockout of Billy Brown in Leicester on 16 April, then, on 7 May, a six-round knockout of Jan de Bruin, although the Dutchman had knocked Turpin down.

Now Turpin was regarded as a serious contender for Sugar Ray Robinson's World middleweight title. The only stumbling block was the Australian Dave Sands, and there was talk of a final eliminator between the pair. In 1949 Sands had won the middleweight Empire title from Dick Turpin, but then he had left Britain and had fought only a few meaningless bouts over the next year. Now it was thought he could be ordered to defend his title. Meanwhile, if that little problem could be overcome, Turpin was expected to fight the winner of Robinson and La Motta. The winner was Robinson.

[1] Jimmy Wilde, 'Bar these Ten a Penny Champions', *Empire News*, 28 January 1951.

Walker Smith, as Sugar Ray had been born, arrived in France on 2 May 1951, getting up at dawn to catch his first glimpse of the coast of Europe. He had become Ray Robinson after he attended an amateur tournament when he was too young to hold a licence. The promoter threw over to him the licence of the real and unknown Ray Robinson saying, 'Hey, kid, you use this for tonight.' Later Robinson added the Sugar. 'He's a sweet fighter, as sweet as sugar', said a woman spectator, or so the story goes. At the time he was regarded as possibly the best pound-for-pound fighter in the world.

Initially there was talk that Robinson would come to London to face Ernie Roderick, something which was quickly knocked on the head when the British boxer was heavily punished by Robert Villemain in Paris in February 1947. Badly cut, Roderick failed to come up for the tenth round. In the event Robinson would not travel to Europe for four years.

Prior to the 1951 trip, he had defeated Holly Minns on points over ten rounds, and on 10 April in his long-running 'bum a fortnight', he had knocked out Don Ellis in the first round in Oklahoma. Four days after his arrival in France he commenced what passed for training, interrupted by a reception for him and his entourage, hosted by the American ambassador. He also attended the unveiling of a plaque to the great French middleweight Marcel Cerdan at the Palais des Sports, and presented to Madame Auriol, the wife of the French President, a cheque for four million francs on behalf of the Damon Runyon Cancer Fund. The American papers were shocked to learn that she, a white woman, should have embraced a Negro.[2]

He was shown a list of candidates from whom he could

[2] See Nat Fleischer, 'Sugar Ray in New Role, the Idol of Gay Paree', *Ring*, August 1951.

choose his next opponents. They included Kid Marcel, stopped on 21 May in five rounds in Paris (after which Robinson gave his entire purse to the Runyon charity), and Jean Wanes, defeated on points in Zurich five days later. Then came Jan de Bruin, who was stopped in eight rounds in Amsterdam on 10 June, followed six days later by a knockout of Jean Walzack in Liège. These were little more than exhibitions.

By the time Robinson fought Turpin he had lost only once in 127 contests. The contest with Gerhard Hecht on 24 June in which he was disqualified for kidney punching did not count. There had been rioting at the ringside after the decision, and within a matter of hours the Boxing Commission had changed the decision to one of no contest. This was a problem Robinson was going to have to face: European and British referees were by no means as tolerant of kidney punching as were their American brothers, where it was legal, provided the blow was neither delivered in a clinch nor was the boxer holding on with an arm or glove.

On 1 July Robinson knocked out Cyrille Delannoit in three rounds in Turin. Subsequently, the proposed contest in Milan with Livo Minelli was banned by the Italian Federation of Boxing.

In his contests with Kid Marcel, Jean Warnes and Jan de Bruin, it was evident Robinson could have put his man away anytime he cared to, but his aim, as he explained it before the bouts, was not to show up the European champions by knocking them out, but to give the fans a chance to see him in action as long as he felt he was not in danger.[3]

On 4 June, Jack Solomons announced that he hoped to stage a contest with Turpin against Robinson. He had originally been looking to promote Turpin against Dave Sands, but the Australian would not sign the contract. London had not been on the schedule of the great man's European tour, but money was money and perhaps he could be tempted over. His manager George Gainsford came to London the next day and things were soon settled. The venue would be the Earl's Court arena; the date 10 July. That left almost two months for partying and nightclubbing in Paris, something at which Robinson was well practised. Had he sneaked into London on 5 June and sat at the back of the hall to watch Turpin dispose of Jackie Keogh in seven? No, said Robinson, but it was all part of the hype. Not that hype was really needed. Earl's Court could only hold 17,000 and within days there were applications for 51,000 tickets.

Despite demolishing Keogh, was Turpin really ready for Robinson? T. F. G. Jones of Uttoxeter was horrified:

> May I take this opportunity of deploring the matching of our middleweight champion Randolph Turpin with Sugar Ray Robinson. At the moment he is little more than a novice and has never been called upon to travel the full distance of 15 rounds.
>
> Randy is altogether too young and inexperienced to fight this superman . . . why should we pin our hopes on a possible knock-out victory (for this is the only way he can hope to win), when in a year's time he should be a much improved fighter?[4]

Mr Jones was certainly correct in one respect: Turpin had never gone more than eight rounds. As for the more general

---

[4] Letter in *Boxing News*, 4 July 1951.

misgivings, there were indeed many who thought Turpin was being overmatched. But a title shot is a title shot is a title shot.

It was true, as well, that Britain had a great tradition in middleweights. Jock McAvoy had grown too heavy before he could have had his deserved shot at the title. Tommy Milligan had the misfortune to run into Mickey Walker at the peak of his career. Ted Moore had fought the almost as talented Harry Greb (Berg spelled backwards); Frank Moody and Jack Hood were two more highly talented British middleweights. Overall, British boxing at this time had some real contenders. There was Jack Gardner, Don Cockell, then a light-heavyweight, and welterweight Eddie Thomas. In August 1951 *Ring* rated Eddie Thomas seventh amongst the welter-weights; Cockell four; Gardner not at all and Turpin as number one contender for Robinson's crown.

'But the most sensational . . . is middleweight Randy Turpin,' proclaimed *Ring*. 'Still by a twist of fate he must be accorded the slimmest chance of winning the title in his class. This is only because the present title holder happens to be the greatest fighter in the world today.'[5]

There was cause for cautious optimism. After all, hadn't Turpin just destroyed Luc van Dam, rated by Robinson as the best he had met on his continental tour in the winter of 1950–1. 'Turpin is a youngster who started out believing that the only necessary requirement for ring success is a wallop. Following losses to former British champ Albert Finch and [Jean] Stock he discovered that such was not the case and that some kind of defence was needed in a hurry. Under the tutelage of brother Dick, a better than fair middleweight himself and a former British champion, he's learned his lessons well.'[6]

[5] Ted Carroll, 'British Prestige Booms,' *Ring*, July 1951.
[6] Ibid.

Robinson installed himself and his entourage at Windsor. 'Bang Bang' Webber was his sparring partner, and commented, 'Ray's a gentleman and it's a pleasure being hit by him.' There was also 'a dwarf in a blue T-vest and size-2 dapper crêpe soled shoes', as well as a French chauffeur. The dwarf's role in life was to tell jokes and, as part of the circus, to sit on top of the punch ball when Robinson worked on it. Robinson was, thought the writer Damon Runyon, 'a very smart duck'.[7]

Nat Fleischer thought that Robinson was in condition. Jack Solomons, keen to talk up a good fight, thought, after seeing the champion against Kid Marcel, that Turpin would knock him out. Fleischer did not: 'I've seen Turpin three times and he has yet to impress me as the great fighter the British think they have in him. He can sock with the best of 'em but so can Sugar.'[8]

Frank Butler, then with the *News of the World*, was certainly in Turpin's corner: 'If I were Randolph Turpin due for the toughest fight of my life against Ray Robinson at London's Earl's Court on Tuesday, I would resent being boxing's Forgotten Man. Here I am one of the few Englishmen good enough to battle for the world's middleweight crown, and I feel like a prophet without honour among my own people. So let us give Turpin a fair crack of the whip. We shouldn't count him out before he climbs in the ring.'[9]

Later, Freddie Mills wrote that shortly before the fight he had lunch with Turpin and 'spotted the confidence in our champion. For him the other guy was only human; he had a jaw and a body to punch and Randy was going to do it.'[10]

---

[7] *The Times*, 11 July 1951.
[8] Nat Fleischer, 'Sugar Ray in New Role, the Idol of Gay Paree', *Ring*, August 1951.
[9] Frank Butler, *News of the World*, 8 July 1951.
[10] Freddie Mills, *Battling for a Title*, p. 74.

Eddie Phillips, a welterweight from Edinburgh, had been Turpin's chief sparring partner for some time: 'He was hard with his sparring partners. It was just like a real fight. There was no mercy shown and he had no preferences. It was "You're here to do a job." He was a real hitter and he taught me a lot about defence.'[11]

'After two years of sparring with Turpin he decked me for the one and only time while preparing for the Robinson fight. In fact, I remember Randolph being quite excited by that. He said he'd been doing his best to knock me down for months so he reckoned he must have been in good shape for the bout.' Six months later Phillips elaborated: 'Randolph had finally put me down while sparring in one of our last sessions before the Robinson fight. I remember he whooped and said to me "I must have a chance against Robinson now."'[12]

In fact he had more than a chance. Robinson had not been training properly and in the hours before the fight there was sudden money for Turpin. It is a measure of the fashion of the day that, at the ringside, Robinson's wife Edna May and her sister wore fur stoles and hats with half veils. Turpin arrived more modestly. He came on a train from Leamington, weighed in, could not find a hotel at which to rest, and so had to go with his brothers to the cinema, before taking the underground to Earl's Court. Len Harvey had told Turpin at the *Boxing News* annual luncheon: 'I see no reason why you cannot beat this Robinson. Remember he's only the same as you. He's no superman. He's two arms, two legs and a pair of fists. So have you. Just get in there and let him know who's the boss and you'll win the world's title.'[13]

[11] Conversation with author, 30 June 2003.
[12] Edinburgh *Evening News*, 20 January and 11 July 2001.
[13] *Boxing News*, 10 July 1951.

This is exactly what he did. He came out fast and won four of the first five rounds. From then he rarely looked back. To dispel any lingering doubt, he took rounds twelve, thirteen and fourteen as well. *Boxing News* thought he had won nine of the fifteen rounds. It was a stunning display.

By the final round the crowd knew Turpin was clearly ahead and they were going wild, Amazingly, however, the vastly experienced commentator Barrington Dalby had Robinson well in front. There was a tendency in those days to make sure that the radio audience thought something was happening in every second of the round. Of course this was scarcely ever the case. In most boxing matches there are periods of inactivity. Dalby, anxious to give the audience a rousing commentary, picked Robinson as the champion but, blind in his favour, picked the wrong man. Robinson's left eyebrow needed eight stitches after the fight. When Turpin's hand was raised, the crowd began to sing 'For he's a jolly good fellow' and, it is said, King George VI left a dinner party to hear the result. Barrington Dalby had his knuckles rapped over the commentary.

Ring was not happy with Robinson's performance at Earl's Court. Nat Fleischer wrote: 'Had he fought against La Motta as he did against Turpin he would not have gone 10 rounds. He left his fight in France where social engagements, golf, night entertainments and long hops by car to engage in exhibitions and bouts had taken their toll . . . . I cannot conceive Robinson again being as bad as he was in the London fight.'[14]

Fortunately for Robinson there was the then customary rematch clause in his contract, and he would next fight Turpin in New York, but this time Robinson would be in full training.

[14] Nat Fleischer, 'Highly Trained Robinson Would Beat Turpin in New York', *Ring*, October 1951.

According to booth fighter Harry Legge, Turpin was at a fair at Aldershot the night after the Robinson contest. Surrounded by admirers, he made his way to the almost deserted boxing booth and offered to referee the next contest to pull in the crowd.[15] At the weekend Turpin was back boxing in Mickey Kiely's booth. He had agreed to appear and he honoured his agreement. It may seem incredible that the world champion should appear at a booth, but this was something he really liked. Now £20 was offered to anyone who could stand up for three rounds with him. No one could.

Turpin went back to north Wales, where the local councillors met him and Leslie T. Salts at the railway station. Turpin was now firmly under the influence of Birkenhead-born Salts – artist, councillor, chorister, shrewd if unscrupulous businessman and antiquary. Later, Salts acquired the title of 'Count', and liked to be addressed as such. He was also quite content to be referred to as a millionaire. Turpin's return and the beneficial publicity he attracted for the town was, said the local paper, thanks to the generosity of Salts. Turpin had regularly eaten in Minnie Wright's Rendez-Vous Café in Rhyl whilst he had been training in north Wales, and there was a grand reception for him there, again attended by council members. The local paper was rather miffed that it had not been told until it was all over. That would have been both good copy and more publicity for the town.[16] Already the vultures were circling and taking random pecks.

On 12 July Turpin travelled to the Midlands for a civic reception. First, there was a motor parade with Turpin in an open-air car sandwiched between the mayors of Leamington and

[15] Harry Legge, *Penny a Punch*.
[16] *Rhyl Journal*, 19 July 1951.

Warwick, in the latter instance the Earl of Warwick. At Clarendon Road they were joined by the band of the local sea cadets. Outside the town hall, Randolph Jnr, then aged three, had a bunch of cerise sweet peas for his father. It would be one of the few times the boy would see him, now that his parents were separated. A Vampire jet did a victory roll. If Mills had been obliged to endure patronising speeches by the gentry, it was nothing to those suffered by Turpin on the balcony of the town hall. The local paper, pulling its forelock, wrote: 'With a smile and a happy air of informality, Lord Warwick quietened the crowd with a wave of his mayoral hat and explained that the "poor champion" had been working all afternoon – "perhaps not harder than on Tuesday night". (Cheers).'

And with Turpin getting more cheers for his, 'Well you realise what I mean to say in my own language' in reply.[17]

The illuminated scroll commissioned by the Council was not ready and would be presented in September or, if Turpin was not back from America, then in October. In the evening the Mayor of Leamington gave a dinner party to celebrate the victory, over which Lord Willoughby de Broke presided at the Manor House Hotel. The management presented a large iced cake with two boxers in the ring in their corners, and with the two nations' flags.

Turpin was by now a major celebrity. He modestly attributed his win to his sparring partner Mel Brown. He had, he said, learned more in sparring twenty rounds with Brown than in all his previous fights. No, he had not bet on himself, even at the attractive odds on offer. This was Turpin's far, fierce hour and sweet.

A possibly unhelpful, if well-meaning, piece of interference

---

[17] Warwick and Warwickshire *District Advertiser*, 13 July 1951.

came when the Mayor of Leamington tried to effect a reconciliation between Turpin and his wife, who acknowledged
each other in the street, but no more. Telephone calls were
made to invite her to the mayor's home, where she was given
a glass of sherry. Turpin promised to call when next down
from Wales. In the end, nothing came of it.[18]

Within days, Turpin was back in training for his rematch
and the popular press was naturally interested in how things
were going. Turpin said he had a lot of fun with the animals
at Pets' Corner at Gwyrch Castle. He liked knife-throwing
and archery – 'I've got my own set at home' – going to the
pictures, listening to the gramophone and reading. 'Nothing
highbrow, you see – as a matter of fact I've just been reading
Tarzan.'

Turpin also liked reading about Robinson's famous car and
his 'circus'. 'To me all that only seems a shocking waste of
money, but if he likes to spend it it's his affair.' Turpin had
opened the display of boxing trophies and gloves on display
at Gwyrch Castle, some of them bought from pawn shops
and others sold by their owners. He was disapproving of
their extravagances in parting with their trophies: 'Those
fellows didn't realise it was their day. This is my day and I
must make the most of it.'[19]

W. Capel Kirby suggested Turpin should earn around
£80,000 in the next two years. He was, however, not so
sanguine about the rematch, and went on to predict Robinson
would win in twelve.[20] Jimmy Wilde was playing the part of
Cassandra. Recalling that Tommy Milligan had been stopped
in ten by Mickey Walker, he wrote, 'Can Turpin improve on

[18] *Reynolds News*, 29 July 1951.
[19] *Empire News*, 8 July 1951.
[20] Ibid., 29 July 1951.

that against the man most people rate higher than Walker? I doubt it – very strongly.'[21]

Training was very much a local affair. Turpin could be seen doing his roadwork on the A55, and before the sessions started the Penmaenmaws Silver Band entertained the crowd. He was hard on his sparring partners and knocked out two heavyweights whilst wearing sixteen-ounce gloves. His much lighter brother Jackie was there for speed, and after a continual battering he put on a pair of knickers, bra and lipstick and scrawled, 'Please don't punch hard here' on his body. The crowd was delighted and this became a regular feature of the open sessions. The rounds spent sparring with Mel Brown were more serious, and Brown did his best to eliminate what he saw as a flaw in Turpin's style: his one-punch complex.

Salts, who perhaps had control of his protégé because he made him feel like a champion, and who was another of Turpin's expensive nemeses, was in charge of the photography. There was a large picture of Turpin in the local paper extolling the castle's amenities – the monkey house, the aquarium, dancing to the Hammond organ and so forth. Special buses were available from Abergele station. But then the council put a block on the whole thing. Amazingly, Turpin was told he would be in breach of planning permission if he sparred. He could only skip and train. Salts appealed but the council meeting was not until 20 August whilst Turpin was due to sail on the fifteenth.

Nevertheless, thousands of visitors had their picture taken with the champion. This was not, of course, merely to swell the Salts coffers, although it no doubt did that handily. It

[21] Ibid., 8 July 1951.

was, so Salts said, to develop Turpin's crowd consciousness. Salts was also in charge of the gate, charging spectators a shilling each to come and see Turpin's workouts, with children at half price. There was no question of the money going to Turpin, or to charity. It went to Salts. In return he lodged, fed and watered the boxers. 'They were our guests,' he said in a television film on Turpin's life. It was estimated that at any one time, 10–15,000 people came to see Turpin work, but Salts was keen to point out that whilst he would rather have had Turpin than not, the castle had already attracted up to 28,000 visitors on one day.[22]

W. Capel Kirby found the champion no different from the pre-champion: a quiet chap, beloved by all the staff for his simple tastes, friendliness and unassuming demeanour. Unlike so many boxers, there was no trouble getting him out of bed. He was always up early doing his breathing exercises on the battlement overlooking the Irish Sea. He was a stickler for personal hygiene and would brush his teeth six times a day.[23] All in all Turpin was, as racehorse trainers say of their winning charges, 'Kind as a Christian.'

There were, however, distractions. It was not always early to bed, there were commitments to be honoured. On 25 July he boxed an exhibition in Portsmouth on a bill topped by brother Jackie against Teddy Peckham. Turpin's brother-in-law, Michael Stack, was also on display, boxing Bos Murphy, whom Dick Turpin had beaten for the British Empire title.

There were also women. Elizabeth Finn, the daughter of a Rhyl hotel manager, recalls meeting Turpin at the railway station: 'I was seventeen at the time. I'd missed the train and was in the buffet. He was with Jackie and Eddie Phillips. I

[22] *64 Day Hero*.
[23] *Empire News*, 22 July 1951.

went out with him but he wasn't very interesting, I preferred Eddie Phillips and I went out with him more. If you're meant to be training for a world fight and you're meant to be focused on only that, he certainly wasn't. I remember being with Eddie, going into Randy's bedroom at the castle and he was still in bed holding court. I sat on the edge of the bed. He had at least one other girlfriend apart from me.'[24]

Even before the council intervened, there was also a bit of a worry about one of Turpin's ears, which had temporarily halted sparring, and had produced a news blackout from Gwyrch. It was nothing really, reported W. Capel Kirby: 'The damage was apparently superficial, nothing that could not be put right by a little supervised blood-letting to ease a slight swelling.'[25]

There were now discussions as to who would make up the Turpin party when it sailed. Naturally George Middleton and Leslie T. Salts along with their wives and daughters and possibly Minnie Wright from the Rendez-Vous Café would travel. There would be no question of anyone tampering with Randy's food. She would do the cooking if she could get a plane ticket.

With his ear lanced, Turpin left for New York on 15 August on the *Queen Mary*. Turpin did not take Williams or Mel Brown with him: apparently there were financial questions to be resolved with Brown.

Before Turpin sailed there was a reception for him at the Lockheed Ballroom in Leamington where, as three buglers from the Royal Warwickshire Regiment sounded a fanfare, he was presented with a silver salver and rose bowl. Jack Solomons was there, along with Prince Ras Monolulu, the racing tipster who, in full feathers, bounded on to the dais

---

[24] Conversation with author, 9 April 2003.
[25] *Empire News*, 5 August 1951.

to give his predictable selection. The jockey Gordon Richards, who had been riding at Birmingham that day, sent a whip as a token 'from one champion to another'. Wishing Turpin well, Alderman R. R. Davidson made something of a sanctimonious speech: 'We should be above undue partisanship and willing to acclaim the winner with enthusiasm. Whatever the outcome of the fight I sincerely trust that the occasion will prove to be one more bond to cement the friendship between our two great nations.'

The entertainment ended with dancing and a cabaret. Dick Turpin was not at the gathering and there were rumours that things were not well between the brothers.

Mel Brown, who had lost to Dave Sands in a supporting contest on the Turpin–Robinson bill at Earl's Court, had offered advice to Turpin and his camp even before the first bout: there were fixers in America. He himself had been offered money to take a dive against Robinson. He had refused, and the match had never come off. The claim, unsurprisingly, was hotly denied by the Robinson management. Brown also feared that the water bucket and better still the water bottle might be contaminated with drugs. Then if the boxer were to lick his sponge in turn he would be contaminated. He would box badly, have another lick at the end of the next round and would be in a downward spiral to defeat. Another trick was putting a liniment pill in the last meal the boxer had before the contest. This would produce a dry, burning sensation which would only be aggravated by water.[26] It is difficult to know whether Brown was being paranoid or if his fears were justified, but certainly they would have played on Turpin's mind. And his concerns cannot have

[26] 'I warn Turpin: watch the fixers,' Mel Brown, *Empire News*, 22 June 1951.

been eased when he attended a party given by a local sportsman the night before Turpin sailed. Tommy Farr is said to have taken Turpin into a private room and warned him that the Mafia would try to introduce a woman into the camp who would interfere with his training. The woman would be on the *Queen Mary* and Turpin should be on his guard against any such siren.

The next day Turpin, dressed in a blue suit and wearing a black beret, was given a civic send-off by the Leamington council. Jimmy Wilde was sorry he wasn't taking either Williams or Mel Brown with him. On the voyage over, Turpin did irregular workouts, on Saturday 18 August knocking down the Tottenham heavyweight Danny Sewell to general satisfaction. There were worries, however, that he was being brought along too quickly. There were also fears that he had left England later than he should. New York was going to be a big surprise to someone who had previously never been further than Paris.

Turpin evidently had not listened to Tommy Farr's advice about the siren call of women, Mafia-connected or not. Almost at once he encountered two well-dressed women. The younger of the pair, Adele Daniels, has, over the years, been variously described as a showgirl and a clerk. Whichever is true, she was certainly good looking. The brothers were invited to a breakfast party and, in Dick Turpin's words, 'It went on from there.' George Middleton thought she seemed 'a very nice person'.

After landing, Turpin trained at Grossingers', a leisure complex owned by the eponymous Harry and Jean in the Catskill Mountains, 150 miles from New York. Spectators at his workouts were charged a dollar admission, in aid of the Damon Runyon Cancer Fund for Cancer Research and the

Sunshine Homes for Blind Babies, the latter nominated by Turpin.[27]

It was not an ideal training camp. There were far too many distractions in the form of celebrities and women, and there were continuing worries about Turpin's programme. It was quite apparent that, however good Jackie Turpin and Eddie Phillips might be, they were insufficient to give him the required work. More worrying, there was an edge on him, something unusual in a fighter not yet in peak condition. It had been raining and Turpin, who had learned to play Lotto on the boat, kept himself amused. Thankfully, soon there came some good news for the Turpin camp: the financial squabble had been resolved and once Mel Brown had fought Duggie Miller in Birmingham he would come to New York. Meanwhile, Robinson was giving his senior sparring partners, Dave Green and Baby Day, a hard time at their training camp at Pompton Lakes. He was not going to make the same mistake twice.

A Sunday newspaper reported, 'Turpin looks terrific.'[28] But rumours were filtering back to England that things were not going well at all. There were stories that he was holding, or at least attending, wild parties; that he was drinking into the early hours; and that he had been seen in nightclubs. These were denied, as far as possible. Yes, he had been in a nightclub, but only once. No, the person seen drinking was brother Dick. There were continuing suggestions that the brothers were becoming increasingly estranged, and allegations about a deterioration in Turpin's relationship with Middleton. Publicity pictures were released of Turpin playing table tennis to improve his hand–eye co-ordination; of his trying his hand at softball, but none of the shopping trips into town, which

---

[27] In November 1951, Turpin handed over a cheque for £233 to his charity.
[28] *Empire News*, 26 August 1951.

were covers for his visits to Adele Daniels. The estranged
Mary Turpin sent a telegram wishing Randy luck. In return
he sent back a message to his son, 'I wish I could have you
over here. Look after your Mummy.'[29]

In England the hype was wound up with enthralling stories
about Turpin's relatives in British Guiana. His uncle Adolphus
did not hear of his nephew's win over Robinson for some
time; he had been prospecting for gold in the Potaro River
at the time of the triumph. Uncle John Leslie had known
Turpin would win and his only disappointment had been
that the boy had failed to knock out Robinson. This time it
would be done in eight rounds, he predicted.

On 11 September two 'Turpin Special' flights full of
supporters flew to New York via Prestwick. The first was
inauspiciously late taking off. Amongst its fifty-five fans,
mainly from Manchester and Birmingham, a number were
stopped by Customs, and excess currency was confiscated
before they were allowed to board.[30]

The match took place at the Polo Grounds, the home of
the then New York Giants, on 12 September 1951. At the
weigh-in Dr Samuel Swetnick, who examined Turpin, was
reported as saying, 'I have never seen a boxer in finer condition. He was very calm and not the type to become excited.'[31]

There was, however, a small cloud over the contest. Over
the years there had been a number of fatalities in professional and amateur rings in America and at the end of August
George Flores had died in a contest at the Garden, after being
knocked out in forty-six seconds of the final round by Roger
Donoghue. Contrastingly at the time, according to Teddy

[29] *Warwick and Warwickshire District Advertiser*, 14 September 1951.
[30] *The Times*, 12 September 1951.
[31] *Empire News*, 9 September 1951.

Waltham, there had been only two fatalities in the English ring since the war. In 1946 Alex Murphy died following a bout with Emile Famechon, and in 1948 Mickey Marley died after his contest with Jim Stimpson. Poor Bert Veale apparently did not count. Teddy Waltham attributed it to a virtually foolproof system of medical examination.

As for the fight itself, Peter Wilson thought it wasn't great. There was a great deal of mauling and some slow handclapping from the crowd. *Boxing News* thought Robinson had shaded the first round. The third was even, but Turpin clearly won the fourth, making Robinson miss and landing some heavy punches. The next three were even, and Robinson won the eighth. Possibly Turpin was ahead by the ninth, which he won clearly. Robinson came away from a clinch with a badly cut eye and was happy to hold and keep out of more trouble for the rest of the round. The consensus of opinion is that Robinson's eyes would cause a stoppage sooner rather than later, and so it was something of a last-ditch effort when Turpin was knocked down with a lightning right. He had been hurt earlier in the round, and had managed to hang on. This time he was knocked down and for a moment lay, starfish-like on the canvas. He pulled himself together to beat the count but Robinson moved in for the kill. With Turpin trapped on the ropes and shipping all sorts of punishment, from straight blows to rabbit and kidney punches, the referee stopped the contest.

From outside the ring, particularly since the critic is not the one taking the shellacking, it is easy to question a boxer's decision, but many thought Turpin should have taken a count to give himself a rest. It is also easy to criticise a referee, and some thought that, with the death of Flores in his mind,

Goldstein panicked.[32] Just as there had been in the first Mills–Lesnevich fight, there was criticism that he had stopped the contest prematurely, particularly since there had only been eight seconds to go in the round. Under American rules, the referee could have begun the count when a boxer was holding the ropes or resting helplessly against them. Now it was suggested that the referee had erred on the side of caution.

Back in England, Teddy Waltham supported the referee: 'It was proper. I would have done the same. Randy was defenceless. Too bad it had to be that way, but the referee did the correct thing.'[33]

Fleischer was not impressed with Turpin: 'For those who had been accustomed to seeing British boxers demonstrate cleverness, science and strict adherence to the rules of ring technique, Turpin was a disappointment.'[34] Nevertheless, it was certain there would be a third meeting.[35]

Later, Robinson would say that he thought Turpin had got up too soon from the knockdown. He should have taken a longer count and had a breather.[36]

As for Turpin himself, he said he thought he could have won, had he been allowed to continue. Years later, his brother Jackie wrote that he had said in the dressing room, 'A champ is entitled to die in the ring before they take his title.'[37]

Now the recriminations started. Harold Mayes wrote, 'I had always maintained that Turpin's victory had been just one of those boxing accidents. Robinson has probably gone

[32] *Daily Mirror*, 14 September 1951; *Boxing News*, 19 September 1951.

[33] Nat Fleischer, 'Robinson King Again!', *Ring*, October 1951.

[34] *Ring*, October 1951.

[35] Daniel M. Daniels, 'Randy-Ray Set for Third', *Ring*, November 1951.

[36] Sugar Ray Robinson, 'Turpin's Error Cost Him the Title', *Empire News*, 25 January 1953.

[37] Fred Burcombe, 'King Randy by His Brother Jackie', *News of the World*, 28 July 1991.

over the hill. I know that even he won't doubt that.'
Nevertheless, he added there was a 75 per cent chance
Robinson could still beat most of the middleweights. He
thought Turpin had been foolish to stick to the ninety-day
return clause. As the champion, he could have ducked and
dived and stalled until it suited him. Too many people had
told Turpin that Robinson was no better than he was in
London. An American trainer should have been brought in
for the last four days. Maurice Seamon, 'Whitey' Bimstein
and Ray Arcel were all available and $500 would have secured
their services. On the night Turpin's corner men had looked
clumsy. They had been late getting his stool in at the end of
the round and had been uncertain when to push him out
for the next round.[38]

There were also stories of parties thrown in adjoining rooms
to keep Turpin awake, but these may have just been echoes
of the complaints that Robinson made of his pre-weigh-in
night in London.[39] There have also been persistent suggestions that Turpin, afraid of the power of the Mafia, had indeed
thrown the fight. The story, as told by Clark Mellor, who
worked as a wrestler with Turpin, was that Randolph had told
him the night before the fight that a man dressed in a striped
suit, black shirt and white tie had threatened Turpin, saying
there would be four men dressed like him at the ringside and
Turpin would not leave the arena alive if he won.[40] Orig
Williams, who promoted Turpin both as a boxer and a wrestler
in his last years, says, 'I often asked him [about whether he

---

[38] *Empire News*, 16 September 1951.
[39] He complained he had been kept up with the yelling of customers and the
pounding of their glasses on the bar as well as strains of the juke box. (Jack
Birtley, *The Tragedy of Randolph Turpin*, p.47.)
[40] Orig Williams in conversation with author. The story was repeated in *Randolph
Turpin* by Eryri Productions, 2001.

had dropped the fight] because he was so far ahead at the time, but he always denied it.'[41] Looking at the footage of the ninth round, it is difficult to see how Turpin could have thrown the fight. The beating he took looks far too real.

Despite such talk, Turpin was still a huge celebrity in Britain, and could look to a half-million-dollar gate against Rocky Graziano, or a lucrative match with the still absent Dave Sands.

In the meantime, it was on to a series of exhibitions with Dick, with whom things had apparently been patched up, and a stint on the music halls. This had been arranged before Randolph had left for America, and he was said to be on a weekly four-figure sum. Asked by a reporter what he was going to do on the stage, he replied he was going to scrub it. In fact, in his week in October at the Trocadero in Elephant and Castle, he topped the bill over the Beverley Sisters, sparring and boxing with Jackie and Mosh Mancini. *The Times* saw him as a 'diminutive light-brown figure' and seemed to have been most impressed with Reco the Clown. In Glasgow, Turpin appeared with such acts as Betty Driver, the Peterson brothers and Rob Murray. In Liverpool, one of his chief supporting acts was Victor Julian and His Pets. The local paper thought that whilst it was impossible not to like Turpin, for non-boxing enthusiasts it was a bit boring and it would have been better if some of the local middleweights had taken up his offer to spar with them. The paper particularly liked one of the supporting acts, Woods and Jarrett, who 'set feet tapping with their dusky rhythm'.[42]

In his act, Turpin once more shadow boxed, gave a display

[41] Conversation with author.
[42] *The Times*, 23 October 1951; Liverpool *Echo*, 20 November 1951; *Birmingham Mail*, 2 November 1951; *The Times*, 2 November 1951.

on the bag and the punch ball, and boxed a few rounds with brother Jackie and with Eddie Phillips. 'Even those less interested in the sport can appreciate his lissom agility as he goes through the gamut of training,' enthused *The Stage*. Birmingham boys were more lively than Liverpudlians, however, and a week at the Birmingham Hippodrome nearly ended in tragedy. In the second house on the Thursday night, Francis Zibea, one of the local boys who took up the challenge to box Turpin in sixteen-ounce training gloves, stepped out of the ring in the second round and collapsed. At first it was thought that he had fractured a bone at the base of his neck, but then it was suspected he might have damaged a nerve. Other one-night stands followed at Moss Empires, including a November Saturday at the Winter Gardens, Morecambe. But then it was the pantomime season and the tour was over.[43]

As for opponents, Ron Pudney was the Southern Area champion and there were vague thoughts of matching him with Turpin. Mismatching would have been the word. There was also a suggestion that Solomons would put Turpin in with Charles Humez, the Lion of Flanders, at Earl's Court in March 1952.

---

[43] *The Stage*, 15, 22 November 1951; *The Visitor*, 13 December 1951.

13

Randolph Turpin
Meets a Lion

1952 began with the suggestion that Turpin should move up to light-heavyweight. A match had been spoken of for some time, against twenty-six-year-old Alex Buxton, the most talented of the Watford family of boxers. He had won 62 of his 75 contests, 42 of his wins coming inside the distance. His pedigree might not have been top class but it was certainly good enough for a match to sell to the ever-gullible public. Buxton had boxed Dave Sands twice in Australia, both times losing on points. He had also knocked out Jimmy Davis – as had Turpin five years earlier – and had scored a points win over the well-thought-of South African, George Angelo.

Buxton and Turpin were matched at Harringay on 12 February, in the first of what would be a series of three contests between them. Possibly with the idea of revving up interest, *Boxing News* wrote that Turpin would have to be on his very best form to win. It might even be that whoever landed the first good punch would take the other out.[1]

The fight itself proved that displays in theatres and exhibitions around the country are no substitute for serious training. Turpin looked dreadful. Buxton caught him around the ears far too often and the crowd was jeering and stamping by the time the referee Jack Hart stopped the contest in the seventh round, after Buxton sustained a bad cut over his left eye from an accidental clash in the first. *Boxing News* felt sorry for both men. Buxton for the cut and Turpin because he had been so awful. Although it was early in the year the paper thought it might be a leading contender for the Most Disappointing Fight of the Year award. Turpin accepted, 'I didn't know my left from my right. I tried too hard.'[2] Nevertheless, the exhibitions continued.

Old friends were still in the background. In March, Sugar Ray Robinson disposed of Carl Olson. Robinson was now being talked about as the next challenger to Joey Maxim for the light-heavyweight title. With it the dream of Robinson's rubber match with Turpin faded. In the labyrinthine world of boxing politics there were, however, still possibilities. If Sugar Ray were to beat Maxim, he would probably immediately retire undefeated. Turpin would then be a logical contender for either the middleweight or the light-heavyweight crown. But, if Robinson lost to Maxim, he might give Turpin another shot. All that, however, would be far in the future.

In the meantime, Turpin signed to box another British 'Great White Hope' of the period, Don Cockell, who had finally put an end to the run of Lloyd Marshall over British boxers, knocking him out in one round. He had also beaten Albert Yvel and the Turpin brothers' old opponent, Albert

[1] *Boxing News*, 6 February 1952.
[2] 'Turpin Too Bad to be True', *Boxing News*, 20 February 1952.

Finch, in seven. Unfortunately, he had then been stopped by another American, Jimmy Slade, in December 1951. With the defeat, out of the window had gone the quite serious talk of a match with Joey Maxim. Now rehabilitation, if not redemption, might come in the form of a win over Turpin.

This was an attractive-looking match for Solomons' White City promotion. On the line were Cockell's British and Empire titles against a blown-up middleweight, albeit a former world champion. Throughout his career, Cockell had had weight trouble, and he had boxed Slade weighing twelve stone twelve. The Board of Control, whilst approving the Turpin contest, ordered Cockell to have an interim contest, with the proviso that he must make twelve stone ten.

Meanwhile, Turpin was scheduled to box Renato Tontini. In fact, it was Cockell who went in with the Italian champion in the end. Tontini was injured before his contest with Turpin and Jacques Hairabedian, the Frenchman, took his place. Now something of the pre-Robinson Turpin, in his most masterful form, knocked his opponent out in three rounds. As for Cockell, he went in with Tontini and although he won, he was rather worse than he had been against Jimmy Slade.

Turpin v Cockell on 10 June quickly became something of a massacre. By the fifth, Turpin was grinning at the crowd as he drove Cockell around the ring with a series of dazzling combination punches. He knocked him down in the third, and again in the eleventh, this time for a count of six and another of nine. He then caught Cockell again, at which point referee Tommy Little saved the Londoner with a minute and fifty seconds left of the round.

It was a vintage Turpin performance. He now held four titles; two at middleweight and two at light-heavyweight and, under the Board of Control's rules, he was going to have to make up his mind which he would keep. But not quite yet. George Middleton announced Turpin was going on a cruise to forget about boxing, but in the back of everyone's mind was still the possibility of a third match with Robinson.

Sugar Ray was attempting to box at light-heavyweight, and on 25 June 1951, when the temperature reached 104 degrees and the tarmac on the roads melted, so too did Robinson, who failed to come out for the fourteenth round against the heavier and stronger Joey Maxim. He was not the only retiree that night. The original referee Ruby Goldstein collapsed, also suffering from exhaustion, and was replaced by Ray Miller at the beginning of the eleventh. Robinson was now also pursuing a temporary, very successful career, as a song and dance man on the vaudeville circuit and there was pressure on the great man to make up his mind whether the stage or the ring was to hold his future. Later Robinson would say he rather wished he had retired immediately after regaining his title from Turpin.

Later in the year, on 21 October, Turpin took the British Empire middleweight title, defeating George Angelo on points over fifteen tedious rounds. It was said of the South African that he would have won the Back-Pedalling Championship.

In December, Sugar Ray finally announced his retirement and Turpin gave up his light-heavyweight titles. In future he would box as a middleweight. Once more he was a world championship contender for the title Robinson had left vacant.

Freddie Mills, meanwhile, was apparently promoting successfully at the Empress Hall, London, Bristol and Southampton. Certainly he was having a bit of luck. Despite the fact that he was five days outside the time limit for submitting a purse offer for the final lightweight eliminator between Tommy Barnham and Frank Johnson, and the fact that his purse offer was £200 shy of the one submitted within the time limit by Pioneer Sports, he was successful in his bid.

It is said that the middleweight division has had something of a jinx attached to it. Back in 1895 the 'Nonpareil', Jack Dempsey, died from tuberculosis at the age of thirty-three. Later, Stan Ketchel was shot and Billy Pepke committed suicide. Les Darcy died at the age of twenty-one from, it was said, a broken heart. Harry Greb, 'The Human Windmill', died in Atlantic City on 22 October 1926 following an operation on his nose, and the next year Theodore 'Tiger' Flowers, who had taken the title from him and successfully defended it, died after an operation on his eyes on 17 November in New York.[3] Eddie McGoorty died at the age of forty in 1929, and Marcel Cerdan died in an air crash in 1949. The most recent victim of the 'curse' was the Australian Dave Sands, who had died in a road accident in 1951.

The retirement of Sugar Ray Robinson in 1952 left the middleweight division in something of a state. There were a number of rival claimants to the title. It was not the first time there had been chaos in the division. In 1910, when Stan Ketchel had been shot and killed on a Missouri ranch, it had taken three years to sort out the contenders.[4] Finally Frank

---

[3] For an account of the Greb–Flowers contest, see Charles Lesemann, 'Harry Greb, The Human Windmill', *Boxing News*, 16 April 1954.

[4] Ketchel began his career in Butte, Montana, taking on the local champion Kid Tracey and knocking him out in the first round for a purse of $50. In all he won 59 out of his 63 fights, 49 of them by knockout. Towards the end of his career, he fought Jack Johnson, even though he was to be outweighed by forty pounds. Johnson refused to train and Ketchel lasted until the twelfth round, but the beating he took ruined his health. He went to Conway, Missouri to stay on a friend's ranch and there became involved with one of the cooks, Goldie Smith, who was also seeing a Walter A. Kurtz, a deserter from the navy. Kurtz apparently accepted the love triangle for a time, but finally one morning he came into the dining room, where Ketchel had his back to the door, and ordered him to put up his hands. When Ketchel refused, Kurtz shot him in the back. Kurtz was sentenced to life imprisonment and was released in 1934.

Klaus beat Billy Pepke on a disqualification in Paris on 5 March 1913. It was thought that Pepke, realising he was being beaten, had deliberately fouled Klaus. Things had gone smoothly until, in 1931, the champion Mickey Walker decided to give up the title and concentrate on heavier divisions. From then on over the next decade, there was a proliferation of champions supported by rival organisations until, on 28 November 1941, Tony Zale defeated George Abrams on points at Madison Square Garden. Order was once again restored.

Now, in 1953, as the man who had defeated Sugar Ray Robinson, it was accepted that Turpin was a very real contender. It was proposed that he should fight the rugged and durable Charles Humez, the Lion of Flanders. The Americans, however, had their own agenda, wanting to see their own men get a crack at the title. They would not recognise the winner of Turpin v Humez as world champion. It had a good deal to do with the purse. The world champion could claim 60 per cent for a defence, successful or not. It had also a good deal more to do with promoting and refereeing. First, the Americans could see the title staying in Europe for some time and were concerned about the according loss of revenue to their promoters. Then there was the problem of refereeing. American referees gave boxers a great deal more latitude. In some states there was even a no-foul rule, something looked at askance in Britain at the time. The referee simply gave the victim time to recover. An American boxer, in Europe in general – and in Britain in particular – would have to mind where he landed his punches and would have to break when told, however hurt he might be, or he would face disqualification. No title, no American pay-day.

In the end, despite considerable manoeuvring by Jack Solomons and the British Boxing Board of Control, as well as a suggestion that Olson fight Humez, with the winner to meet Turpin, things were worked out, as they usually are in boxing – if not always to the satisfaction of the boxers. Under the arrangement, Turpin was to meet Humez and, in America, the light-punching Paddy Young was to fight the equally light-punching Hawaiian, Carl 'Bobo' Olson. The winners were to meet each other. Turpin should not have been displeased. He was expected to defeat Humez, and neither Olson nor Young were regarded as devastating punchers like Robinson. However, Olson in particular had a respectable record. He had only been beaten five times, including twice by Robinson and twice by Dave Sands. Even though there were signs that the press and public were calling an end to their unquestioning love affair with Turpin, he was still good copy. He hit out at his critics and denied that he was slipping.[5]

In his personal life, Turpin was now locked in a bitter divorce case in which his wife, Mary Theresa, was alleging cruelty, something Turpin denied. The proceedings ground to a halt on 23 March 1953, when Mr Justice Karminski ruled that Turpin's wish to claim that his wife condoned his cruelty would have to be specifically pleaded. Condonation could, in those days, occur by just a single act of sexual intercourse. Of course, there was no question that amending his defence could be done there and then; the law was far too majestic for that to happen. The case would have to be adjourned and Turpin would have to pay all the costs wasted.[6]

The previous autumn Turpin, against strong family advice,

had purchased with Salts the Great Orme complex at Llandudno for a reported £12,000. Some say the purchase was £15,000, of which each found a half. Once a nine-bedroom hotel with an eighteen-hole golf course on a windswept headland outside the town, it had been requisitioned by the RAF in the war, when it had become a temporary radar station.

On Easter Monday 1953 the Welsh former world champion flyweight Jimmy Wilde opened Randy's Bar at the Great Orme International Sporting and Holiday Centre. Messages of congratulations came in from the runner MacDonald Bailey, Denis Compton, Godfrey Evans and Bruce Woodcock. Freddie Mills had been expected, but instead he too sent a message of congratulations. There was also one from Sugar Ray Robinson. After the formalities, Wilde, Turpin and brother Jackie signed autographs for the fans.

Looking back, it is hard to see how Turpin and Salts thought they would make money from the Great Orme. For a start, there was no bus service to take visitors to the hotel, or, as one councillor called it, 'the great attraction' at the summit. Telephones were also at a premium.

However, Randy was a big draw, and these were the days of the great British seaside holiday, when tens of thousands would come to north Wales' seaside resorts for their week away from the pit and the mill.[7] Turpin announced he would be spending a good deal of his time there, training for the Humez contest.

The year had started well for Turpin, with wins over Victor D'Haes, whom he knocked out in January in Birmingham, and the durable South African Duggie Miller, beaten on points at Leicester a month later. This was followed by a win over

---

[7] In 1957, the crowd in Llandudno on the August Bank Holiday Monday totalled 110,000.

Walter Cartier, who was disqualified in the second round in London. Cartier would, said the reports, have been cut to ribbons by the Licker, had he not persistently held his man. It was not, however, a night of unsurpassed joy. There had, for some time, been difficulties in the Turpin training camp. However talented he might be, Bill Hyam had caused some resentment amongst the other handlers, and finally he left on the evening of the Cartier win. Frank Algar, unlicensed as a trainer by the Board of Control, would now take charge of training, or what sometimes passed for it.

The Turpin v Humez contest in June was expected to be a glittering affair, a fitting sporting occasion for Coronation week; Waterloo re-fought with the British hero knocking out the gallant but less talented Frenchman to the roars of a delighted crowd. Humez was well thought of. He had only lost his welterweight title on a disqualification and he had regained the French middleweight title by beating Gilbert Lavoine. Instead the fight turned out to be a stinker, with Frank Sinatra, then married to Ava Gardner, leading the exodus from the ringside with three rounds to go. There is no doubt that Turpin won, but, 'What should have proved to be a dynamic battle proved to be a dud . . . [It was] a laughing, apologetic affair in which after almost every punch the contestants would step back, laugh or grin at each other, then return to the business of the evening,'[8] *Ring* complained. 'During the last five rounds when it was obvious to everyone, except Turpin and his handlers, that he had nothing to beat, our patience gave way to hope. In the last third of the bout, hope turned to prayer, but again we were denied,'[9] said *Boxing News*.

[8] *Ring*, August 1953.
[9] *Boxing News*, 17 June 1953.

One of the reasons for the fiasco was that Turpin had not been training properly, nor could either man make the weight with ease. Both had been off to the sauna, and Turpin had to go to the scales four times before he eventually made the weight, with two minutes to spare. He had seemed to make the weight on the third attempt, but Humez's manager had protested, and it was back to the scales. If, as was claimed later, Teddy Waltham was not wholly supportive of the champion, it certainly wasn't showing then. *Ring* reported that Teddy Waltham had wiped the scales of any dust, before Turpin made the weight, with seconds to spare.[10] His successor as General Secretary, Ray Clarke, has an interesting story that Jack Solomons took Turpin into a cubicle and 'performed an act on him' before he was able to make the weight.[11]

Turpin also had another excuse for his poor showing. He had again damaged a hand. Now asked whether he had any preference for London as a venue to meet the winner of Olson–Young, he told reporters:

> I did until now. But I've made up my mind. They don't want good boxing here such as I gave them tonight. They want murder. I hurt my hand in the first round when I crashed it against his arm and that prevented me from using it effectively. The attitude of the crowd has caused me to change my mind. I'll willingly fight the American winner in New York. Mr Middleton will arrange for that. Whether it's Olson or Young, I'll whip either and I'll stop those squawks. Those who don't

[10] *Ring*, August 1953. It may have been that for some reason the scales were weighing heavy. At the same time Frank Johnson failed to make the weight for his lightweight title contest with Joe Lucy.
[11] Conversation with author.

think I'm the champion will soon find out. I'll show
who is the boss.[12]

This may have been a liberal interpretation of what Turpin
actually said. It is certainly a much more articulate voice than
the one which had delivered the 'thank you' speech at
Leamington Town Hall two years earlier to the patronising
glances of others on the balcony. But he was right in one
way: fight fans have never much prized skilled boxing over
knockouts and blood. Even so, Nat Fleischer doubted that
Turpin would have beaten either Olson or Young in his
present form: 'With careful training and the help of an
American second to handle Turpin, the British may see their
man regain the world crown. He has what it takes to defeat
Olson or Young but will not, in my opinion, turn the trick
with the kind of training he followed for the Humez battle.'[13]

In fact Turpin and Freddie Mills were both in the courts in
the middle of June 1953. On 12 June, Turpin was divorced
by Mary Theresa Turpin of Queensway, Leamington. He was
granted reasonable access to their son as, in the pompous
way the Bar has of putting these things, 'The father has a
certain amount of glamour for the son and the wife is quite
willing to continue access,' although when it came to it, there
was virtually no communication between father and son
during Turpin's life. Quite why it was thought necessary to
spend the money instructing Queen's Counsel for what was
now an undefended hearing is not clear. But no matter, Turpin
would pay. The divorce was said to have cost £8000, a very

---

[12] *Ring*, October 1953.
[13] Ibid.

substantial sum in those days, but Turpin thought it cost him over double that figure.

Turpin was still a star. That week his fight with Humez was on show at news cinemas around the country, second only on the bill to 'Elizabeth is Queen', narrated by the former barrister Leo Genn. His finances, though, were, even then, in a hopeless mess. He had, it is true, put £7500 into Great Orme, but apart from that, most of his money from the second Robinson fight – claimed by him to be £30,000 but grossed at £68,145 – was gone. He earned a gross of £13,938 from the Humez contest. Out of that, however, he had to pay a tax to the Board of Control, training expenses, and Middleton's customary 25 per cent cut. This left Turpin the tidy sum of £9582. Unfortunately he had borrowed £7500 from Solomons, Middleton had advanced him £400 to finance his contested divorce, and he owed income tax in the region of £4500. He was, therefore, nearly three thousand pounds in the red.

On 19 June, Olson outboxed Paddy Young, cutting him and winning easily. But, ominously, he failed to show a powerful punch. *Ring* returned to the theme: 'Despite the fact that he has lost much of the fighting skill he displayed in his first bout with Robinson in which he won the title, he's nobody's fool when it comes to boxing and hitting. Many of the punches and slaps which Olson landed on Young won't find their way onto Randy's anatomy if the Britisher gets himself in fighting trim.'[14]

The big word was the 'if'. The retired Robinson, however, thought that Olson would beat Turpin: 'It's a matter of styles.'

Meanwhile, there was some excitement on the north Wales

---

[14] Ted Carroll, 'Turpin Tries Again', *Ring*, September 1953.

coast. There was a story that the Turpin v Olson match would be in London and that Turpin would train at Gwyrch, whilst the American would have the use of Great Orme. It turned out to be just a rumour. The fight was arranged for New York – it was Turpin who would be doing the travelling.

As he sailed, *The Turpin Story, the Life Story of our Local World Champion* was showing at the Plaza, Rivoli and Roxy cinemas in Coventry. It is not recorded whether Turpin received any of the profits.

14

Randolph Turpin Tastes Forbidden Fruit

When Turpin sailed for New York to meet Olson, his mind must have been in a turmoil. In the previous few months, he had suffered a bitter and expensive divorce suit. There were troubles at home, in that he was also half engaged to two other women. He was being urged by his mother to give up boxing. *Ring* painted an appropriate picture of Beatrice: 'Partially deaf, almost totally blind with toil-worn hands that bear mute testimony to the desperate battle to keep her brood intact during its bitter early years.'[1]

It was unsurprising that his training was not going well. Indeed the Board, which at the time effectively meant Teddy Waltham, was so unhappy at the state of Turpin's affairs that on his advice the President, J. Onslow Fane, spoke to the boxer before he set sail. The *Empire News*, which had Turpin

[1] Billy Williams, 'The Turbulent Turpins', *Ring*, October 1953.

under contract, reported, 'I've been homesick. I don't know why but it seemed to get worse and worse.' Another article in the *Empire News* had his mother pleading with him to give up boxing.[2] Turpin was also receiving letters asking him what was wrong. In all he had a postbag of 3000 before the fight and many of the writers were criticising him.

Training methods have changed over the years – almost entirely for the better. Just after the First World War, when Kid Harris from Barbados came to England, he was matched by Alf Denhart with Eddie Beattie in Newcastle. A condition of the contract was that if he could not make the agreed weight of ten stone seven he would forfeit £20 from his purse. Six days before the contest Harris was still twelve pounds over the stipulated weight and Denhart was calling him a lazy trainer. He had him tied to a butcher's cart, whose driver was instructed to keep up a good clip around Regent's Park. Harris had the choice of running or being dragged. He was then wrapped in a twelve-hundredweight wrestling mat, and sweated off a further four pounds trying to get out. The rapid, and forced, loss of weight does not seem to have done him any great immediate harm. He was ahead in the eleventh round when he was knocked down by a low blow. The referee, however, refused to disqualify Beattie.[3]

Training in Turpin's day was not the same as today. Now, the bigger and better gyms have dieticians on staff and sweating to make the weight is completely out of favour. Every trainer had his own methods, but a rough schedule for a championship contest would have the boxer doing road-

---

[2] *Empire News*, 18 October 1953.
[3] *Thomson's Weekly News*, 8 February 1919. Joe Fox, who later sparred with Kid Harris, took off twenty-two pounds in fifteen days for his contest with Tommy Harrison. (*Thomson's Weekly News*, 1 March 1919.)

work, running four miles or around forty minutes early in
the morning. Then it would be home to change, rest and eat
and probably take a mid-morning walk. In the afternoon or
early evening it would be into the gym for six to eight rounds
of shadow boxing, work on the bag, the speed ball and
possibly open sparring. This would begin six to seven weeks
before the match, though it was anticipated that the fighter
would be in some sort of condition already. In Turpin's day,
as there had been for years, there was much more emphasis
on sweating weight off the fighter, who would be bundled
up in sweat gear to do his work. If that wasn't bringing the
weight down sufficiently, it would be hot baths and the now-
outlawed sauna. He would also be told to cut back on liquids.

The point of the exercise is to bring the boxer in at the
correct weight on the day of the weigh-in – which was then
the day of the contest, not the day before, as it is now. So a
week before the fight, he might be two to three pounds over.
On the morning of the contest he might be a pound over,
but shadow boxing and sweating would bring off the excess.

Sparring would be done with a number of partners, often
at different weights, to develop speed and stamina. In the
first couple of weeks it would be easy sparring and thereafter open sparring. A week or so before the contest the boxer
might have a full fifteen-round workout, with one or more
sparring partners, simply to test his ability to go the distance.
Sparring would finish three or four days before the contest
and then it would simply be gym and roadwork. Sundays
would be a day off. The other aspect of correct training was
the mental preparation for the contest, something which, in
later years, Turpin certainly lacked.

In New York Turpin was being called 'The British
Pretender'. Harold Mayes wrote, 'Turpin has trained for

stamina, he will need it all.' There were worries that he had
made the weight for the fight too early. Mayes thought that
the longer the fight went on, the better it would be for the
tireless Olson. 'Why all the smiles in Turpin's camp?' asked
the paper.[4] Although, as recommended by just about
everyone in boxing, Turpin had appointed an American,
Jimmy August, to work on the strength, 'he might just as
well have been a casual observer'. August wondered whether
there had ever before been a camp where the fighter was
boss. Tips had to be passed on to him through his sparring
partners, and since he was averaging less than a round a day
they were not in a position to pass much on. They
complained they were getting rusty. As for George Middleton,
'the manager who is managed' was the unkind but accurate
assessment of his position. When eventually Turpin did spar
in public – two rounds each with Irwin Steen and Eddie
Dixon – it was reported that 'some of his swings were more
like those you see in a YMCA gym'.[5]

Dick Turpin was forthcoming: 'If anything goes wrong this
time they won't be able to pin it on me. I took some of the
can back because he was overweight but I haven't trained
him this time. Half the time I haven't been able to get near
Randy. Algy [Frank Algar] has been so busy taking him cups
of tea. I think he took him a dozen yesterday.'[6]

The truth is that things were going seriously wrong. The
Daily Express writer Desmond Hackett and its cartoonist Roy
Ullyett had been out to the Grossingers on two occasions, and
the most that had been seen of Randy was his backside

[4] Harold Mayes, 'Why All the Smiles in Turpin's Camp?', *Empire News*, 18 October 1953.
[5] Ibid., 'Turpin's Manager Cracks the Whip', *Empire News*, 25 October 1953.
[6] *Empire News*, 18 October 1955.

Randolph Turpin's
Lonsdale Belt.
*(By kind permission of
Thomas Mellis of Horsham)*

Strongwoman
Joan Rhodes tests
Freddie's muscles
at the Earlham
Street gym.
(George Douglas)

Randolph Turpin's
grave. *(Dock Bateson)*

Len Harvey after defeating Jock McAvoy. *(Popperfoto)*

Programme for Bruce Woodcock v. Freddie Mills. *(Courtesy of Derek Whitfield)*

Programme for Eddie Maguire v. Freddie Mills. *(Courtesy of Derek Whitfield)*

Plaque to Freddie Mills
at St Michael's School.
(James Morton)

Randolph Turpin's
statue in Warwick.
(Courtesy of Dennis Slade)

Freddie Mills
in training with
Nat Seller for his
winning 1948 World
light-heavyweight
title against Gus
Lesnevich. *(Popperfoto)*

Randolph Turpin with
his mother at her
Warwick home in 1951.
(Popperfoto)

Freddie Mills and his
daughters Amanda and Susan.
(Popperfoto)

Goslett Yard, where Freddie Mills' body was found. *(Popperfoto)*

The end: Randolph Turpin knocked out in the second round by Yolande Pompey. *(Popperfoto)*

Randolph Turpin signs for his London wrestling debut with promoter Joe D'Orazio. *(Courtesy of Joe D'Orazio)*

Randolph Turpin tops the bill on an unlicensed promotion.

Leslie Salts, co-owner with Randolph Turpin of the Great Orme Hotel, Llandudno. *(News of the World Picture Library)*

Freddie Mills shows how to box in Nat Seller's book for boys. *(Hulton Archive)*

Freddie and Chrissie Mills. *(Hulton Archive)*

Don McCorkindale, Chrissie Mills' first husband, before his bout with Primo Carrera. *(Popperfoto)*

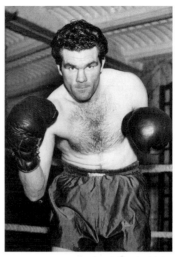

Freddie Mills in his prime. *(Popperfoto)*

Randolph Turpin, Jackie Turpin and Frank Algar, his trainer, land in Southampton after Randolph's losing fight against Bobo Olson. *(Popperfoto)*

Turpin's triumphant reception after beating Sugar Ray Robinson in 1951. *(Hulton Archive)*

Randy, about to be taken down by Cyril Knowles. *(Mirrorpix)*

disappearing in a taxi. Ullyett called it Turpin's 'Non-Training Camp'. The cartoon read: 'We did meet George Middleton his manager, who says he doesn't know what to say about Randy, and Mr Robert Christenberg, New York's Boxing Commissioner, who knows, but is too much of a gentleman to express an opinion.'[7] The displeased Turpin later physically took a swing at Hackett, whom he blamed for some of his misfortunes.

Another report in the *Express* said Turpin had come out of hiding and had boxed six rounds. Five days later, it was said that he was sticking to roadwork, afraid he would lose the edge if he did too much fighting. Two days before the fight, Dick Turpin commented, 'Our Randy is spending less time in his own room. He joins in the games and likes to have people around him.'[8]

Boxers have always had something of an ambivalent attitude to the value of abstinence from sex before a fight. Heavyweight champion Lennox Lewis believes: 'Mentally, you have to be very focused. Sure, the aspect of looking forward to being with your woman afterwards gives you strength. I agree with not thinking about your woman, having that little edge, otherwise it can take your energy away. Having an orgasm is like running up the stairs. That's as much energy as you use. I think three weeks before the fight is a fair time to kind of just cut it out.'[9]

The highly respected manager Dennie Mancini thinks the period should be longer: 'Going with a woman the day before can't be beneficial. It's better to abstain the old fashioned way from four to five weeks before the fight. It's a one-to-one combat sport and you need all the strength you can muster.'

[7] *Daily Express*, 12 October 1955.
[8] Ibid., 19 October 1955.
[9] Melissa Mathieson, 'Lennox', *Sunday Telegraph Magazine*, 5 May 2002.

Brendan Ingle, the manager of many champions over the last forty years, thinks six or seven weeks is better: 'If a boxer has one girlfriend there is a problem. If you have two you've plenty of problems.'[10] Turpin unfortunately had at least three and probably a considerable number more. He was, as people say, sex mad. He thought that abstaining for three weeks at most was sufficient and after that a kiss and cuddle was in order. At least that is what he told the newspapers. Shortly before the fight there were suggestions that his girlfriend Gwen should come over, but Turpin forbade it.

Then, in the week before the contest, came the news that he was being named as co-respondent in the divorce suit brought by a certain Pamela Valentine's husband. The allegation was that Pamela and Randy had met whilst she worked at Gwyrch Castle, and had continued their relationship at the Charing Cross Hotel in London. Turpin maintained he thought she was single. He had been astonished to hear she had a daughter and gave her £2 to buy a dress as a Christmas present for the child. The next year he was ordered to pay the costs of the suit.[11]

The *Empire News*, reiterating that Turpin was the boss, noted that if anything went wrong on Wednesday, he would have only himself to blame.[12] The Liverpool *Echo* was convinced that this would be a 'muddleweight' contest, and one of the dreariest on record to boot.[13]

At least the special correspondent of *Boxing News* offered some optimism, writing just before the fight, 'Our champion will give of his best tonight . . . he aims to win inside the

[10] Conversations with author.
[11] *Daily Express*, 11, 12, 16 and 19 October 1953; Desmond Hackett, 'The Great Untamed', *Daily Express*, 1 December 1972.
[12] 'Why All the Smiles in Turpin's Camp?', *Empire News*, 18 October 1953.
[13] Liverpool *Echo*, 16 October 1953.

distance but may adopt the same tactics as he did against Charles Humez and go for a conclusive points victory'.[14] As for Turpin, he and the *Empire News* were still writing a good fight. 'I never jibbed. I won't start now,' he claimed.[15]

Better still, from Turpin's point of view, it was thought that Olson was having weight trouble, but it was Turpin who caused a minor sensation at the weigh-in when he was found to be well under the weight limit. He immediately went out to odds of three to one.

Now the fear was that he had left the fight in the training camp. Once the fight started, though, initially these fears seemed misplaced. Ringsiders thought Turpin had won the first three rounds readily enough, but then he lost three of the next four, with one drawn. In the fourth, he was clipped hard and immediately went into a clinch from which maul he emerged with a cut eye. Later, Turpin would claim that was the moment his brother Dick left the corner. Dick said it was because he had stomach ulcers. However Turpin won the eighth, so going into the ninth the pair were even. It was then the wheels really came off the Turpin wagon.

His left eye was now swelling badly and he was shipping punishment at close quarters. With a matter of seconds to go before the end of the round, Olson trapped him on the ropes and hit him with a series of lefts and rights to the head. Turpin went to the canvas and the count had reached four when the bell rang. The referee failed to hear it and went on counting the kneeling Turpin. The tenth and eleventh were more of the same, with Turpin taking punishment from the fortunately relatively light-hitting Olson. In round thirteen Olson cut Turpin's mouth, but now he too was flagging, and

[14] 'Turpin in the Mood to Win', *Boxing News*, 21 October 1953.
[15] *Empire News*, 18 and 25 October 1953.

Turpin held his own in the last two rounds. There was, however, no doubt whatsoever who was the winner – the two judges and referee were unanimous in their verdict. Turpin seemed happy it was all over. From his dressing room he said, 'If I had been as well mentally as I was physically the result would have been different.' It was said he would soon make an important announcement. Salts, who had not travelled with the party to New York, had 'not the slightest doubt it would come'. His mother felt sure he would retire and go back to work for Parver, by now a councillor. Some thought he would farm in north Wales 'in a big way'. But no announcement came.

Back at his hotel he started passing blood and was wrapped in a sheet filled with ice cubes. No doctor seems to have been sent for and piecing things together it seems he was soon off to the apartment of his American girlfriend, Adele Daniels.

Criticism was almost unanimous. Few were pleased with the performance, certainly not *Boxing News*: 'If ever a fighter went into the ring mentally unprepared it was Turpin. The undeniable fact is that Turpin has gone back a long way. He has things on his mind more important than boxing and when that happens a fighter has "had it" to use a well understood expression. No fighter could possibly deteriorate to such an extent unless he was mentally unequipped for the job.'[16] Later, Turpin's second Mick Gavin would say that the boxer had returned to his corner several times and said he had had it. He was told that Olson looked worse and he must go out again. It was noted that, apart from the knockdowns, there were some sixteen occasions when he had been in trouble on the ropes and had not easily or quickly escaped.

[16] *Boxing News*, 18 October 1953.

Garvin thought that unless someone could snap him out of his present state, Turpin was finished.

The *Empire News* thought he had staked everything on a quick knockout and the gamble hadn't come off. *Ring* thought that Turpin had definitely let the British down by his lack of training. Olson had won because he was in peak condition. This was echoed by Jack Solomons, who thought the better fighter lost because of lack of condition. The American trade paper thought: 'He [Turpin] had trouble making the weight until some 10 days before the fight. Then he weakened himself and, at the weighing in, tipped the beam at 157. Far too low for Randy.'[17]

Turpin may have been bowed but certainly Jack Solomons back in England was unbroken. He was promoting Yolande Pompey against Ray Barnes in November and already had plans for Turpin to meet the winner. If that match did not materialise, then there was always Paddy Young or Joey Giardello. When Turpin came through these preliminaries, there would be a rematch in London with Olson on 1 June 1954. The promoter said, 'I repeat I refuse to believe that this fine figure of an athlete is played out. He has undergone a bad patch, that's all. We must therefore play him for all he's worth'.[18] And play Randy, Solomons would.

In fact he gave away two and a half pounds to Olson. Still, he came out with just over £20,500, less Middleton's cut from the fight and the money paid to Adele Daniels. Why to Adele Daniels? One explanation of his poor performance came after Turpin was arrested on 2 November 1953, shortly before he was due to board the *Queen Mary* to return to England. He appeared at the Upper Manhattan Magistrates'

[17] *Empire News*, 25 October 1953; *Ring*, January 1954.
[18] Jack Solomons, 'I Believe in Turpin', *Everybody's*, 14 November 1953.

Court to answer a complaint by Adele Daniels, described as a Negro clerk in the State Department of Labor, that he had belted and kicked her around her penthouse apartment at 750 Riverside Drive and W. 125 on the edges of Harlem more than half a dozen times since his arrival for the Olson fight. No one questioned what a clerk in the State Department for Labor was doing in a penthouse apartment.

Turpin had, said the flamboyant J. Roland Sala, Miss Daniels' lawyer, promised to marry her. This would have been a somewhat complicated exercise since at the time he was still married, possibly engaged to a Welsh girl, had recently been named in the police officer and his wife's pending divorce action, and was involved with a number of other women in shorter-term relationships.

On his return to America for the Olson contest, said Miss Daniels, Turpin and she had picked up their relationship where they had left off after the Robinson fight and, she said, Turpin had been training on her at her apartment. She claimed he had assaulted her on the 22, 23 and 24 September, all before the fight, when he should have been tucked up safely at the training camp. Although she had 'loyally nursed him' after the Olson disaster, on 23, 24, 25 and 26 October he 'did strike her a number of violent blows about the face and body with clenched hands, and kicked deponent with his booted foot'.

The principal aim of Turpin's lawyer was to get him on the boat home and in what was described as 'as novel a defence as ever was made for a champ', Lew Burston, foreign representative of the International Boxing Commission, commented, 'Even if this guy can't punch, certainly she should have marks on her body as a result of the numerous beatings they allege in the complaint.' Sala wanted Turpin held in custody for mental reports, claiming that he was 'definitely mentally ill, psychopathologically. This man is bestially primitive.' But Turpin was released into the custody of his elderly lawyer, Saul Strauss, and the case was remanded until 4 November, with the promise of an early hearing so he could indeed catch the boat. Then the simple assault charge was withdrawn and Turpin deposited $10,000 so that the boxer could sail that day. Adele Daniels said she had withdrawn the charge voluntarily and had neither been threatened nor offered money to do so. Sala, who had resisted the judge's suggestion on the previous hearing that the case should be withdrawn, denounced Turpin on what were described as 'international grounds': 'Randy is anti-American. He should be everlastingly grateful to our American system of democracy – a system he has maligned and defamed openly and notoriously.'

Sala promised to launch a civil suit within forty-eight hours and prophesied a substantial pay-out for his client. George Middleton was defiant, 'I invite Mr Sala to make the state-ment on English soil.' The eight-strong Turpin party caught the boat in time and the newspapers speculated that $10,000 might be the sum Miss Daniels would eventually receive, less anything trousered by Mr Sala.[19]

Turpin gave at least some explanation to the British press at the time: 'Adele's not bad. I met her after my fight with Sugar Ray two years ago. We've been writing ever since. It was such a shock to me that she should raise such a charge like this. There's no reason. She has always been so quiet and

[19] Sala was described as wearing a black suit, grey double-breasted vest, a white shirt with Barrymore collar and a red tie and black Homburg, the last presum-ably not in court. A number of British journalists were said to be visibly impressed. He regularly had his own troubles with the courts and in the year of the Turpin fight was himself arrested for non-payment of parking fines. The *Daily News* did not comment on Miss Daniels' costume. 'Girl Says Boxer Turpin Practised Punch on Her', *Daily News*, 3 November 1953; 'Sala lets Turpin Go, Sets up 100G rematch', *Daily News*, 5 November 1953.

friendly. We certainly did discuss marriage but when I came out to the United States the last time I told her it was over. I said, "Forget about me."[20]

Over the years he gave conflicting accounts of when he had told Adele about his proposed marriage. Now, he said that it was the night before he was due to sail, when he took her to a nightclub. She had been hinting that she wanted him to take her back to England and he had wanted to tell her about Gwen. In another version he had told her from the time of his arrival in New York. In yet another version he denied ever having spoken to her of marriage

Before the case, there had been suggestions in the newspapers that Turpin, despite the defeat, had enough left in him to be an attractive proposition in the New York rings. Now the Commission suspended him indefinitely, although they had lifted this by the end of the year. The British Boxing Board of Control considered taking action, but decided to let the matter lie for the present.

It was not, however, a happy team that arrived back at Southampton. Randy was shut in his cabin and would not emerge. He had not spoken to Dick for the last four days because, it was thought, Dick had refused to give evidence for him at the hearing. There was a run-in with the press. A little charade was carried out as Turpin was driven past the hotel in Southampton in which a Gwyneth (Gwen) Price, described as a friend of Turpin's, was staying. Gwen was rather more than a friend. She had met Turpin on 22 March 1952 when he was in training at Gwyrch Castle. She had asked him for his autograph and he had bargained it for a date. She had then missed her bus and Turpin gave her a lift home. They had, as she put it, clicked. She now greeted him on his return in 'I Love You' stockings.

The pair were soon holed up in Devizes, and Gwen was claiming to be just a girlfriend. Turpin poured out his troubles to Maurice Freeman of the *Mirror*, saying that mentally he was 'just out of this world'. He was, he said, no longer interested in either boxing or marriage, at least until his troubles were cleared up.[21]

Days later, Turpin announced his proposed marriage to Gwen. They were married on 15 November at the register office in Newport. The bride and groom arrived an hour after the registrar and left quickly, with the windows of the car greased to keep out the cameras. The next week Turpin took his new wife to see his mother, who was not pleased with things. She was not pleased because she had not been invited to the marriage – none of the Turpins were – and she was not pleased because of her son's divorce from Mary. Nevertheless, she was the only one of the family who really adapted, and warmed to Gwen.

On 9 December 1953, with J. Onslow Fane in the chair, twenty-one stewards met to consider the allegations of Teddy Waltham, their General Secretary, that Randolph Turpin had not trained adequately for his last contest and as a result had brought boxing into disrepute. George Middleton also faced allegations that he had not fulfilled the duties expected of a manager, and that he was a party to Frank Algar, who held only a second's licence, acting as a trainer while knowing that the latter was incompetent. Algar was also called to answer the allegation that he had acted as an unlicensed trainer.

---

[21] Maurice Freeman, 'I am Fed Up with the Bright Lights', *Daily Mirror*, 2 November 1953.

Waltham gave evidence, claiming that he had been told that no training schedule had existed and that Turpin had decided when, and how, to train. A proposed six-round session had been stopped after four, when Turpin appeared tired and had said he wanted no more boxing. Turpin had assured Waltham there would be two further workouts. As for the fight itself, he considered Turpin had outclassed his opponent for three rounds and then had 'perceptibly tired more and more as the contest proceeded'. Privately, Waltham had told the Board that Turpin and Algar would lock themselves in a room in an afternoon, refusing to come to answer the door. The implication was that there was a homosexual liaison going on between the men. It was not, however, a matter which was raised at the meeting.

George Middleton had the task of refuting Waltham's allegations. He said Turpin had trained hard, completed his roadwork, had not left camp after 4 p.m. on any day, and had never been further than three miles from the camp. Algar was described as merely a friend.

Turpin himself said that he had begun his roadwork in July and commenced serious training in the third week of his stay at Gwyrch Castle. He felt more confident when Algar was present, as he had done before the Humez fight. He had boxed fifty-four rounds before leaving for the States and he confirmed Middleton's evidence about his conduct in America. This, however, cannot have been correct. Had the Board wanted, they could have called *Express* journalist and cartoonist, Hackett and Ullyett, who were in a position to give contradictory evidence. Turpin told the Board that the knockdown was as a result of blows and that he had had no intention of quitting halfway through the contest. The Board concluded that Turpin should have employed a professional trainer, as advised by the President of the Board, before his departure for America. He had not followed this advice. The minutes of the meeting noted that, 'After a careful enquiry the Board accepted Turpin's explanation but reiterated the advice that he should not in future train himself.' Algar was not to allow himself to be described as Turpin's trainer, or to train him unless he became licensed.

Turpin said he was pleased it was all over. He had been intending to box an exhibition in Brussels that weekend, but the Board's doctor advised him that it would be unwise because he had an infected cyst on his right eyelid.[22]

Meanwhile 24-year-old blonde, Pamela Eunice Valentine, the wife of the policeman who had cited Turpin as co-respondent in the divorce case, said she had been receiving poison-pen letters. She was cross-petitioning and she thought that it was worry over the case that had upset his training.

This at least gave Turpin the opportunity to enjoy married life with his new wife, Gwen. Except, of course, that a mere two months earlier he'd been heading to America in eager anticipation of a reunion with Adele Daniels. Mosh Mancini recalls that just before he had set sail, 'Turpin brought out a little red negligee. It was very, very pretty and he said, "I can see Adele in that." I asked who Adele was because I knew that he was courting Gwen, and he said, "She's a smashing American girl."'[23]

The *Empire News* may have had Turpin under contract, but that did not stop them featuring Miss Daniels to give her side of the story on the very day he married Gwen. Daniels

[22] Minutes of the meeting of the Stewards of the British Boxing Board of Control, 9 December 1953; *The Times*, 11 December 1953.
[23] Conversation with author.

had 'enjoyed the confidence' of Turpin's manager, brother and other members of the party, she revealed, but Randolph himself 'was so strange and irritable and used to bark at me every time I opened my mouth. When I mentioned it to those in his party they told me not to answer back but to do my best to humour him. I begged them to have him examined by a doctor because I thought he was a sick man. I still do. After his fight with Olson he was worse.' She had first known something was seriously wrong between them – one can only presume she saw the court case she brought against him for assault as a blip – when she saw a picture of Gwen Price at Southampton in the 'I Love You' nylons which she had bought Turpin in New York. He had told her he wanted them for his sister, Joan.

She had been continually buying him things such as a crossbow because he had not realised how expensive things were. Turpin had admitted to her that he had once been out with Gwen, but said that had been a long time ago and things had been finished between them before he had come to New York.[24]

But soon J. Roland Sala was claiming that Miss Daniels had not been able to work following a neck injury and he had given her money to help her. Sala said he was trying to get the girl reinstated with the Labor Board. At the beginning of January 1954, Turpin's lawyer in New York, Saul Strauss, applied for an order that a doctor be appointed to examine Miss Daniels. Finally, at the end of the following year, the civil case resumed. Now an allegation of rape had been added which, if proved, would no doubt have pushed

[24] John Sampson, 'My Broken Romance with Randy: the Truth', *Empire News*, 15 November 1953.

the damages nearer to six figures. Turpin went back to America for the hearing, which began at the end of November 1955 and ran for four days.

It was now accepted that he would have married Adele Daniels back in 1951, but for the impediment of the first Mrs Turpin. He agreed that, having written her a number of love letters – one hundred and fifty, said Miss Daniels, all of them containing an explicit proposal of marriage – he had also given her cash and presents to the tune of around $2,000. She had given him a combined comb and clipper. On his return to New York for the Olson contest he had told her she could forget about marriage. As for the allegation of rape, this had been on 24 September, when Turpin should have been safely tucked away at his training camp. Instead, claimed Sala, he had forced his way into her bedroom, put a pillow over her face and raped her.

She claimed that Turpin told her they would be married immediately after the Olson fight, but that day he had tried to choke her. When she regained consciousness, Turpin was sobbing hysterically, saying he must have been mad. After the Olson fight, he had been determined to go back to her flat, and when she refused his suggestions – whatever they were – he punched and kicked her. Sala claimed her injuries were worse than death itself. She thought that as a result of the punishment he had taken in the Olson fight, he had become a 'maniacal and dangerous person'. As for her injuries, she had suffered nervous and psychiatric upset, and a 'paralysis of the left hand side of the face which caused her to have a twisted expression when she had occasion to smile'. She may have over-estimated the damage she suffered but it all sounded horribly like the allegations in the petition lodged by the first Mrs Turpin.

On the second day of the trial, Sala walked out of court. He had repeatedly clashed with the trial judge, O. McGivern, who described his examination of Miss Daniels as 'a monument of impropriety'. On the fourth day, the case was settled after an hour's discussion between the lawyers. Miss Daniels, now described as 'shapely', had begun to wilt under cross-examination. She accepted that within hours of the alleged rape she had been with Turpin in a restaurant and had then gone with him to see Orlando Zulueta beat Paddy De Marco at the Polo Grounds. Turpin had been fêted at ringside. She denied that the next day she had turned up at his hotel with a suitcase packed, ready to go to his training camp with him. She also denied that she had received money from him for rent and food. Re-examined, she said she had only gone to the Zulueta fight because she feared Turpin. She was able to elaborate on the incident after the Olson fight. Turpin had said that she was like all Americans, 'trying to push me around. I am the master and in England when I say move they move.' He had told her, 'If you make one step to call the police I'll break your neck and if I don't others will.' She asked him what that meant and he replied, 'You know what I mean. I have friends and connections in the boxing world.'

The 'push me around' remark certainly echoed an article under Turpin's name in the *Empire News* earlier in the year. In the article he claimed that his relatively poor performances had been caused by a fallen arch in his right foot. Had he not found an osteopath who had cured him, he would have had to quit boxing within the year. The article was headlined 'I'm Tired of Being Pushed Around'. The piece had been accompanied by an assessment of Turpin's character by Dr Eric Singer who, after analysing his signature, said it showed 'intelligence, ambition, speed, good memory, logic, dexterity, accuracy and a faculty of observation'.[25]

However, Ms Daniels was now wilting, and the $100,000 claim was finally settled for $3,500. The Turpin camp felt vindicated. His lawyer, Saul Strauss, issued a statement saying his client continued to maintain his innocence. Sala was disappointed his client had settled against his advice. As for Randolph himself, he rather ungallantly commented, 'That girl was too much for one man. I had to get rid of her.'[26]

So, what exactly was the truth of the rape allegation? '"Randy wasn't half as black as he was painted, if you'll pardon the pun," said British sportswriter Tex Hennessey, who has close ties to Turpin's widow and children. "The rape case in America was an enormous cover-up which only came to light a few years ago. His older brother Dick was in America with Randy at the time of the alleged rape. Randy was between marriages then but Dick was happily married. According to what I've learned from knowing the family, Dick was the culprit."'[27]

In the television film *64 Day Hero*, Gwen Turpin comments, 'He said it was a set-up. He never said Dick actually assaulted her, but that he never touched her.' Others, at the time and indeed later, were not convinced by this. They pointed out that Randolph, still the star and bankable, had to be protected; Dick was expendable in the eyes of the press and public: hence the starting of the rumours. Not, fortunately, that it did Dick any harm.

[25] 'I'm Tired of Being Pushed Around', *Empire News*, 15 March 1953.
[26] See, *inter alia*, *Amsterdam News*, 7 and 14 November 1953, 7 December 1955; *New York Times*, 5 December 1955; *The Times*, 30 November, 1, 2 and 3 December 1995; *Empire News*, 4 December 1955.
[27] Nigel Collins, *Boxing Babylon*, p. 100.

15

**Randolph Turpin
Is Destroyed**

From the New Year of 1954, when the court case with Adele was still nearly two years in the future, life only went downhill for Turpin. He was fined £2 at Abergele Magistrates' Court on 2 January for possessing a rifle without a firearms licence. The previous August, Turpin had been found with an unregistered .22 Winchester, although he did have a licence for his .22 BSA. Now his new gun was confiscated. Perhaps the worst part of the affair was that he had to stand close to the witness box so he could hear the evidence given by the police officer. This was reported in the local and national newspapers, but the Boxing Board did not wish to know.[1]

Then Turpin was back to training in Warwick, with the suggestion of another world-title fight, or at least an

---

[1] Rhyl *Journal*, 7 January 1954. Deafness was not an insuperable handicap in boxing. One fighter had a series of lights in his corner so he could work to agreed signals.

elimination contest – possibly with Yolande Pompey. He was definitely to defend his European title against the light-punching Tiberio Mitri. Turpin was the only remaining British holder of a European title and *Boxing News* thought it would be disastrous for the sport if he lost it. It was generally accepted, win or lose, that it would be his last appearance as a middleweight. He was having trouble with the scales and it was now apparent that he would not be getting a return with Bobo Olson, at least in this country. The new and punishing entertainment tax would see to that.

Training was interrupted one Saturday morning in January, when Turpin appeared in Oxford Magistrates' Court, charged with dangerous and careless driving. He was not known for his safety behind the wheel. 'He was a mad hatter driver,' says Maria Mancini. On this occasion he was only found guilty of careless driving on the Oxford to Henley Road, when he had tried to overtake a bus in fog and had hit an oncoming car. In the quaint currency of the time he was fined fifteen guineas, with five guineas costs.[2]

In the meantime, a warm-up was scheduled between him and the unknown Swedish middleweight Olle Bengtsson. The contest scheduled for 30 March was the chief supporting contest at the top of the bill between Cockell and Roland La Starza. It was something of a triumph for Cockell, who dealt severely with the American.

It was considerably less of a triumph for Turpin who struggled to a points win over ten rounds, of which, according to the referee, he won five, lost two and drew two. He did knock the tall Swede down for a count of eight in the fourth, but he was unable to do so again, and he finished with cuts

2   Warwick and Warwickshire *District Advertiser*, 22 January 1964.

over both eyes following an early collision of heads. Even worse was that during the last few rounds Bengtsson was beginning to control affairs. Desmond Hackett commented: 'Turpin had courage all right. But the right-hand exterminator that was once Turpin's passport to world championship had gone. I doubt if it will return.'[3]

As always, Jack Solomons put as good a gloss on things as possible. Turpin was ring rusty; after all he hadn't fought for six months. Anyway, the crowd wanted nothing less than a knockout from him. His judgement may have been wrong but he was still the best middleweight in Europe. Cockell, Turpin and Pompey were all still in line for world-title bouts. If nothing else, like any top-class promoter, Solomons talked a good contest.

On 2 May 1954 Turpin went to Rome to meet Mitri before a crowd of 27,000. The contest lasted less than a minute. Neither boxer struck a blow in the first half minute, then Turpin landed a light left. The counter by Mitri was short. Next, with the first real punch of the fight, Mitri hit Turpin with a left hook high on the cheek but under the right ear. Turpin hit his head on the boards as he went down. He was partially up at five and then stumbled on to the ropes. He hauled himself up and when Mitri came forward was in no position to defend himself. The referee stopped the contest. *Il Messaggero* suggested that either Mitri had developed a murderous punch, or he must have struck some vital centre of Turpin's nervous system.[4] Later, Turpin claimed that he had been blinded by a flashlight, that the Spanish referee was wrong in stopping him and that he had suffered double vision. Everyone was out of step but our Randy.

[3] *Daily Express*, 1 April 1954.
[4] *Il Messaggero*, 3 May 1954.

This time there was a thorough medical examination of Turpin which was instigated not by the Board, but by the boxer himself. On 11 May the Board issued a statement through their chief medical examiner, Dr Phil Kaplin: 'At Turpin's request he was examined by an eminent physician and surgeon oculist. After a prolonged investigation including X-rays, blood tests and special visual examinations he was proved to be in excellent physical health and in their opinion he is fit to continue his boxing career.'

Years later Jackie Turpin revealed that he thought his brother's eyes were out of alignment, and that he should have been prevented from boxing there and then. His former trainer Bill Hyam recalled that his right eye showed no pupil. It turned up and only the white showed. His former sparring partner, Peter Price, said that in 1952, six years before Turpin retired, he told him he feared he was going blind in his left eye. Jonah Spencer, another sparring partner, said, 'Randy had double vision. One night after sparring in 1956 or 1957 I saw his eye had a turn in it. I said "What's wrong with your eye?" He swore and said "Did you notice it? I've got double vision."'[5] Jack Birtley blamed the Boxing Board of Control for not taking a stiffer line: 'They covered themselves by getting some pro-boxing doctor to say "This man is fit to carry on."'[6]

The next problem was Turpin's weight. George Middleton wrote to the Board saying that Turpin was having trouble with making the middleweight limit. Accordingly, the boxer was surrendering his British middleweight title. He would retain his Empire title for the present and was ready to defend his Empire light-heavyweight title.

[5] *Daily Mail*, 22 July 1966.
[6] *64 Day Hero*.

The light-heavyweight division was not strong at the time. Again, the name Yolande Pompey surfaced, along with Alex Buxton and the Canadian Yvon Durrell. A final date of 30 April 1955 was set for Turpin to defend. There were, however, other offers. Harry Levene, later the nemesis of Solomons but then managing Eddie Smith – the cruiserweight champion of Bermuda – offered a £500 sidestake for Turpin to meet his man. It was declined.

In the meantime, there were exhibitions to be undertaken, with longed-for moments of glory for the opposition. Larry Parkes from the Potteries boxed a three-round exhibition at the Victoria Hall, Hanley. Nearly fifty years later he would recall: 'Before the bout Randy came into the dressing room and told me what to do. However, when he'd gone my manager Benny Jones told me to forget what he'd said and try to knock him out. But we were wearing big 16 ounce gloves and the only time I caught Randy was when he decided to let me hit him. He was a six-footer like me, but so good and powerful. He was out of this world compared with the boxers I was used to meeting.'[7]

There were now also signs of difficulties between Turpin and Middleton. The manager wanted Turpin to return to the Midlands to train. Turpin wanted to stay in Wales where he was happy. When it came to it, though, he agreed to come back to Leamington to complete his training. He put all his possessions, including a washing machine, in a taxi and moved across the country.[8]

He received a hero's welcome from the crowd of nearly 5000 when he reappeared against the Luxembourg champion

---

[7] Stoke *Sentinel*, 30 September 2000. Earlier Parkes had also appeared with Turpin at the travelling booth run by Charles Hickman.
[8] Jack Birtley, *The Tragedy of Randolph Turpin*, p. 106.

Ray Schmit at the Embassy Sportsdrome in Birmingham on 15 February 1955. Schmit had the reputation of being durable and had never been knocked out. But he was open to a right-hand punch, something Turpin either failed to appreciate or could not execute. Turpin boxed with his left hand but, probably because of the long lay-off, his timing was out. He knocked Schmit down in the fourth round, and was moving solidly but unimaginatively to a victory when Schmit was disqualified in the eighth round for holding. He had been warned in the previous round, but ringsiders thought the decision was harsh. Turpin was booed as he left the ring.

The next month, he met another continental champion, this time the Spaniard José Gonzales, over ten rounds at Earl's Court. Turpin could still pull in the crowds: the attendance was close to 18,000. In the fight itself, either Gonzales mistook the count of referee Jack Hart, or he had lost interest, for he was making no great effort to get to his feet when he was knocked out in the seventh. Until then it had been more left hands from Turpin and the final blow had seemed to some to be more like a push.

There were no signs from these showings that Turpin would beat the then British light-heavyweight titleholder, Alex Buxton from Watford, whom he met at Harringay on 26 April. Of course, Turpin had defeated Buxton in their first meeting three years earlier after the loss of his title to Sugar Ray Robinson, stopping him in seven rounds. Now, he stopped him in five rounds less. But the bout was disappointing. Both men wrestled their way through the first round and at the beginning of the second, they were told to make a contest of it by referee Ben Green. They rushed at each other, Buxton fell to the canvas, and he was counted out. No one could actually say which punch had caused the damage.

Buxton said in a post-fight interview, 'I don't know what hit me.' The press was not entirely clear either. Some thought it was a body punch, some a right to the jaw, or a head. Turpin was naturally happy, but no more enlightening, 'I felt fit enough. I saw the chance and let him have it.'

Turpin may have been happy, but Solomons was ecstatic: 'Last night proved wrong the people who said that Turpin was finished and that his punch was gone. It also proved that champions do come back. Turpin has come back and I am doing my best to see that he gets a world title fight. I shall be flying to Las Vegas on Monday to see Charlie Johnson, the manager of [Archie] Moore, and I hope to get a fight between Moore and Turpin for London this year.'[9]

Moore had outpointed the durable, if ageing, Joey Maxim for the world light-heavyweight title, and then successfully defended it against him twice. In another defence, he had knocked out Bobo Olson in three rounds. Now he was moving up a weight division to box Rocky Marciano for the heavyweight title. The thought that Turpin should go in with Moore was horrifying.

It is often said that if a fighter has one last fight in him, it should be with his manager. In Turpin's case, it should have been with his promoter, because a match with Moore would certainly have been his last. But at the time Solomons' only concern seemed to be whether Moore would beat Marciano. In the unlikely event that he did, the Moore–Turpin bout would be a non-starter.

Meanwhile, Turpin had his appendix out, and on 19 September he outpointed Eddie Smith in Birmingham. There was, however, no sidestake to make this match. On 21

September Marciano stopped Moore in nine rounds. Solomons could now see no obstacle in the way of a fight between Moore and Turpin. His boxer would top the bill at Earl's Court against Moore at the beginning of 1956 – 10 January was the date set.

Turpin could not expect to concentrate solely on training for the Moore fight in the interim, though. Solomons had slots at major venues to fill, and so his big draw would have to fight again in 1955. This was justified by saying that Turpin had to guard against ring-rustiness, but of course the primary reason for it was to make as much money out of Randolph as possible. Turpin was matched with the Canadian light-heavyweight Gordon Wallace. This seemed safe enough: Wallace was not regarded as a big puncher, and the only highlight on his record was that he had outpointed the respected Johnny Sullivan.

The crowd at Harringay in October certainly got excitement for their money. Turpin knocked Wallace down in the second round, but the blows did no great damage. By the end of the round, Turpin had himself been down twice. In the third, he caught the Canadian twice with right hands to the jaw and knocked him down again for a count of five. But the writing was on the wall: Turpin might be able to knock the man down, but he could not keep him there. By the end of the fourth round, Wallace had survived and was doing the better work. In the fifth, Turpin took a punch to the jaw and went down for a count of eight. He was unsteady on his feet when he was knocked down again, following a barrage of blows ending with another right to the jaw. This time, although he pulled himself up and was standing holding the rope at the count of ten, it was all over.

Ernie Halford, who had grown up with Turpin, remembers

sitting with Dick Turpin at the ringside: 'He seemed out of
form and in about the second round his brother Dick sitting
next to me, got up saying, "That's it" and left. Afterwards I
asked Dick what was wrong and he said Licker had received
a nasty letter saying, "Get out and give a white man a
chance."'[10]

Turpin had displayed courage, as he always did, but it was
clear he could no longer take a decent punch, and that his
own was not what it had been. It is said that the last thing of
a boxer's to go is his punch, and Turpin's had seemingly gone.

Solomons did not bother to catch the New York flight.
George Middleton took a correct attitude with his boxer and
the press, announcing Turpin's immediate retirement: 'If
Randy were to change his mind, he would have to look for
a new manager. I persuaded him that it was time to pack in
the game and I will not say anything which might help him
to alter his mind. You can see the result. We are disappointed
but our decision is final. Randy Turpin is finished. He will
fight no more.'[11] Turpin said he could see the punches
coming, but he could not get out of their way.

A month later, though, it was a different story. Turpin
would not retire, nor would he be getting a new manager.
'We had a long discussion and have examined the matter
from every angle, and this is our decision,' said Middleton.[12]
The truth was, of course, that Turpin could not afford to
retire and Middleton could not afford to let him. But it was
acknowledged that Turpin wanted a break, so he relinquished
his British and Empire light-heavyweight titles, rather than
face a Board-ordered defence.

[10] Letter to author, April 2003.
[11] *Daily Herald*, 19 October 1955.
[12] *Sunday Chronicle*, 12 December 1955.

The title was now to be contested between Ron Barton from West Ham and Turpin's old adversary Albert Finch, to whom he had lost and then beaten on points eight years earlier in 1948. In March 1956, Barton stopped Finch. In April, Turpin had his comeback fight, again in Birmingham, this time against the Italian Alessandro D'Ottavio, who was stopped at the end of the sixth round with a cut eye. No one was impressed: D'Ottavio had come in overweight and had paid forfeit for being so.

Boxing News reported, 'On this showing he [Turpin] has lost the killer instinct. He was told by his advisers to be careful and careful he was.'[13]

There was better to come, however, against an unranked Frenchman, Jacques Bro, whom Turpin knocked out in five rounds on 18 June in Birmingham.

Despite his going backwards in boxing terms, Turpin was, in fact, creeping up the ratings and was now ranked tenth in the world. Yolande Pompey was ranked his number-one challenger; Gordon Wallace five; Barton six; and Alex Buxton seventh. In British terms Turpin was number-four challenger to Barton, Albert Finch, and Buxton.

After that, in an effort to climb the rankings, Turpin visited Hamburg on 21 September to meet Hans Stretz, ranked four in the world, over ten rounds. A win would again move Turpin into the position of a serious challenger. In three contests Turpin had never won abroad. Indeed, he had never survived the distance.

For much of the contest he looked as though he would end that run: he was clearly ahead after six rounds. But then all the old problems resurfaced: his legs went, his timing was off and

---

[13] *Boxing News*, 20 April 1956.

he could not take a punch to the jaw. With the German making a grandstand effort at the end, Turpin was again knocked down, taking a count of eight. He lost on points. There were suggestions that the referee Max Pipow had been harsh in not allowing Turpin to work at close quarters, and all the correct noises were made by Middleton, who called for a rematch in England with a British referee. But it was obvious that far too often Turpin had stood, his arms down and his mouth open, inviting a punch, which wobbled him when it landed.[14]

In the *Evening Standard*, George Whiting, one of the few reporters with whom Turpin remained on good terms, was severe: 'No doubts now – Turpin is just another fighter . . . the whiplash punch and the split-second timing that once gave him world supremacy have gone. And Turpin must not blame us for noting their passing – with infinite regret.'[15]

By now, Turpin was finding it more and more difficult to commit himself to training. The light-heavyweight Stan Cullis recalls:

Randy had training problems. He'd be supposed to be at the gym at 6 or 6.30 and Mo [Mosh Mancini] would send people out to find him at 7.30. Jimmy Linus – I was at school with him – would say, 'It's going to be a bloody hard night.' And he was right. He'd do three or four rounds with Jimmy and Jimmy would hit Turpin with everything he had. Sparring with Turpin was like a war.

Sometimes Middleton would say to Mo, 'You bloody train

14 'Randy Fails to Last the Pace', *Boxing News*, 28 September 1956. In the summer of 1957, Stretz took up wrestling after an eye injury in his contest with Dagomar Martinez. He had held the German cruiser- and middleweight titles.
15 *Evening Standard*, 22 September 1956.

him.' Randy would listen and then he'd take no notice. Keeping his sparring partners was the hardest thing in the world. Michael Stack must have sparred more rounds than anyone else. He never fought for the British title and I think maybe that's why.'[16]

Turpin was now getting bad headaches. Stan Cullis recalls:

He got lots of them in 1956–7. We all get the headaches. It depends on how many will stand up and say so. It was like a migraine times ten. They're easy to forget but when you have them . . .

Everybody knew when he had one. He didn't have to say. Had he had a brain I think the guy would have seen a doctor or a brain surgeon. So far as he was concerned it was a pain in his head and it was there. It's hard to say but any sane person would have gone to the doctor. His hangers-on weren't going to tell him there was anything wrong. There were too many people making money. He knew they were but he didn't know how to stop them.[17]

Meanwhile, Ron Barton was forced to give up his title to undergo an eye operation, and it was time for another round of musical chairs of promoters and fighters. A match between any two of Howard, Buxton, Finch and Turpin would have been acceptable. Howard was tied to a contract with Harry Levene and Buxton really wanted to box in London. For a few

---

[16] Conversation with author.
[17] Ibid.

days it looked as though Buxton would box Howard. In the end, it was Buxton against Turpin. A win meant a cherished Lonsdale Belt outright for either man and possibly a step back up the world rankings. Buxton was clearly on the way down, but even so there was no unanimity in the press about a Turpin victory. 'Third Time Lucky' for Alex?' asked *Boxing News*.[18]

The one-sided contest on 26 November 1956 took Turpin little further. Buxton already had two psychologically scarring defeats by Turpin and, even at his best, he was not in the same class. He was knocked down for a count of five in the first round and took five counts in the fifth before the referee Frank Williams stopped the contest. A disinterested or even a humane observer should have noted that Turpin could not put Buxton away. The Coventry *Evening Telegraph* was, however, cock-a-hoop: 'Last night Turpin showed that he still has the merciless punch that once put him on top of the world's middleweights. Fighting with a power and fury that no-one thought him capable of, he had a packed hall acclaiming a great comeback.'[19]

The *Daily Express* was equally happy: 'Turpin was superb. He has never fought better. He was supremely fit, confident, ice-cool – the Turpin of his world middleweight days.'[20]

Jack Solomons could see his goose was laying again. Turpin would now fight Archie Moore. But *Boxing News* was sceptical: 'Disregard all the grandiose schemes and plans that were tendered on behalf of Randy Turpin . . . in our opinion at least [he] is still only a shadow of his former self. He had

---

[18] *Boxing News*, 23 November 1956.

[19] Coventry *Evening Telegraph*, 27 November 1956.

[20] *Daily Express*, 27 November 1956. Curiously this report did not appear under a signed byline and Jack Birtley thought perhaps it and the report in the *Evening Telegraph* had been written by the same man. (*The Tragedy of Randolph Turpin*, p. 114.)

nothing to beat in Buxton . . . It is nonsense to suggest that, on the night's form, we can now hope for great things from Turpin. Whatever it was this will go down in history as one of the worst title fights in the cruiserweight calendar.'[21]

The next realistic step was for Turpin to meet Arthur Howard to fight the British light-heavyweight title. The contest was planned for the following March. However, Turpin injured a hand whilst sparring, and the promoter Alex Griffiths at first delayed the promotion but then, when the injury did not heal immediately, brought in Johnny Sullivan. At four days' notice – and with Turpin at the ringside – Sullivan did nobody any favours by outpointing Howard in a non-title bout over ten rounds. The fight was regarded as a cracking one.

Turpin was ready for his match with Howard by the summer, and they met in Leicester on 11 June. A curious incident occurred in Howard's dressing room before the contest. Dick Turpin came in and told Howard that he hoped he would beat his brother – once again the bad blood in the Turpin family became evident.

Dick's wish was not granted. Turpin beat Howard on points over fifteen rounds, but it was not an easy contest. Howard knocked Turpin down five times. As usual there were mixed reports. Naturally, Middleton was positive: 'Last night Randolph beat the toughest Englishman he is ever likely to meet.' Desmond Hackett may have been politically incorrect by today's standards but he was more realistic: 'But this was an unhappy sepia shadow of the old Turpin. Apart from a slight buckling at the knees and a few falls that did not even merit a count, Howard clearly advertised that Turpin no

[21] *Boxing News*, 23 and 30 November 1956.

longer carries the destroyer punch that made him world menace number one.'

Boxing News thought that whilst Turpin had generally controlled the contest, Howard had thrown away three great chances: 'Fifteen furious, fantastic always exciting rounds. Fifteen rounds of slog, swipe and slam. It was often ridiculous. It was often too bad to be true but it was a fight every second of it AND Randy Turpin is still light-heavyweight champion of Great Britain.' As for Howard: 'He had time to look in the mirror and try the crown on for size in rounds five, twelve and thirteen.'[22]

For Turpin the year ended with a string of contests against unranked Europeans, all of which ended in stoppages.[23] There was now talk of Turpin moving up a weight and boxing heavyweight Joe Erskine, who had narrowly outpointed Henry Cooper in September. Finally, the long delayed Turpin v Pompey bout was, said Solomons encouragingly, a final eliminator for the world light-heavyweight title.

Then came something of a bombshell. The Midlands promoter Alex Griffiths announced that the number-four-ranked light-heavyweight, Willie Pastrano, was to be matched with Turpin in the coming February. He and his partner were not sure whether the fight would be in Leicester or Birmingham. There was also talk of a rematch at Madison Square Garden. It was not a contest which appealed to the press. Pastrano was very highly thought of. On 22 October, weighing thirteen stone six, he had completely outboxed the Welsh heavyweight Dick Richardson. A month later Turpin, weighing twelve stone seven – his heaviest ever – had made

[22] *Daily Express*, 12 June 1957; *Boxing News*, 14 June 1957.
[23] Ahmed Boulgroune in nine, Serio Burchi in two and Uwe Janssen in eight.

hard work of defeating the German Uwe Janssen. If the match took place Turpin would be giving away at least a stone, or bulking up – something which would do him no good at all. He was also eight years older than Pastrano. All in all, there was the possibility of a seriously bad beating. *The Times* accepted that Turpin still had a punch but asked: 'Who can imagine he will land it to good effect on the fleet-footed Pastrano before he is battered by a stream of cutting left jabs? This seems a match which could do nothing but harm to boxing.' Let alone Turpin. *The Times* thought the Board should step in, and it did. Under Regulation 20, it had the power to prohibit the match as not being in the interests of boxing. Roused from its then customary torpor the Board duly did so.

Naturally there was dissent from the promoters. Turpin said he thought he had an even chance and the promoters thought they should appeal against the decision. They did, and after a hearing in London on 8 January, Griffiths and Middleton emerged, without a contest on their hands but unbowed, 'We lost on points,' said Griffiths. 'The Stewards said that no reflection was cast on any of us.'[24]

Turpin was still the British champion as 1958 dawned, but just how far he was slipping was demonstrated by a mauling ten-round win against the Dutchman Wim Snoek in Birmingham on 11 February. Even the *Evening Telegraph* could not see a shining light at the end of that performance: 'It is always sad to see the decline of a champion. But unless Turpin can do better than this, then the writing is all too clearly on the ex-world title-holder's wall.'[25]

Two months later Turpin made hard work of defeating Eddie Wright over seven rounds at Leicester on 21 April, but on 22

[24] *The Times*, 9 January 1968.
[25] Coventry *Evening Telegraph*, 12 February 1958.

July Redvers Sangoe was stopped in the fourth round after taking a number of counts. This was the problem for Turpin and his management. He was still too good for the run-of-the-mill British and European light-heavyweights, as Mills had been, but in the terms of world boxing he was a spent force.

Turpin was finally matched with the Trinidadian Yolande Pompey in the open air at the Alexander Sports Stadium, the home of the Birchfield Harriers, on 9 September 1958. The match was made at twelve stone nine. Turpin weighed in at twelve stone seven, with Pompey three quarters of a pound over twelve stone.

Pompey had already had his chance with Archie Moore, but had been stopped in ten rounds at a half-empty Harringay Arena. *Boxing News* reported that Pompey had been ahead in the first half-dozen rounds, but manager Dennie Mancini thinks Moore was toying with him. He had watched him train with Arthur Howard as his chief sparring partner at Windsor and knew that Moore had been forced to lose a stone in three and a half weeks to make the weight. 'Moore was eating a steak, spitting the meat out and swallowing the blood. Afterwards he smoked a cigar and had a drop of brandy.' As for the fight itself: 'Pompey didn't know what to do. He was in awe of him. In the second round Hart [the referee] ordered them to stop boxing and told Moore that he wanted more action. Moore looked at him in disgust. Moore then did Pompey over and then stood back.'[26] Pompey was cut in the ninth and took three counts in the tenth before the contest was stopped.

The Turpin *v* Pompey match was a contest which would have been of real interest five years earlier, and although both

[26] Conversation with author.

had gone backwards since then, it still attracted considerable attention. The overall feeling was better late than never and, with the hype which surrounds almost any worthwhile boxing match, it was suggested that the winner would walk into a world title contest before the end of the year. Only Gordon Wallace of Empire-based fighters had defeated Turpin, but there were thoughts that Pompey could become the second. Despite the general interest in the match, the Board refused to allow it to be broadcast, fearing that it would interfere with the show promoted by Stan Baker at Streatham.

The long-time champion of Freddie Mills, Peter McInnes of *Boxing News*, thought Turpin could still do it. Pompey's form had been disappointing in recent bouts and he had not won for almost a year. Better still for Turpin, Pompey's punching left a lot to be desired. He had taken a long time to deal with Johnny Sullivan who was, after all, a blown-up middleweight. 'Randy is still a good clouter but no more than that . . . When both were at their best we would have plumped for Turpin. With the bloom removed we would still fancy the verdict going to Randy.'[27]

It did not. He had the better of the first round and Pompey dropped to one knee, but he rose without a count. It was then, astonishingly, that Turpin touched gloves, instead of going in for the kill. It was his last opportunity: he was knocked out after ninety seconds of the second round. A right hand caught him flush on the side of the jaw and dropped him flat on his back. His head hit the canvas as he fell. Turpin made desperate efforts to get up, but his legs would not hold him. When he was partially up he skidded along the canvas and was counted out. This was Pompey's

[27] *Boxing News*, 5 September 1958.

world championship. His supporters swarmed into the ring and carried him on their shoulders to the dressing room.

'The day cannot be far off when Turpin calls it a day,' said *Boxing News*.[28] He did so in some style. In October 1958 Jack Solomons promoted his final show at Harringay Arena before it was redeveloped as a warehouse. To commemorate the evening he brought together many former champions who had boxed there, having them introduced into the ring before the main contest. They included Jack Petersen, who later became president of the BBB of C, and his German opponent Walter Neusel. Freddie Mills was a notable absentee. He was billed to appear in Leeds in Dickie Henderson's *Road Show* and thought it would be wrong not to turn up. Instead, he sent a telegram which, to his regret, was not read out. Randolph Turpin took the opportunity to announce his final retirement. *Boxing News* was pleased: 'For the third time he relinquished the British light-heavyweight title without conceding defeat. This time he has made a final decision.'[29]

But where was he to go now? With luck he could live off his ring earnings. He had, by any reckoning, earned a minimum net of £133,251 from his career, the equivalent today of many millions. But, in fact, most of this money had gone; squandered on poor investments, uncollectable loans – thousands to a man to buy a pig farm, hundreds to a man to buy a Chevrolet – lawsuits, cars, presents, and a series of women.

---

[28] Ibid., 12 September 1958. Pompey was matched on 14 October against the Nigerian Dick Tiger, a contest which Tiger won readily. With the defeat went Pompey's world title contest. Possibly the reason was that Pompey had been obliged to boil himself down to make the weight. He was due to pay a substantial forfeit for every pound over weight. Tony Vairo, 'How I Put One Across Harry Levene', *Sunday People*, 18 March 1962.

[29] *Boxing News*, 31 October 1958.

16

Freddie Mills in Arcadia

Mills in retirement was as enormously popular as he had been in the ring. At the *Boxing News'* luncheon in October 1950 he received a cup for the 'Gamest loser of 1949' and made a typically joking speech in acceptance. 'Last year I came here and got a belt – then I got a belting from Joey Maxim. My wife is going to go crazy over this [cup] when she comes to clean it every Friday.' He also received a certificate from America for his sportsmanship.[1]

Eight years after Mills retired, the journalist Peter McInnes, who had taken such an interest in Mills' early career and idolised him, wrote: 'The Chinese restaurant is even more flourishing today than it was in the days when Mills was an active glovesman. It is certainly true to say that his fame and popularity have increased rather than diminished. Add to this fact that for some years now he has contributed a weekly

[1] *Boxing News*, 29 November 1950.

boxing column for a Sunday newspaper and you can see that Mills is just about as successful as "A Man of Business" as he was "A Man about Boxing".'[2]

He certainly did well enough in the housing market. Chrissie Mills wanted him to put his money into property and Bill Bavin, an estate agent and insurance broker who had handled some insurance matters for him in the summer of 1947, found him a row of small houses in Straightsmouth, Greenwich. He also sold him a house in Stansted Road for letting out, and another property in Bromley Road, Catford, which was converted into one-bedroom flatlets. Bavin did well for him and by 1957 Mills had an income of around £3000 a year from the properties.

One venture which was not quite such a success was a café, jointly owned by Mills and Bavin, in Peckham. It was managed, in theory, by an ex-Guardsman. Unfortunately he had difficulties in getting up early enough to cook and serve the breakfasts and he had to go. Shortly afterwards the café also went, but at no great loss.

Additionally, they still owned the detached family home, Joggi Villa (pronounced Dog-Eye, it stemmed from a name Chrissie called a dog as a child). They had moved there on 26 June 1947. Mills had been in South Africa when she cabled him to say it was on the market. It had a stone bird on the roof, to which Freddie would say good night.

Immediately after his retirement, and for some years thereafter, Mills was in great demand in the entertainment world. His broadcasting career started with an appearance on *In Town Tonight*, and took off on television with Al Burnett in *Kaleidoscope*, when he sang 'April Showers'.

2   Peter McInnes, 'Knight of the Roped Square', *Boxing News*, 26 September 1958.

On one radio programme he was used as the straight man for comedians, playing the 'manager' of the diminutive comedian, 'Killer' Askey. He was a guest on *Sports Report*, as well as *The Name's the Same*. He appeared as a mystery guest on *What's My Line*, and on *The Forces' Show* with comedians Jimmy Jewell and Ben Warriss. He was Buttons in a television version of Cinderella. He played a good old Britisher comically defeating a bunch of Oriental supposed judo experts. He was a teddy boy; he dressed in drag as a char.

By 1958 he was writing his own boxing column and appearing regularly on television in *6.5 Special* with Jo Douglas and Pete Murray. He had his own twenty-four-part keep-fit series and had appeared in five shows with Dickie Henderson. In 1958 he toured in the *Dickie Henderson Road Show* and the next year did a summer with him in Blackpool, billed as Special Guest Artiste in sketches with the diminutive Jimmy Clitheroe. He also did a good impression of the Inkspots, something he had perhaps learned from Sugar Ray Robinson. He appeared with Frankie Howerd in *Fine Goings On* and advertised the Philishave electric razor with Freddie Trueman and Benny Hill – there was a boy's punchball with Freddie's face on it. He cut a record which included the song 'Two Lovely Black Eyes'. There was a Freddie Mills' *Boys Boxing Annual*. For some years it seemed as though you could not switch on the television without seeing Freddie Mills in some guise or another.

He crowned beauty queens, picked champion babies, attended cricket, football and darts matches, opened fêtes, fought his way out of a strengthened paper bag and even 'knocked out' Jack Solomons in a match with Tommy Farr. Much of this was for charity. The boxer Nosher Powell recalls, 'He'd always pull the stops out for charity. He was always the first there.' But was he making money for himself?

The comedian Bob Monkhouse recalled: 'My partner Denis [Goodwin] and I wrote a sketch for *Calling All Forces* in which Ted Ray interviewed Freddie. Freddie used to go off the script doing cracks of his own and you could see it disconcerted Ted for an instant. The audience loved it. He was very, very good at doing comedy. For an amateur he had a good delivery.'[3]

Already there was a hint of desperation to this constant activity. He appeared sliding on his bottom on the bill for an ice show and on television as a clown, with Charlie Caroli in the water bucket and trouser routine. This was, of course, good old sport Freddie – anything for a laugh – demonstrating a fine line in self mockery. Whereas Turpin's subsequent wrestling career was merely degrading.

He was certainly seen as an easy touch for spongers. Birtley recalls the story of a man who hung about near Solomons' gym and had been tapping Mills for years. One days Mills, wound up by his wife, asked the sponger to give one reason why he should not put the ten shillings in his own children's money box.

Mills hadn't abandoned the sport for showbiz altogether, though. He was also promoting boxing, beginning in Bristol with an open-air show on 28 May 1951. It featured two local boys, Terry Ratcliffe and Gordon Hazell, who boxed Gilbert Ussing and Bos Murphy – seen off by Dick Turpin conclusively some years earlier.

Nosher Powell believes that Mills promoting was not a sensible move. He recalls: 'I remember when he was

[3] Conversation with author.

promoting and not doing too well at Earl's Court I boxed Joe
Bygraves for him. I was doing my own managing then and
I went in to see him and his advisers. They made an offer
and behind their backs he was pointing to the ceiling, "Ask
more." He was a fighter's promoter.[4]

Mills also visited prisons and on his second visit to
Dartmoor to talk to the inmates and give an exhibition, he
appealed to the prisoners to donate blood. Six hundred of
the inmates did so. They may have been inspired by the film,
Emergency Call, which Mills had made in which he boxed
Powell, who recalls:

I'd made several films and was a friend of Lewis Gilbert.
He decided he was going to make a boxing film, *There
is Another Sun*. In fact, it was the springboard for Laurence
Harvey's success. I got a call from Lewis to go and have
a lunch with him at Shepperton. What he wanted was
a big name in boxing to give it more authority and I
thought he meant me. Instead, I was to be the technical
adviser.

I put Freddie's name forward and Lewis wondered if
he'd even take it. To the outsider Freddie was still the
king. We had a guy who was an actor to box Freddie. I
got in the ring saying, 'Do this, don't do that.' The left
hand don't work for an actor like it does for a boxer. Lewis
said to me, 'He's not shaping too well. How about you
playing the part? I'll cut the dialogue.' I said, 'That's a lot
of confidence you have in me.' Freddie had a nice few
lines of dialogue and he shaped well and the boxing
sequence went well too.

[4] Ibid.

When the bell went we were off, and they were so engrossed that the round didn't stop after three minutes or four or five. I was getting banged. Freddie didn't know how to pull a punch. I said, 'Cut,' myself and that they'd have to do it in one-minute takes. He'd have been the British equivalent of 'Slapsy' Maxie Rosenbloom. That man must have made a hundred films in Hollywood. He was working till the day of his death.[5]

In fact, over the years, Mills appeared in twelve films altogether. Apart from two *Carry On* films, *Regardless* and *Constable*, none of them was in any way noteworthy. His parts were generally limited to the likes of 'Lefty', 'Jewel Thief', 'Tiny' and in *Joey Boy*, completed the year of his death, 'Sergeant'.

In January 1953 Mills moved his promotions to the Empress Hall in Earl's Court. His doings were still news, particularly in the boxing fraternity. That month he announced he would be taking a team of boxers, including Randolph Turpin and Tommy Farr, to Korea to entertain the troops, but it never got off the ground.

Just how much of Mills' promotion was his own and how much he was fronting for Jack Solomons is open to question. Certainly the Board did not want one promoter tying up too many venues at once and Mills would have been a good front man. But if he was just a front, he took things very seriously. He opened an office at Joe Bloom's gym in Earlham Street little more than a hundred yards from the restaurant and announced he would be selling tickets direct to the public. This was, on

---

[5] Conversation with author. 'Slapsy' Maxie Rosenbloom held the World light-heavyweight title in the early 1930s. He was said not to have a punch but even without one he defended the title eight times in four years. He had 106 fights and a sequence of 16 straight wins and a non-losing run of 22.

the face of it, public-spirited indeed. At the time, tickets for a Solomons' promotion were hard to come by at face value for ordinary members of the public. The bulk of the tickets would go to friends and partners of Solomons, who would sell them at a 50 per cent mark-up. But this did not always work according to plan. A good example was the first Mills *v* Woodcock contest. Tickets had not been available to the general public for the fortnight before the fight, but on the evening it rained and the scalpers caught a cold as they tried to unload five-guinea tickets at a guinea.

The problem with a Mills show was that, although he had good main and supporting events, his promotions would not necessarily sell out. Powell remembers: 'Freddie had just retired and he wasn't doing too well at promoting. He was a very, very honest man. Everyone got paid but Freddie didn't. He didn't want to see young fighters get took on as he had been when he was young. He paid over the odds.'[6] He was far too honourable to negotiate downwards and, instead of coming to an arrangement with the boxers' managers, as so many would have done, he ensured they were paid out of his own pocket. His career as a promoter ended in 1954. Of promoting, he later said, 'I didn't lose money but I nearly lost my sense of humour.'[7]

As if dealing with promoters were not enough, around this time he also took on journalists. This time he won. Mills, along with Solomons and Broadribb, won damages against the Manchester *Evening News*, complaining that they had been libelled over a comment in November 1951 that, 'Tonight's fight, in fact, is just about the most meaningless bout since the Joe Baksi *v* Freddie Mills carve-up.'

[6] Conversation with author.
[7] Freddie Mills, *Daily Mail*, 26 July 1965.

The three claimed that 'carve-up' meant a fix. The paper published an immediate clarification and apology, saying that what they meant was that Mills had been carved up. This did not satisfy the plaintiffs and a good deal of fun was had by counsel and judge before the financial settlement was agreed. Solomons announced in court that he would give the balance of his winnings after expenses to charity.[8]

Three years later came one of Mills' proudest moments, when he appeared by request in an exhibition bout with Johnny Williams at Buckingham Palace on the grass of the Rose Garden. Ironically a photograph of the bout would be used a decade later as the cover of the programme for 'The Freddie Mills Night in Aid of the Dependants of the Late Freddie Mills'.

---

[8] The contest in question was between Roy Ankarah and Tommy McGovern. Manchester *Evening News*, 26 November 1951; *The Times*, 16 June 1953.

17

Randolph Turpin
Meets Doctor Death

Unlike Freddie Mills, there were no heydays for Randolph Turpin after his defeat by Pompey. The reality was that he was broke and had no real way of putting his finances together again. From time to time during his life, Turpin gave explanations about his lost money. In 1947 he had, he said, opened a deposit account and for the next four years spent £3000 and saved £6000. Then, on 10 July 1951, he opened a current account to which he transferred £26,000. In 12 months the whole amount was gone. £4000 went out in the last three weeks of December of that year alone. The suggestion was that someone had been signing cheques in his name.[1]

Later, Turpin would blame George Middleton for his financial position, saying that he had never received the money he was owed. It was a repeated complaint and one Middleton

---

[1] Randolph Turpin with Sam Leitch, 'With Hate in my Heart', *Sunday Mirror*, 15 April 1962.

steadfastly denied: 'Up to 1951 the system was that I countersigned cheques for Randy to draw money. Coming back from the second Robinson fight he said he wanted to handle the money himself from then on. I know there are people who will always say George Middleton did all right and Randy didn't. They are ignorant people. Randy was like a son to me. I can go anywhere in the world and hold my head up.'[2]

For now, it was straight to work – first in George Middleton's scrapyard and later in one owned by Bertie Harrison. Again, unlike Mills, there was no career for Turpin on the radio or on television when he retired. For a start he had a speech impediment, secondly he had learning difficulties and thirdly, and perhaps most importantly, he was black. There may have been little colour prejudice whilst he was growing up in Leamington, but by now there certainly was. In the 1960s black people did not star on television and radio. True, there were exceptions, such as Hutch, the pre-war nightclub entertainer who appeared in cabaret, and Edmundo Ros, who hosted a radio show from his nightclub in Regent Street. And, of course, there were other entertainers, such as Billy Daniels, but, on the whole, there were no black newscasters nor sports commentators; black people were not invited to give soundbite opinions. Enoch Powell had yet to make his 'rivers of blood' speech, but it was in the offing. Even if Turpin had wanted a career in show business, unless he sang or danced, which was what was expected of black people at the time, he would still have been marginalised in the world of showbiz. The closest he ever came was on stage in Llandudno, where he'd shadow boxed a little and answered questions. He had done this with some success after the second Robinson contest. But that had been seven years earlier, when he was still a top name. The entertainer Bob Monkhouse remembered:

> This would be 1959–60. Terry Scott was appearing for the season and I went to the castle [Gwyrch] with him. Turpin had been offered pretty good money to appear at the local theatre and do ten or twelve minutes. I said I'd look at his publicity material for him and he could have a few shills in the audience to ask questions to get things going. He said 'What?' And I repeated it. 'That's the problem,' he said. 'I can't hear what they're saying. I've had so many blows to the ear.'
>
> He told me how Joe Louis used to sit outside a night club in one of the hotels in Las Vegas signing autographs at a table. 'I never want to be seen doing that,' he said, 'flogging autographs at a few shillings a time.' I liked him. He was very polite to me and he had a nice nature. Terry thought he was a tragic figure.[3]

So, instead, Turpin went to work from eight until five in George Middleton's yard breaking cars or driving a lorry, and he seems to have been relatively happy doing it. He had the consolation of weekend visits to London, where he spent money on women as if he was still earning tens of thousands. Bertie Harrison would later say: 'He was a good worker and liked. We'd go out at the weekends and nights, every night. At weekends we'd go to clubs and pick some birds. We'd have a good time. He was generous. He'd give birds anything.'[4]

3 Conversation with author.
4 *64 Day Hero.*

There were still appearances in the boxing booths, and boxing on unlicensed shows continued. For that, Turpin could not expect any favours from the Board's General Secretary, Teddy Waltham. So one of the greatest humiliations in Turpin's life, and there were a number, came in July 1961 when the then British middleweight champion, Terry Downes, challenged the American Paul Pender for the world title. Pender had ended the reign of Sugar Ray Robinson when he outpointed him on a split decision on 22 January 1960 at the old Boston Arena, defeating him again in the rematch on 10 June that year. Downes had already lost once to Pender, retiring with a badly damaged nose. Now there was a rematch, and it was suggested that Turpin could teach Downes a good deal about defence. The British Boxing Board of Control refused permission for him to spar. This was odd because at the time there was not much check on who was or was not a sparring partner, nor what their credentials might be. Instead, Turpin was allowed to give Downes what was called some 'pointers'. Downes later said he thought Turpin could still hit: 'Just a round at half speed for the photographers proved Randy a smashing whacker. He tucked me a punch up the ribs to make me realise what a good champ he must have been.'[5]

For these 'pointers', Turpin received £40.

Overall, he spent a good deal of time in Wales, where the

[5] Terry Downes, *My Bleedin' Business*, p. 164. Through no fault of Downes, the contest left a sour taste in a number of mouths. The Boston promoter Sam Silverman was beaten up on 12 July as he left a nightclub off Piccadilly. He had been with his friend, Elliot Price, a big-time gambler, after Downes beat Pender. Six months earlier Downes had been stopped in seven, but this time Pender stayed on his stool at the beginning of the tenth round. The contest had not been a hard one. There were slight cuts to both men and Pender had taken the ninth round. Pender's trainer Al Lacey said his eye was too bad to continue. Later

Great Orme complex was steadily going to rack and ruin, and his money was ebbing away. Salts maintained that the complex was not being run properly and he would have nothing to do with it. He claimed later he had given Turpin good warning of his views. What he had to say in November 1957 about the prosecution of the manager of the gift shop at Randy's Bar over selling what were euphemistically described as '61 novelty items, 34 educational toys and 11 inscribed plaques,' is unrecorded. Back in August, Constable John Jones had purchased a rubber figure of a woman and later a plaque. They had, said the manager, been bought from firms in Liverpool and Rhyl and he had been assured they were all right. The goods were forfeited.

At one time, in charge of the complex had been Turpin's sister Joan and her bricklayer husband John Beston. She would say that they had cleaned the place up, whitewashed the buildings and opened the slot-machine arcade. But they did not have the control they claimed. Turpin would come back from the Midlands or London with hangers-on and waive all their bills. Gerald Williams, who delivered soft drinks to the Orme, was making money on the side from the bottles and maintained others were as well. 'I could sense what was going on,' he told Gordon Williams. Joan Turpin and her husband eventually went back to the Midlands, leaving the tradesmen unpaid. Gwen Turpin paid some £2000 out of her own account to settle the debts. Turpin was not

---

Lacey said that Pender had had a series of injections for flu and was not fit to continue. The Soho villain Albert Dimes lost a large amount of money backing Pender. The next morning at the Carlton Towers Hotel, Silverman's face was more bruised than Pender's and the promoter had bruises on his ankles. He recognised Dimes, but would not name him. (Frank Butler, *The Good, the Bad and the Ugly*). Pender retired from the ring in 1963 and died on 12 January 2003. He had been suffering from Alzheimer's.

happy and tried to get John Beston to return to the complex to sort things out. When he refused, Turpin broke his nose. 'I've nearly killed him. It's the first time I ever kicked anyone,' he told his wife.[6]

Finally, Turpin sold Great Orme to pay off some of the tax he owed. He lost some £5000 in capital and an unknown amount in running costs. For the twelve months before the sale, the premises had been managed by one of his former sparring partners, Tommy Ennifer, whose previous managerial experience had been on a demolition site. Again, there have been allegations and counter-allegations about the final home for the money. Turpin would say that some £2500 was deducted by the bank and applied to an overdraft of Salts. The entrepreneur would say that he never received a penny back his investment.[7]

One career open to black men in the 1960s was wrestling. They would usually appear as a villain, such as Black Butcher Johnson; sometimes as a comic, like his half-brother Johnny Kwango; or as an acrobat, like Masambula, whose trick was to walk around the top rope of the ring on his hands.

Turpin was fortunate in that wrestling throughout the country was increasingly coming under the grip of Joint Promotions, who controlled the top venues, owned the most famous names and had something of a lock on television shows. There were, of course, smaller promoters in smaller halls, some of whom were close to organised crime. The public simply could not get enough wrestling. There were shows every night of the week in London and soon

---

[6] Unless otherwise stated the quotations regarding the Great Orme are from *64 Day Hero*.
[7] 'Turpin Just Burned Up Money', *News of the World*, 23 July 1966.

there were several breakaway independent groups looking to challenge Joint Promotions' monopoly. The largest and most successful of these was Paul Lincoln Promotions, possibly because he, himself, wrestled as the hated villain, the undefeated masked man, Doctor Death. He fought in a series of battles, often with his close friends Ray Hunter or Judo Al Hayes, both of whom were regular masked White Angels.[8]

Another rival to Joint Promotions was Matsport Promotions, run by George Kidd, the former World lightweight champion, Eddie Cappelli and Joe D'Orazio. They needed a star attraction. Kidd knew Turpin, and saw him as a potential top-of-the-bill and crowd-puller. Former wrestler and promoter Joe D'Orazio recalls: 'At that time in America former boxers were becoming a draw as wrestlers and we thought Turpin would be an attraction. George went down to the Castle and there he was – unshaven and reading comics. Randy come down to my office which was in Brixton a few days later. He'd still got his clothes from when he was earning money boxing and when I first saw him it depressed me to see how he looked. It seemed as if he'd a cast in his eye.'[9]

There have been plenty of role models for well-known boxers – now down on their luck – turned wrestler. Jack Johnson, Primo Carnera, Joe Louis, Jersey Joe Walcott, 'Two Ton' Tony Galento, Jack Doyle, Larry Gains, Muhammad Ali, Chuck Wepner and Mike Tyson are just a handful of those who have become involved in wrestling in one way or

[8] In the North of England at smaller halls Doctor Death was often Ted Beech, whom Turpin wrestled regularly.
[9] Conversation with author.

another.[10] Not all boxers turned wrestler have done badly. Carnera, who in fact had begun his career as a weightlifter before becoming a boxer, was one who prospered, at least for a time. But then his critics, and there were many, said he was never really a boxer.

In contrast, Joe Louis' career as a wrestler was not such a success. In 1956, with the Revenue at his throat, Louis received an offer of $100,000 from promoter Ray Tabani. Louis then made his most often quoted remark: 'Rose [his wife] was real upset. She said it was like seeing President Eisenhower washing dishes. I told her it damn sure beat stealing.' Later, in his book he added: 'I honestly didn't feel there was anything dishonourable about it, but then when you're broke who can see straight?'[11]

On 15 March, Louis made his mat debut in Washington against a man who would be one of his regular opponents – 'Cowboy' Rocky Lee. The referee was none other than Jersey Joe Walcott. Unsurprisingly, Lee did most of the work, and behaved badly as well. At the end of a match, which lasted ten minutes, Walcott pulled Lee away from Louis, so giving the former champion a clear shot at Lee's jaw. The Cowboy was knocked out of the ring and counted out, to the huge delight of the crowd. Later, it would be Lee who was Louis' last opponent and the one who ended his career in Columbus, Ohio. He accidentally stood on him, damaging muscles near

---

[10] Not all appeared for financial reasons; recently Lennox Lewis announced he wanted to fulfil his boyhood dream and appear in a wrestling ring possibly as a guest referee. (*Evening Standard*, 18 October 2002.) Others simply liked the idea. Both Jimmy Saville, the entertainer, and Harvey Smith, the top show jumper, appeared in the ring. Occasionally it has worked the other way round. In 1933 Larry Gains introduced a former wrestler Pat Delancey to the boxing ring, where he met with some success. George Godfry hopped back and forth in the 1930s, and in the same period Paul Berlanbach boxed, wrestled and then boxed again.
[11] Joe Louis, *My Life*, p. 233.

to his heart (the cowboy weighed 340 pounds). Louis' licence to wrestle was withdrawn.

Boxer v wrestler matches have been popular spectacles over the years, as have most boxers turned wrestlers; the public still want to see them punch: 'Tony [Galento] looks pretty sad whenever he gets into any sort of trouble. His knowledge of wrestling is the same as was his knowledge of boxing, namely a left hook to the jaw.'[12] Turpin's first matches were of that variety and, to the end of his career on the mat, the crowds would call, 'Box him Randy, box him.' It was the signal for him to raise his fists and for the villain to get down on his knees and start to beg.

Turpin was given basic instruction by the technically brilliant former champion Kidd and his partners, who showed him some of the moves in preparation for his winning debut against Frankie Hughes at the Paisley Ice-Rink in early January 1961. His London debut came at the Poplar Baths on 23 February, jointly topping a bill which featured the Spaniard Victor Catilla, who wrestled as Quasimodo, against Doctor Death.

Turpin's opponent before the capacity crowd was the film and television star, Yorkshireman Brian Glover, then wrestling as 'Leon Arras from Australia'. The match was made over ten four-minute rounds, with Turpin wearing gloves. Both men would fight to their own rules. Naturally Turpin won. He hit Glover under the heart in the first round and, to the delight of the crowd, knocked him out in the second. In fact it was an unlikely result. In wrestler–boxer matches, the wrestler who can either take one punch or avoid one wins in a matter of seconds rather than minutes.

---

[12] *Ring*, January 1949.

Joe D'Orazio recalls:

He was a very lovely fellow and we did good business. We never had him on a percentage but he was paid ten times more than the other wrestlers. We had him do a few boxer v wrestler contests and all the time we were teaching him to be a wrestler. He fought Spike O'Reilly with us and Leon Arras and Frankie Hughes. We could charge double for him for a while. He did a couple of shows a week, no more. He knew we weren't going to put him on the dustcart. He was going to have a full-time career as a referee with us when he retired.[13]

On 5 March 1962, Turpin made his home debut at a thousand-seat cinema in Warwick, where he wrestled Rocky Steve Burnett, described as a Canadian lumberjack, at a Cape Promotions tournament. This was a time when cinemas were failing all over the country, and bingo evenings and wrestling tournaments were being put on in them in an attempt to bolster the flagging audiences. That week the owners of the cinema said that they were just about breaking even with wrestling and bingo, but they would look at any sensible offer for the place. Turpin was topping a bill which included such luminaries as The Mighty Ursuss (Masked Monster) v Henri Pierlot, and El Medico v Bill Tunney, who became one of Turpin's regular opponents. In the audience were his wife and their two daughters, Gwyneth, then aged seven, and Annette, who was two years younger. Later Turpin would have two more daughters – Charmaine and Carmen.

Turpin won by two falls to one.

[13] Conversation with author.

He was back in Warwick by November, this time topping the bill on behalf of Jack Taylor's International Promotions, against the rather better-known Pat Kloke. Also on the bill were such stalwarts as Black Butcher Johnson and Mike Marino, who promoted around the country. The Leamington Spa *Courier* did not report on the bout. Yet when Turpin wrestled for smaller promoters, the company was often even less exalted. At the Radford Social Club in Coventry he wrestled Fred Barnes, a local scrap dealer, billed as the Brazilian Prince Barnu. This match was used by his critics as a yardstick of how far Turpin had fallen. Appropriately, the result was a draw after the pair fell out of the ring and failed to get back and beat the count.[14]

Turpin was with Matsport for about a year but, as always, he was easily manipulated. Joe D'Orazio recalls:

One day we had him on the top of the bill at Caird Hall, Dundee and he just didn't turn up. In the evening someone rang up and said he was a friend of Randy's and he was going to wrestle for another promoter. I couldn't believe it. We had to get a substitute. The lawyers said we had a contract and we could sue him, but we didn't. It wasn't his doing. The other people showed him around for a bit and then they dumped him. Later he would say he was sorry he'd left us. Even after he'd gone we never held it against him. One day we were having coffee and he said, 'Joe, I've been treated better by you and the wrestlers than the big boxers.'[15]

---

[14] This bout is cited as one of the great humiliations for Turpin, but, apart from being a scrap dealer, Barnes trained wrestlers at the city's gym in St Peter's School in Yardley Street, Hillfields, Coventry, in the early 1960s. He also wrote a weekly column for the Coventry *Standard*.
[15] Conversation with author.

Just as in his boxing days, there were hangers-on and manipulators out to exploit Turpin. There was no question of wrestlers needing managers: the promoters met at the beginning of each month, worked out the bills and sent instructions to wrestlers on which nights they were to work. Nevertheless Turpin had a manager. The man in question was a Birmingham businessman who exercised control over Turpin's early wrestling career. One story is that his manager took a quarter of a £1000 signing-on fee with Matsport, though D'Orazio denies any such figure was ever paid. Nevertheless, Turpin used to give him 10 per cent of his wrestling earnings. There was no need whatsoever. 'The man was a blagger,' recalls another promoter. 'He became a referee and he wanted £10 a time just to referee the one Turpin bout and that was at a time when a referee got 30/- for the whole evening.' But no manager, no Turpin. 'Anyone who latched on to Turpin saw a meal ticket,' recalls Bill Tunney.

Turpin was, without doubt, a draw in the early days. It is not clear exactly what his earnings were from wrestling. In his statement to the Official Receiver in his bankruptcy proceedings, he said he was paid £250 for his first few bouts, and even when the initial interest in him had worn off, that he was still paid rather over the odds. Mike Hallinan, the wrestling historian, believes that generally Turpin was paid £25 a bout.[16] This may be an underestimation, though. One story that circulated was that the Leicestershire promoter Jack Taylor had paid Turpin £1000 to wrestle on a bill at Granby Halls. Taylor says the story is incorrect: 'I paid him a top of £150, and more usually £100. But he got £120 when he worked Granby Halls. This was a time when I was paying

[16] Ibid.

Bert Assirati £17, and Mike Marino and Al Hayes would work for £10, and they could both wrestle. You could get a decent top of the bill for £10.'[17]

Lightweights were paid a bare fiver. These may seem appallingly low figures, but these men were working – in the trade it is never called wrestling – six or seven nights a week, and they had little in the way of overheads. One man would be deputed to collect the others on a rotating basis. The promoter would pay him for the petrol. Most wrestlers went home in an evening; if they stayed overnight they would find a bed and breakfast where, with luck, the breakfast was suffi- cient for them not to have to buy a meal during the day. It was perfectly possible to save good money, certainly out of the purses Turpin was earning in his first months.

On the road, there were often treats for Turpin's fellow wrestlers, as Jack Taylor recalls: 'Three or four lads would usually travel together and we would stop at a café on the A1 or a hot- dog stall, but Randy would take us to a sumptuous feed at a posh place and he paid. He was generous with his money.'

Or wasteful? Perhaps Turpin felt guilty that he was drawing so much more money than the real wrestlers. But overall he was popular with them – he was, after all, their meal ticket. However, although he was collecting several times the amount they were paid, there was no resentment: they appreciated that, even at the end of his career, he was still something of a draw. Gori Ed Mangotich, who appeared with him in Birmingham, remembers him as, 'A gentleman. I don't mean the accent, because that wouldn't be true, but one of nature's

---

[17] Ibid. To put things in financial perspective, in the mid-1960s, a newly qual- ified solicitor in the London suburbs would be paid around £1000 a year. A four-bedroom house in Warwick with room for a tennis court or croquet lawn cost £8450, whilst a three-bedroom house overlooking Kenilworth Golf Club could be bought for rather less than £4600.

gentlemen.' Bill Tunney, who recalls getting around £6 a bout for matches with Turpin, remembers him as 'a nice man, a good man'.[18] Some said he could be morose, but this was generally attributed to his deafness and by and large he was amiable enough, playing the pinball machines in cafés, relaxing, and sleeping in the dressing room before his bouts, without, seemingly, a care in the world.

Wrestling was then at the height of its popularity. Taylor recalls that when Turpin first appeared at Granby Halls, which had a seating capacity of 1200, he drew a standing-room-only crowd. 'I know Paul Lincoln paid him £500 to appear on a big Granada show,' says the former World wrestling heavyweight champion, Wayne Bridges.

Despite the loss of his licence Turpin was still boxing. Soon, however, he had become more popular as a wrestler than he was as a boxer. Boxing for the Manchester-based North-West Promotions he managed to only half fill the Corn Exchange in Wisbech on 18 March 1963, when around three hundred people watched him knock out Eddie Marcano in the sixth round. Marcano was said to be a 'Top-ranking leading American heavyweight' and the remainder of the card included 'Darky Boy' Johnson, Two-Fisted, All-Action Scrapper v Bill Tunney.' There was, however, no problem with Marcano's work permit: he was actually a general trader in Manchester.

There had been trouble before the promotion with threats from both the British Boxing Board of Control and the wrestling promoter Jack Taylor, who maintained he had Turpin under a six-month contract and didn't want his prize lamb accidentally injured. After all, as a wrestler he had

---

[18] Conversations with author.

recently filled halls in Spalding, Bourne and Huntingdon. The Board's General Secretary, Teddy Waltham, said it was taking legal advice and proclaimed 'Such a match is bad for boxing and should not be allowed.' Threatened with the loss of their licence if they appeared on an unlicensed show, a number of boxers thought better of it. 'Darky Boy' Johnson did not appear and was replaced by the hard-working Buddy Ward, who defeated Tunney but later in the evening was knocked out by local former amateur Peter Brind.

The reporter for the Wisbech *Standard* thought, 'Turpin must have trained hard for this fight because he was remarkably quick on his feet.'[19] An Inspector of the Board who saw the show thought it was a disgrace. Turpin was believed to have received £70 for his night's work.

Turpin had a full schedule. On 15 March he had wrestled in King's Lynn, where he had met Hans Streiger, 'The German Beast', in a £200-a-side, no-disqualification match, and he had been due to box again in Peterborough on 19 March.[20] That would not be against Marcano – the promoters had 'a stable of thirty boxers from whom to choose'. In the event the show was postponed. Although the seats had apparently been selling well, the Wisbech promotion had lost in the region of £150.

The promoters soldiered on and Turpin was finally matched over ten rounds on 9 April at Peterborough's Corn

[19] Wisbech *Standard*, 22 March 1963.
[20] His fight with Streiger was a rematch. According to the hype, Turpin had been saved by the referee in the previous encounter on 15 February. Now he and Streiger were on the undercard to the well-known Abdul the Turk ('He is complete with praying mat and compass') against Boyo Paul, whoever they might be. Streiger, whose real name was Clark Mellor, was from New Mills and had known Turpin a long time. They had first met when Mellor challenged him at Micky Kiely's booth at Chester Racecourse. Turpin would later say that Mellor hit him harder than anyone else. Mellor went on to spar with a number of British champions, and Archie Moore. Regarded along with his friend Levi Walsh, another hardman, as 'a terrorist in his area', he died in 2001.

Exchange, with Con Kelly. 'One of the hardest hitters in the ring today. A most capable opponent. A master of ringcraft,' said the posters. The local newspaper said that a decent house might lead to the return of licensed boxing in the city. The Boxing Board said it would not be held responsible for the events of the night.

At the last minute, the contest was called off and it was announced that instead Turpin would box a fifteen-round exhibition with Frank Bell, billed quite correctly as, 'The only man to k.o. Tommy Farr'. Inquiries as to why the switch had been made proved fruitless when no one answered the telephone at North-West Promotions. Then, at the very last minute, the tournament itself was cancelled.[21]

Contrary to popular belief, this was not, however, the end of Turpin as a boxer. On 14 December that year he appeared at St Gregory's Hall in Cheltenham Spa promoted by Dennis Granville, billed to box Bob Murphy, an American serviceman based at Brize Norton. Instead he knocked out Gordon Corbett of Birmingham in five rounds. It was regarded as the highlight of a disappointing evening, which began forty minutes late when two pairs of gloves were lost. It was evident that 'although [Turpin] is now over 40 he still has more than a touch of his old skill,' said the local newspaper.[22] Corbett, who had been a decent light-heavyweight, would soon be Turpin's regular opponent on unlicensed shows.

On 22 August 1964, Turpin boxed on a Paul Lincoln mixed boxing and wrestling promotion in Malta, stopping the local idol Charles 'Lets' Seguna, who was cut in the second

[21] Peterborough *Courier and Advertiser*, 13 April 1963.
[22] Gloucestershire *Echo*, 16 December 1963. Corbett was a late replacement for Dennis Granville, a former Northern Area lightweight champion who claimed to have been a contender for the British welterweight title. He also said he had boxed over two hundred contests, winning sixty of them by a knockout.

round. The *Times of Malta* was sorry the bout had ended so soon. Turpin's 'craft and ring experience was appreciated by one and all'.[23]

The wrestling promoters now had another problem with Turpin. After he had made one or two appearances at a venue, he could no longer necessarily rely on the drawing power of his name. Wrestling fans are not boxing fans, so he had to develop an identifiable personality. But Turpin lacked both skills and charisma, nor would he work at learning the game. He had been taught the bare minimum by Kidd and D'Orazio and he could not be bothered to learn more. Jack Taylor says: 'If a wrestler don't click, you get rid of him. Several times I suggested, "Why don't you come and have proper tuition?" but he wouldn't. He'd be carried by people like Harry Bennett or Leon Arras. They were the villains. I put him on against Lord Bertie Topham and his valet Ponsonby at the Sportsdrome, Birmingham. That was the scene of his boxing triumphs and that was why we put him on there but Bertie did the work, him and the valet.'

Turpin was stiff in his movements, and because of his deafness it was difficult to work with him. Because he had not learned properly, he did not fall well and there was always the danger that he would accidentally injure an opponent. As the pulling power of his name declined, so did his earnings. Despite less money coming in, his spending carried on regardless. Then, of course, there were the women. And the money went on them just as easily as in his boxing days – a big white Ford Zephyr 6, with a red-bench front seat and a record player in the dashboard, to take him to the venues. 'The best thing since sliced bread for pulling birds,' recalls

[23] *Times of Malta*, 23 August 1964. In fact, the paper was far more interested in the drawn wrestling bout between Mike Marino and Ray Hunter.

one fellow wrestler, a trifle enviously. 'Randy was his name and he lived up to it. He always had gorgeous girls with him, no two ways about it. You'd get to know a girl he'd come with and next time it was an entirely different girl. It was uncanny how he attracted them. He drew them like a magnet,'[24] remembers Jack Taylor.

This sort of lifestyle was not cheap, though, and ever on Turpin's heels was that worldwide scourge of ill-managed sportsmen and actors, the Inland Revenue. Back in July 1962 Turpin appeared at his bankruptcy examination at the Shire Hall. Now he was wearing a hearing aid because of his increasing deafness. He had assets of £1204 and liabilities of £17,126, leaving a deficit of £15,922. He would not, or could not, bring himself to admit that he had ever received the £130,000 earnings from his boxing career. His money had, he said, always been handled by his manager or an accountant and, so far as he was concerned, the income tax had been paid up.

There is no doubt Turpin was reckless with money. His ring earnings had been in the region of £133,000, and he used Middleton as a private bank, much as Mills did Andy Ho and the restaurant. One story is that he came home one night and, throwing money around the room, asked his sister Joan and Frank Algar to count it. The total was in the region of £17,000.

It seems that the Inland Revenue believed Turpin had made money from a film, or a film project, in America, which he had given to a friend to garage for him as a hedge against tax. Later that supposed friend informed the Inland Revenue. In *64 Day Hero*, Gordon Williams discovers one of Turpin's letters, in which he claims that a Mr S owed him money. This is a clear reference to Jack Solomons and the implica-

---

[24] Conversations with author.

tion is that Solomons informed the Revenue when Turpin was pressing him for the money. The reason that Turpin could never claim the money through the courts is that he could not account for its acquisition in the first place. In fact Turpin had been less than discreet, writing in the *Sunday Pictorial* that he had received large sums of money in cash after the Robinson fights.[25] It was no wonder, Solomons apart, that his affairs were under scrutiny.

Apart from the question of the hidden money, which was never raised at the examination, cash was simply pouring through Turpin's fingers like water on to sand. The divorce from Mary had cost £8350, a fairly modest figure in today's terms, but a small fortune back then. There was the expensive divorce action by the police officer, for which Turpin as co-respondent paid all the costs. There was the more modest $3500 wasted over Miss Daniels in America and a gross loss of £10,500 on the Great Orme Hotel. Money was lent to a man to pay off a mortgage; £3000 was given to another in Wolverhampton to hold for Turpin. Mosh Mancini recalls going with Turpin to Birmingham to retrieve money lent or lodged.

The bank had also taken some of the proceeds from the Great Orme sale to pay off a quite independent loan to Salts. Turpin must have been one of the few men to lose consistently in the property market, for additionally there was a loss on each of five houses, and a series of what he described as 'working men's cars', each of which had cost around £1000.

There were all these outgoings, plus the fact that, despite what the Inland Revenue said, over the years Turpin had paid a considerable amount of tax. He also had an accountant, Max Mitchell, who had pleaded with them on

[25] Randolph Turpin with Sam Veitch, 'With Hate in My Heart', *Sunday Pictorial*, 15 April 1962.

his behalf and apparently succeeded in reducing a tax bill of around £100,000 to the one of £17,500. Later Mitchell would read out part of his plea to the Revenue: 'As time goes on, the punching power of a boxer is enfeebled the longer he pursues his profession. His brain through constant pummelling becomes bemused. His eyes are affected. Deafness overtakes him. And in effect he is lucky if in the prime of his manhood he doesn't turn into a two-legged vegetable.'[26]

At his bankruptcy hearing Turpin said: 'It is rather useless of me trying to think about these things, because I thought I was doing the right thing to hand the tax papers to my manager, who then passed them on to my accountants.'

Eventually the amounts Turpin owed and had earned were cleared up, with one exception: the Registrar Mr E. L. Proud was unable to discover what Turpin had done with £1000 from a short series in the *Sunday Pictorial*. Lamely, he explained that he had paid 'a very dear friend' £250 for a car, written off some debts and bought some gifts for his wife and children. The hearing was adjourned for three months and on its resumption Turpin explained that he had paid a Mr Harrison £250, repaid a great friend Mr J. Row of Woking £300 and £150 to a man Adams who had worked in the bar at the Great Orme. Adams had, said Turpin, taken a cut in wages to stay with him. 'Mr Adams was such a good barman, I promised that if he would stick with me he would get what was coming to him in due course.' He had been afraid to disclose this at the first hearing in case the Revenue had gone after these three men: 'Others who have been in bankruptcy have told me that the court would get the money back from the people or take stuff out of their houses and I felt morally obliged to pay them back.'

'I feel bound to say that I feel a certain sympathy for the man who prefers his friends to the Inland Revenue. Perhaps I should not say so but I can see him doing it,' responded the Registrar.

The final stage of an examination determines how creditors are to be repaid. Turpin did not think he could pay more than £2 a week, and that was provided he kept on wrestling. He said he was earning £25 a show but that he was not having twenty bouts a month, as had been reported. He also added, 'When you go out with the wrestling boys, you can spend up to £10 to £15 a night.' In fact, many wrestlers did not socialise, but they were paid cash in hand immediately after their contest, and Turpin was a man for whom cash in hand meant money to spend. No one was looking after his finances. Kent had come and gone. Nor had he paid tax on the wrestling earnings. At this point, the Registrar ominously remarked that Turpin might well be finding himself back before him again. Turpin replied, 'No sir, I do not think that is possible.' The Registrar thought it a great pity that PAYE had not been applied, 'If it did, a great number of theatrical and sporting bankruptcies would be avoided.'[27]

As the months went on, Turpin declined in health and in his commitment to his wrestling bouts. He worked in the October and November of 1964, appearing in Aberystwyth and Lampeter. He could be found in Tamworth in February 1965 wrestling Leno Lazarri, but he was not used again at the venue. After that, his bookings became more and more infrequent. Former World heavyweight champion Wayne Bridges

---

[27] Leamington Spa *Courier*, 20 July and 18 October 1962.

remembers Turpin in his later wrestling days. By then, he was suffering with pain in his back and his legs and he was becoming increasingly disorganised and unreliable: 'I used to drive him to Bournemouth or pick him up in Leamington and go to, say, Stoke, so I got to know him quite well. It wasn't that he didn't want to turn up. He was becoming absentminded. Randy didn't read or write terribly well and if you didn't ring and remind him you were picking him up, he just forgot.'[28]

After Turpin's death, a book was published which suggested that towards the end of his life Turpin was drinking, and suffering from the effects of a long career in the ring and on the booths. It brought protests from the family and was amended, but the truth was Turpin was undoubtedly starting to drink, and his speech was slurred from the blows he had received over the years. In the terms of the trade, he was 'punchy'.

His wrestling career seems to have come to an end in the early summer of 1965, with matches at the West Bromwich Adelphi. Many promoters finally dropped him completely but one who persevered was Welshman Orig Williams. It was he who took Turpin on a ten-day tour of Ireland in a mixed boxing and wrestling show towards the end of his career. Turpin would box his regular opponent Gordon Corbett, whilst the rest of the bill included the Red Indian Thunderbirds tag-wrestling team and two midgets – 'Gorgeous' Fuzzy Kaye, who was a friend of the Kray Twins, and his opponent, the Irish leprechaun, 'Tiny' Tim Gallagher.[29] Orig Williams remembers:

---

[28] Conversation with author.
[29] For more of the interesting life of Kaye, whose real name was Royston James Smith, see Patricia Kelly, *The Barmaid's Tale*, and George Tremlett, *Little Legs: Muscle Man of Soho*. Corbett himself became a wrestling promoter.

The west of Ireland men were huge, tough, strong. After the contests the punters would be in the hotel bar and they'd start whispering in a corner. Then one of them would come across. 'Michael over there reckons he's stronger than yer man and would like to arm wrestle him.' This was a nightly occurrence. When they became a nuisance we would turn round and say Big Michael had to put £20 on the table and then Randy would arm wrestle him. Eventually they'd put in a pile of ten shillings from a whiparound and I'd say that there was one condition: 'Michael looks strong, but he must prove himself by first defeating this man.' And I'd put a hand on Fuzzy Kaye's shoulder. 'You do it or the bet's off.' First there was the indignity, and secondly it can't be done. It's an impossible task to beat a midget. Your hand is so big you'd be pushing his elbow into the table and your arm is in a weakened position. Turpin never had to arm wrestle and we collected the money.

For some, it was all a disgrace: 'Randy penniless became a £25 a night wrestler,' wrote Leo Hickman. 'I remember interviewing him about his new career in Hereford. The shame was on him and his bruised eyes never met mine.'[30]

There is, however, the alternative view expressed by Orig Williams: 'When we had him, the newspapers formed the idea that the former world middleweight champion had lowered himself to box and wrestle for small money in small halls, not understanding at all this was all he knew and enjoyed, and that he made far more money by doing this than selling cups of tea in Leamington.'[31]

[30] Leo Hickman, 'Boxing: When Randy ruled the world', Birmingham *Evening Mail*, 10 July 2001.
[31] This, and previous Williams quote: conversation with author.

And as Turpin himself pointed out, 'Fancy talk doesn't buy nappies for the baby. Wrestling does.'[32]

But, of course, it was far more demeaning than Freddie Mills sliding on his bottom in an ice show. That was show business.

[32] Randolph Turpin with Sam Leitch, 'With Hate in My Heart', *Sunday Pictorial*, 15 April 1962.

18

Freddie Mills
Descends Avernus

By the end of 1964, things were going wrong in Mills' life. Some were long term and some short. The most immediate and important thing was that his elder daughter Susan had been seriously ill with peritonitis. She was taken ill shortly after she returned from holiday in America with a school-friend. At first it was thought that she had picked up a virus which had been sweeping the private school she attended. However, soon it became clear that she was suffering from appendicitis. Despite plaintive requests by Chrissie Mills, the family were unable to get her treated at King's College Hospital, though Mills had regularly opening fêtes and jumble sales there. Eventually she was admitted to St Thomas' and remained there for two months, for much of the time seriously sick.

Mills also had financial worries. The Chinese restaurant had not been doing well for some time, probably for at least the previous four years. Even before then, Mills had, it appears, been borrowing from the restaurant's kitty, asking Ho for £50 or £100 at a time. It had come to the point where the other directors objected and the matter was raised at a board meeting.[1] Additionally, now that Chinese restaurants were spreading around Soho, Mills' was no longer unique. It was decided to give the place a face-lift and turn it into a nightclub. Work began on 1 January 1963 and was estimated to cost £6000. In fact it came to almost double this. Mills had intended to call the new club the rather clumsy 'Sumanda', after his daughters, but it reopened on 9 May 1963 as Freddie Mills' Nite Spot, with Albert Marks and Arthur Haynes as the cabaret.

Nosher Powell, who was working on the door and holding the cloakroom concessions at Isow's The Jack of Clubs, thought Mills was paddling in shark-infested waters: 'I don't know if Freddie was unlucky or just bad at business. When Freddie went into his nightclub he was up against real opposition – Isows, where I was on the door and which had top grub, then there was Churchills, the Embassy, there was a lot of them.'[2]

Nor was the Nite Spot at the top end of the market. The writer Dea Langmead recalls being taken to the club as a young woman: 'I seem to remember some black ties and also suits, no hard and fast rule, apparently – I know I went with a suit – and tables and a small dance floor and a live band. There were girls sitting at the bar and cute waitresses and various brawny, muscular men, and a strange air of it not being quite a top class venue. I think I felt a bit shivery and daring in being there at all, as if rubbing shoulders with the

[1] Jack Birtley, *Freddie Mills*, p. 168.
[2] Conversation with author.

underworld, and if it had been a bit pricey I wouldn't have been invited.'[3]

For the first twelve months, Chrissie would work in the club and Mills would arrive there around 10 p.m. to glad-hand the customers. He took to having a sleep in his car in Goslett Yard around midnight. He would then be woken and would introduce the cabaret and perhaps sing a song. For a time, there were plenty of celebrities happy to be seen in the club, something which itself would draw the punters.

Unfortunately, as Powell says, there were a whole host of rival clubs, many in better positions and many indeed in the hands of underworld players. As a rule, the clubs provided pricey, low-grade meals, expensive drink, a cabaret of varying quality and the opportunity after dinner to sit with 'one of our charming Embassy/ Churchills/New Bagatelle hostesses'. In some clubs, the girls were genuinely freelance and might or might not go home with a punter. In others the hostess routine would be little more than a front for prostitution, often run by the head or a senior waiter. The girls were often required to sleep with the client who picked them, or face the sack and be blacklisted by the head-waiter mafia.

The Nite Spot was no real exception. The club, like all the others in and around the West End, had been hit by the new tax law, which disallowed entertainment as a business expense. By July 1964, the club was employing hostesses selected by a Mr Smith who told a reporter, posing as a potential hostess, that he had worked in a top spot for twelve years. The girls received no food and no pay. They were obliged to make do with what they picked up as tips, possibly

[3] Letter to author, 25 February 2003.

around £6 a night, and the £15 or even £20 they could make if they went home with a customer when the club closed at 3 a.m. However, Mr Smith, who selected which girls were to sit at which tables, thought the £20 was a bit much: 'We are not in the West End. Clients are mainly middle-class men who are prepared to spend £50 on a good evening out. But that £50 must include everything.'

As for the girls, they were expected to drink two bottles of champagne a night. Many clubs did not allow the girls to leave with the punters, but required them to meet in a taxi outside. Mr Smith did not think that was a good idea. He had heard of twenty girls being done for soliciting. It was much safer for the girls to leave the Nite Spot with the men. After all, he pointed out, how could the police prove they were not genuine girlfriends? He told the would-be hostess: 'If you've got brains you'll do well. We sack girls only if they can't drink the required amount or if they upset the customers or fail to satisfy them.'

It sounded very much like organised prostitution and the *People* took Mills to task. Their reporters had picked up a couple of the girls who had suggested they went to a hotel where 'we could all be naughty'. When they had arrived in the room the girls had undressed but, in time-honoured parlance, the reporters had made their excuses and left. At the club they had gone through a plate of sandwiches, half a bottle of gin, the mandatory two bottles of champagne and some mineral waters which, with the girls' hostess fees of £1 each, had come to the now modest-sounding £19 2s. Commenting initially on Mr Smith, whom he urged Mills to sack, Peter Forbes wrote: 'Maybe he thinks a club with a lot of good time girls as hostesses will attract more business. But I can't believe that Freddie Mills will lend his name to such a system.'[4] Reportedly Mills was horrified and contemplated suing for libel, but he was asked by the editor to come to his office, where he was shown proof of the allegations.

Apologists for Mills thought the hostesses were simply that, but it is seriously difficult to believe that he did not know the girls were prostitutes. Mills had mixed in Soho and the West End for years. Even harder to accept is that the worldly wise Chrissie Mills did not know what was happening.

There were also other types of illegality going on at the Nite Spot. Some of the girls were running a version of the corner game. Angela Deacon recalls her husband Robert, who worked as a doorman at the club whilst a law student at University College London, telling her: 'They used to do people. The hostesses would take a fiver and arrange to meet people behind a door which turned out to be a broom cupboard; corks were put in the empty bucket and customers were charged for champagne they didn't have.'[5]

Deacon, who came from Bushey Heath, had taken the summer job through his friendship with Andy Ho's son Tony. There were stories of bad cheques, watches and even a passport taken as security from customers who found they had left their wallets at home. But, whilst Mills may have been a bad manager, what was Chrissie or indeed the experienced Andy Ho doing about things?

According to Deacon, Ho was going home with the takings in one- and five-pound notes and storing them in a shoebox in his fine home in Bushey Heath. Whether Mills knew about this, or received any of the money, is highly doubtful.

A month after the hostess debacle came another piece of

---

[4] Peter Forbes, 'It's Time You Cleaned up Your Club, Mr Mills' in the *People*, 5 July 1964.
[5] Conversation with author.

adverse publicity. On 25 August Mills was denying that he had asked four tenant families to quit Stansted Road. The prospective Labour MP, Joan Lester, intervened on their behalf and Mills told the newspapers: 'I asked an estate agent to sell the property and as far as I am concerned it is now out of my hands. I have not told these people to get out. I understand a property company wants the site so they can build a block of flats there. This is progress. Nice new homes will be going up in the place of this old house. It is either the estate agent or the new owners who have told these families to get out, not me.'[6]

By the beginning of 1965, Mills was haemorrhaging money. His property adviser Bill Bavin had gone abroad and now the management of Mills' properties was in the hands of another company. For some time, unknown to his family, Mills was liquidating his assets and raising money on Joggi Villa. The terraced row in Greenwich and Bromley Road were sold for around £10,000. He sold the property in Brookdale Road, Catford, and took out a £4000-plus bank loan on Joggi Villa. Bavin estimated that he had realised something in the region of £21,000, and in May 1963, even after paying for the refurbishment of the club, he had £14,000 effectively in cash. Two years later it, and any income he had earned in the meantime, was almost gone.

One indication of just how bad things were in the months preceding Mills' death, relates to his maiden aunt, Kate Gray, who lived in an old people's home in Gillingham, Dorset. Mills used to pay for coach outings for the residents. In March 1965, he wrote saying that until business improved he could no longer afford to pay for the outings. The letter began, 'I find it difficult to put pen to paper . . .'[7]

There were also signs that this gregarious man was becoming reclusive. Jack Birtley recalled that Mills spent many evenings at home watching films of his old fights and going through his three scrapbooks, reminiscing with the sports writer Peter Wilson and his friends, Duggie Bygrave and his masseur, Jock Steele, about the good old days on the booths.[8]

The sports writer Frank Butler recalls how, in 1964, Mills had been due to attend the Sportswriters' Dinner, something he always enjoyed. He failed to appear and when Butler telephoned him the next day, he admitted sadly that he had forgotten. Then there were the blinding headaches from which he was constantly suffering. Birtley suggests he was able to keep these from Chrissie but this cannot have been the case: 'At home, it was almost as if I had a big, lovable child as well as a husband, in one and the same person. It was nothing unusual for him to kneel at my feet whilst I was sitting in the living room, maybe watching television, put his head in my lap and say to me: "Cuddle his head, Mummy," (he nearly always called me Mummy indoors). He would wait for me to stroke his head while he promptly fell asleep; yes, while he was kneeling!'[9]

Jan Howard, widow of the underworld figure Billy Howard, recalls that towards the end of his life Mills and Chrissie attended the funeral of her first husband. After the service the mourners returned to her house, where Mills

---

[8] In the autumn of 1944, Mills was in training for his second heavyweight contest with Jack London, this time for the title. His routine was always the same: when Steele had finished giving him a massage, Mills would get up off the table saying 'That was great' and throw a mock punch which Steele would dodge with some ease, until the day he was tagged and finished in the sick-bay. (Jack Birtley, *Freddie Mills*, pp. 182–3.)

[9] Bill Bavin, *The Strange Death of Freddie Mills*, p. 38.

went upstairs and lay on a bed, unwilling or unable to communicate.[10]

In an effort to bolster trade in the failing club, in the spring Mandy Rice-Davies, the one success of the fall-out from the Stephen Ward trial who had earlier debuted her show-business career in Frankfurt, was hired for the cabaret. It was unfortunate that the advertisement in the *Evening News* billed her as 'Mangy Rice-Davies'. The takings were not noticeably increased.

Mills left the management of the place to Ho. McInnes says that he tried to tell Mills things were not right with Ho, but he would not accept it: 'He was a very loyal person.' Journalist Brian McConnell remembers visiting the club in the months before Mills died: 'I'd been in the Nite Spot late in the evening and it was more or less closed, with just the staff and Freddie and a young woman there. I was told later he'd been counselling her after she threatened to commit suicide and he'd talked her out of it. There was certainly no business in the place that night.'[11]

In July, Mills and Ho had each been fined £50 at Marlborough Street for licensing offences; not in itself a great matter, but something which would not attract business and was just one more problem. That week Freddie telephoned Bill Ofner of the Stork Room and other clubs and asked how business was. 'I told him disastrous. He said, "Well, that's some consolation."'[12]

There were also troubles at home. Mills' father-in-law, Ted Broadribb, had remarried shortly after the death of his wife, something of which Chrissie Mills disapproved. Mills, obliged

[10] Conversation with author.
[11] Ibid.
[12] *Daily Mirror*, 26 July 1965.

to take sides, naturally chose that of his wife. Now the ex-boxer and his former manager no longer spoke and Mills ignored Broadribb at the Boxing Writers' Club annual dinner at the Café Royal in Regent Street.

There was also the often-repeated story of Mills' long affair with another woman whom he had met when he had been appearing on the variety stage. Loyally, it is not mentioned by Peter McInnes, but an account first appeared in Jack Birtley's book. Apparently in 1959, when he had been appearing in a summer show, Mills had met and fallen in love with one of the dancing girls, who gave him a key to her London flat. It was an affair which had run for some three years and was spoken of in boxing circles. According to Birtley, Mills became edgy with the children and Chrissie eventually confronted him. Arguments raged and one night she packed his clothes into three suitcases, put them in the garage and locked the front door. When Mills returned he was obliged to throw pebbles at the bedroom window to attract her attention. She told him to go away and take his luggage with him. He returned three nights later and was allowed in.

The matter was finally resolved by a local doctor, who spoke frankly to them and recommended that Chrissie Mills go out with other men. One night she suggested that he go and live with the girl and that if it did not work out he could come home. Mills was horrified at the thought of leaving his children and gave Chrissie the key to the girl's house so that she could dispose of it. According to the story it was thrown, wrapped in a newspaper, to the bottom of the dustbin, with the vegetable peelings.

People involved in boxing of Mills' generation confirm the outline, if not the details of the story, but more recently there has grown the belief that there was never such a girl, and that she was a cover for his homosexual affairs. Nosher Powell recalls: 'I think she [Chrissie] knew how Freddie was going but if she said anything she'd lose the lifestyle, be made to look stupid. He was an item with Mike Holliday. Freddie wasn't good-looking but he was a lion of a man. The girls threw themselves at him, but with Holliday it was different. The man was sympathetic to him, Freddie needed that condolence. I think it was known throughout the West End.'[13]

Holliday was a singer, and a troubled one. On the night of 28 October 1965, he had been in the Nite Spot threatening to commit suicide and had, it seems, been talked out of it by Mills and Chrissie, who offered him a bed at their home for the night. He assured them that he would be fine and left. Following an overdose of Nembutal, Holliday was taken to Croydon General Hospital on the morning of 29 October and died that evening. At the inquest it was revealed that he had left a note for his estranged wife, saying: 'The Income Tax want their money by Wednesday or else. I guess I ain't man enough to take it.' There is little doubt that his death was a great blow to Mills.

There were other stories in the boxing world of Mills' homosexuality. Stan Cullis, the light-heavyweight contender, remembers:

I only had close contact with Freddie at the Becket [gym]. Danny Holland ran the place. I met Mills, say, half a dozen times. I'd come down from Coventry looking for a better manager. Freddie would come in and watch but he never worked out himself when I was there. He said he thought

---

[13] Conversation with author.

I was fast enough and he gave me some general tips. Then he came back again. Whenever he came in he would come over to me and expect me to listen to him. Then one day he said I should have a massage. I said I couldn't afford it. I wasn't even paying gym fees. I was getting £1 a round sparring.

He said I had to have a massage and he took his coat off and massaged me two or three times. I was with some blokes and they were grinning at me when it was over. I said, 'What's so funny'. One of them said, 'Eh, come on Stan. He's got his fucking hands on your arse.' I said he was giving me a massage and they said he'd got one out up and that he liked boys. 'He's fucking queer. He fucks them up the arse.' A couple more of the boys explained. It knocked me for six.

Next time he came over to me I said, 'I don't want to know, keep away.' I blew up. It was in front of a whole load of people. I said to him, 'Leave me alone, I'll look after myself.' Fortunately he turned round and walked away. He could have beaten ten times the crap out of me.

Danny Holland came over to me two or three weeks later and asked what the ruck was with Freddie and said I owed him an apology. I felt smaller than ever but I told him. Danny said 'Whatever they said, remember that man was a world champion and he was trying to teach you something.'

Four years later when I fought Johnny Cole in Bristol, [Terry] Lawless was Cole's manager and in his corner was Danny Holland, who was reckoned to be the best cuts man there was. I well beat Johnny on points and Danny came into the dressing room afterwards and said, 'Well done Stan, I didn't think you'd beat John.' Then he asked me if I'd

ever apologised to Freddie and when I said I hadn't he
added, 'Well there's no need to now anyway.' I never really
knew what he meant. I didn't think anything more of it for
years but then I felt embarrassed for him; embarrassed for
me.[14]

Cullis does not appear to have been the only boxer who
attracted Mills' attention. Powell claims that he propositioned
the fighter Freddie King. He thought as the years went by
Mills became overtly homosexual and he was with him in a
club when a singer came over and said that Mills had just
approached him for a date: 'There are poofs you can take
anywhere and nobody would know they're bent but others
get a couple of drinks down them and it becomes very
apparent. Freddie was in that mould.'[15]

To compound his troubles, shortly before his death Mills
had had a viral infection. Many thought him to be something of a hypochondriac. In his book, Bill Bavin reprinted
a letter he had received from Mills' doctor:

Two to three weeks before Freddie's death he had an attack
of Asian 'flu. I found him swaddled between two electric
blankets sweating his heart out. He was really frightened.
Freddie was quite a baby if he was not well despite the
fact that he was amongst the strongest of men in our
country.

   He held my hand and asked if he would be all right.
I reassured him and gave him antibiotics to prevent
complications. Later that week he rang me in surgery and

[14] Conversation with author.
[15] Dan Slater, 'Kray Gay-Love Secret of Freddie Mills death', *News of the World*,
5 April 1992.

asked me if he could 'have a few quiet words' with me sometime. I said, 'Any time.'[16]

Of course, Mills' name was still in the newspapers. When his world-title belt was stolen from his car in Brixton there was a report not only of the theft, but also of its return. Two days later it had been found hanging over Mills' front garden fence wrapped in newspaper with a note, 'Sorry, Fred.'[17] But he was not getting the work in the media. Perhaps the most galling thing was that as far as those who made decisions in the entertainment world were concerned, he was passing his sell-by date. He was becoming yesterday's man. Very few can sustain a career of more than a decade in the eyes of producers, and Mills had been going a long time. By the middle of 1965, he had not worked in the media for some six months, and when he put his name forward as a commentator on the forthcoming Clay v Liston bout, he was told there were enough boxers on the programme already. It was a decision which badly hurt him.

In the weeks before his death the stone bird blew off the roof of Joggi Villa in a storm.

[16] Bill Bavin, *The Strange Death of Freddie Mills*, p. 38.
[17] *The Times*, 17 and 20 October 1962.

19

Freddie Mills Is Shot

Freddie Mills was found in his car in Goslett Yard at the back of his club on the night of 25 July 1965.

The last day of his life was commonplace enough. He cleaned his open-air swimming pool. After lunch he went to the bakers in Half Moon Lane, Herne Hill and then to the off-licence for a week's supply of cigarettes. In the afternoon he trimmed the hydrangea bushes in the front garden, took a nap and had haddock for a late tea around 8 p.m. He and his wife watched television with the two girls and their babysitter; the Beatles were appearing on the *Morecambe and Wise Show* and the girls were allowed to stay up late. He had, it appears, been in good spirits after the programme, dancing the twist with his elder daughter in the kitchen.

Usually Mills and Chrissie went to the club together, but Chrissie had loaned her mini to Donnie McCorkindale, her son by her first marriage, and his wife so they could go to a party. The loan was on the understanding he would bring it back by 11.30, when she would drive to the West End to have supper with Mills, as she did every Saturday. Mills therefore decided to go on his own to the club in his silver-grey Citroën at 10 p.m. He was wearing a blue suit without a topcoat.

On arriving at 10.30 p.m., Mills told the doorman, Robert Deacon, that he was going to sit in his car. According to Deacon, Mills then said, 'I've had a few drinks and I'm going to sleep it off. Would you wake me in half an hour?'[1] He was looking tired, sitting in the front of the car, but not smelling of drink. Deacon returned at eight minutes after eleven, and the car was now at the end of the yard. 'Mr Mills said he was not going into the club yet and asked me to wake him in another half-hour,' said Deacon. 'He seemed subdued.'

Deacon returned at 11.45 p.m.: 'Mr Mills was on the back seat and I tapped on the window and pushed his arm without effect. I patted his face and noticed saliva around his mouth and nostrils. I went back into the club and called the head waiter, Henry Grant.' The head waiter himself then went to the car, thought Mills looked ill, but made no effort to rouse him. Rather, he called Andy Ho out to the car. In his evidence to the inquiry, Ho then said, 'I met Mrs Mills and I said I thought Freddie was very ill in his car. Mrs Mills got in the car and shouted, "Andy! Andy! Call an ambulance. Freddie's badly hurt."'

Chrissie Mills confirmed Ho's account. Donnie had been late back and so he had agreed to drive Chrissie to the club.

---

[1] The details of the inquest into Mills' death that appear in this chapter are gleaned mainly from the *South London Press*. Letter, 20 February 2003, Clerk to HM Coroner, Inner West London to author: 'The death was in 1965 and enquiries have found that any paperwork is no longer available. Files are maintained for fifteen years by the Archives unless they are of particular legal interest.'

They arrived at about 12.25 a.m. She and Ho were not on the best of terms, and had recently had what she called a tiff, of which there had been a number. When she arrived, Ho took her arm and she thought he was going to apologise. Instead, he told her about Freddie. Chrissie told the coroner, 'I saw Mr Ho, his partner, who took me to Goslett Yard. He told me that Freddie was ill in his car and wanted me to wake him. That was the first I knew anything was wrong.'

The word was round Soho in a flash. Nosher Powell, then on the door at the Jack of Clubs in Brewer Street, heard the news from a taxi-driver:

A Jewish cab driver, Sammy, was dropping a punter off when he said to me, 'Have you heard about Millsie? Someone shot him.' I dashed across the pavement and more or less pulled the poor sod out. I told Sammy I'd pay his fare and he was to take me to the club in Charing Cross Road. When we got there the law was across the courtway. I slung Sammy a few quid and I was past the law before they could stop me. The Superintendent knew me well enough and he said, 'Nosher, come away.' I asked who did it and he said, 'Do yourself a favour, come away.' Freddie was sitting in the back with the gun still more or less in his lap with the barrel up between his legs. The Super said, 'He did it himself.' I couldn't believe a man like him would kill himself but the Superintendent said he'd shot himself twice. He'd put the gun in his mouth and tried to pull the trigger and as he couldn't quite reach he'd had to turn sideways. He was such a brave bastard he'd done it again.[2]

---

[2] Conversation with author.

Mills' mother, Lottie, learned of her son's death from the press. She was interviewed the day afterwards, telling reporters: 'He was a wonderful son. I was expecting him here with his family within the next week or two for part of the children's summer holidays. I can't believe what has happened and can't find out any details. He never forgot me or his friends in Bournemouth. I hope his daughters grow up to be like their father – they'll be really good citizens if they do.'[3]

Andy Ho's daughter Nina, the receptionist at the club, told the newspapers: 'For some time Freddie hadn't appeared on television or opened fêtes or any of the things he used to do. He wasn't happy about that. Maybe he wanted to make the headlines once more when he died.'[4]

Before the inquest at Westminster Coroner's Court had even begun on 2 August, the papers had reported that the police were satisfied that the second of the two shots had killed Freddie Mills and that no one else was involved. The questions to be answered were: what had he done in the six hours after leaving his Denmark Hill home; where did he go during that time, and whom did he see? There was also the question of why he had decided to stay in his car for nearly two hours.'[5]

But the inquest did provide an answer to one thing that had puzzled the press. New evidence was forthcoming about where Mills had come by the gun. He had, it seems, been in the habit of visiting an old friend, a Mrs May Ronaldson, whom he had known since he was a boy, who ran a shooting gallery at Battersea Funfair. Just how close a friend she really

[3] 'Freddie Mills, "Best Son Mother Could Have"', Bournemouth *Evening Echo*, 26 July 1965.
[4] *Daily Mirror*, 26 July 1965.
[5] *Evening News*, 26 July 1965.

was has been the subject of much toing and froing. But there is little doubt that Mills and his wife knew her from the times they took the children there. However, according to McInnes, Donnie McCorkindale would say he had not seen her at the funfair and did not believe she worked there.[6]

According to Ronaldson's evidence, some days before his death, Mills had gone to see her and told her that he wished to borrow a rifle as a prop for his appearance as a cowboy at a fête in Esher. She gave him one, pointing out that whilst it did not work it would serve its purpose well enough. Two days later, he returned the rifle, saying the fete had been cancelled. However, he was back again the next day to say after all it was on again, this time on the Saturday of the following week. Could he borrow the rifle again? He told her he did not like rifles and asked her son to put the gun in the boot of his car. According to her evidence, he also took three bullets from the mantelpiece.

Some years later, she repeated her story to reporters from the *News of the World*: 'Then on the Thursday he called for it again. When I got it back after his death it was working. How he or somebody repaired it, I don't know. It was a semi-automatic, self-loading rifle. You just pulled the trigger and didn't have to cock it after each shot. I didn't give Freddy ammunition but we found later that he had taken three bullets from my home.'[7]

The police, the pathologist, Professor Keith Simpson, and the coroner, Dr Gavin Thurston, were all convinced it was suicide. Simpson thought the wounds were caused by 'delib-

[6] Peter McInnes, *Freddie My Friend*, pp. 222 and 227.
[7] Peter Earle and Charles Sandell, 'Was Freddie Mills Murdered?', *News of the World*, 22 September 1968.

erate self infliction'. There was no real attempt by Chrissie Mills' lawyer to suggest that it had been murder. The only real question raised was, why?

Chrissie Mills told the court that Mills had had a pneumonia virus in the previous weeks: 'He had been worried recently but he didn't tell me a lot. My elder daughter was in hospital with peritonitis and I took such a beating that he kept things from me.'

D.I. Harold Walton told Thurston that a spent cartridge had been found on the back seat and another on the front. There was also a hole through the rear nearside door. After the ambulance driver said the gun was definitely out of Mills' reach, Henry Grant was recalled and asked why he had done nothing when he had first seen Mills. He made the very reasonable reply, 'Does one question an employer's attitude when he says he wants to sleep?'

Thurston, in making his findings, said: 'He had business worries but always put on a good face towards life, although Mr Ho told me that this cheerfulness could be deceptive.' Ho mentioned that he thought Mills had been slightly quieter than usual in the last week.

The funeral was attended by over a thousand people. The Rev. John Nicholls of St Giles told the congregation, 'My task is easy because I am talking about Freddie. All I can say is that if you ask anyone who knew him he would tell you "A great guy" or "A nice fellow".' The comedian Bruce Forsyth gave an address; the pall bearers included Henry Cooper and Jack Solomons.

The tributes had been universal. The *Daily Telegraph* summed things up: 'One didn't have to know Mills to like him. One word of greeting or even a nod or a smile from a total stranger was all that was needed to make that stranger a friend. Utter unselfishness and generosity epitomised Mills.'[8]

The grave at Honor Oak cemetery became an immediate target for sightseers and within a matter of weeks there were complaints about the behaviour of some of them. Families had brought picnics, transistor radios were being played loudly and children were running around out of control.[9]

Immediately after the inquest, Chrissie Mills, who was not in court to hear the verdict, said she felt there was something, 'oddly lacking somewhere'. She said, 'I was absolutely stunned when I heard the verdict . . . very dissatisfied and most distressed'. She was appalled that no one had 'admitted the possibility that Freddie was in fact already dead when they were trying to wake him up' in the car.[10]

In his will, which Mills had made in February 1953, he left his estate to Chrissie. It amounted to £3767 19s. 7d. When all debts had been paid, however, it was reduced to a paltry £387 6s 5d.[11]

[8] *Daily Telegraph*, 26 July 1965.
[9] *South London Press*, 10 August 1965.
[10] *The Times*, 3 August 1965.
[11] Grant of Probate, 16 February 1966.

20

Randolph Turpin's Demise

On 17 May 1966, within a year of the death of Freddie Mills,
Randolph Turpin was also dead.

After the debacle of Great Orme, Turpin had really wanted
a small guest house in Wales, which should not have been
beyond the bounds of possibility. Two years before his death,
at a time when he was still wrestling, a house of seven flatlets
in Rhyl was on the market for £6750, and in Denbigh an
untied freehold coaching inn was £750 less. Instead, never
one to take advice, and despite strong warnings from his
friends, Randolph had bought Harold's Transport Café in
Russell Street, Leamington in 1959, re-naming it after his
wife. The business was in a very poor way and the building
already pencilled in for demolition. One Londoner who went
there described it as worse than ones in Cable Street, which
was saying a good deal. Turpin was already financially
strapped: the taxman was on his back and the Great Orme
was proving a very costly exercise.

Maria Mancini recalls: 'It was a down-and-out café for lorry drivers and dustmen. You wouldn't pass it and go in. There were six or seven long tables. It looked like an institution. Beatrice was a wonderful woman. She was semi-blind but she still worked in his transport café. Beatrice seemed so poor.[1] All she wanted was a little cottage and after Randolph died Mosh got her into an almshouse. She choked on some bread and died a bit later.'[2]

Promoter Orig Williams knew that, 'Turpin hated the café, the half pennies he was making from it and the indignities which went with it. Lorry drivers and other smart-arses were always trying to get him to arm wrestle them or even to have a stand-up with him to prove to themselves how tough they were.'[3]

Bitterly Turpin described his day: 'Up at 6, put the boiler on, make tea, get 50 bacon sandwiches ready for the grill, get the boarders' breakfasts, serve, wash up in café, keep the kids amused.'[4]

The rest of Turpin's family now entered one of their periods of alienation. They did not like Gwen and they did not like the café where, they believed, they were never made to feel welcome. When Kath called to see her mother and had a cup of tea, she was asked to pay for it. Incensed, she told her brother to, 'Stick his café up his arse and his tea.'[5]

On the other hand, the food was not bad, recalls Bill Mills. 'They didn't come any rougher, but you got good value,' says Tom Price-Davies. People went there because of Turpin's name. He was still a good cook and there were plenty of

---

[1] She was paid £3 a week. *Sunday Mirror*, 29 April 1962.
[2] Conversation with author.
[3] Ibid.
[4] Randolph Turpin, 'With Hate in my Heart', *Sunday Pictorial*, 15 April 1962.
[5] *64 Day Hero*.

customers. Turpin remembered the better times with some bitterness. In the café hung a sign: 'That which seldom comes back to him who waits is the money he lends to his friends.'

In the last few years of his life Turpin seems to have lost complete touch with financial reality. Wrestling promoter Jack Taylor remembers: 'At one time he'd got some problem with the council and the café over some ants, and he used to say he could close it down tomorrow because he'd got a castle in Wales. He used to say he'd never needed the café. He went from being reasonably well off to nothing. Turpin was so gullible. He didn't go into partnership with people, he put money up for a share of future profits, and he didn't just put up hundreds.'[6]

Nine months before his death, Turpin wrote to Jack Solomons asking him to try to sell his trophies, and particularly his Lonsdale Belt. He was hoping to get £10,000 for them. He wrote: 'I am in cash trouble Mr J. but I am not begging.' Another letter was sent to the Midlands promoter Alex Griffiths, and this time a price of £8000 was suggested for the belt. Griffiths had opened the negotiations, but no sale was ever made. Turpin must have changed his mind because in a letter to his wife he wrote: 'They are yours. As long as you keep them, you have a part of me. Don't ever sell them.'[7] She did.

Although he was still in demand to present prizes at amateur tournaments, as the months went by, Turpin became more and more reclusive. One of his last public appearances was in aid of an appeal fund for Mick Leahy, the Coventry boxer who had unfortunately ended his career in September 1965, after he had driven into the back of a stationary lorry

[6]   Conversation with author.
[7]   Jack Birtley, *The Tragedy of Randolph Turpin*, pp. 134–5.

and sustained horrifying injuries. Turpin presented him with a pair of autographed white gloves.

Then, as a reminder of his past life, he was invited, all expenses paid, to attend the Emil Griffiths-Manuel Gonzales World Welterweight title match, to be followed by a farewell gala at Madison Square Garden for his old rival Sugar Ray Robinson. The contest itself was not up to much, but Turpin was one of four former middleweight champions in the ring with Robinson. Carl Olson, Gene Fulmer, Carmen Basilio and finally Turpin, all climbed over the ropes into the ring, in their dressing gowns, and each received a great ovation as they posed in a huddle with Robinson. Turpin told the reporters that no other tactician could match Robinson.

But in the early months of 1966 Turpin was back in the café. Two or three times a week he would go to work at his friend Mosh Mancini's car spraying and repair business in an afternoon. In the evening he would join his brother, Dick, and Mancini to train youngsters in the local gym. Domestically, things were not happy and he often slept in the shed at the rear of the café.

Then the inevitable happened. Not only was the council seriously talking about a compulsory purchase of the café, to make way for a car park, but on 14 May came another letter from the Inland Revenue, this time claiming some £200 tax on Turpin's wrestling earnings. On 16 May he accidentally gave his head a bad bang on the corrugated roof of the café's shed. A few days before he had been offered a job at £20 week as a driver for Middleton. He turned it down.

Shortly after lunch on 17 May 1966, Turpin's two elder daughters, Gwyneth and Annette, went back to school after lunch, and he went upstairs to check on his third daughter, Charmaine, who had a cold. He came down, reported she

was sleeping and went back upstairs. His youngest daughter
Carmen followed him. Around 2.30 p.m., Gwen went
upstairs and there at the side of the bed on the floor was
Turpin. Carmen was sitting, crying, in a pool of blood. Gwen
asked Turpin what he had done, believing he had hit the
child, but got no reply. She then ran with Carmen to the
nearby Warneford Hospital where she was told the child had
been shot and gravely injured. By the time she returned the
neighbours had already called the police.

Turpin was found slumped between the bed and some
packing cases. The top blanket and the counterpane on the
bed showed a few blood stains. A note had been pinned to
the door of the bedroom in which Turpin wrote of, 'Having
to carry the can for the money owing to the Inland Revenue.
Naturally, they will say my mind was disturbed but it is not.'
Dr Derek Barrowcliff took swabbings of his hand and told
the inquest later that given Turpin had used his left hand he
was satisfied he had shot himself. This in itself was curious,
since Turpin was right-handed.

Dick Turpin heard of the death of his brother in the early
evening from a neighbour. He took a bus to the café, where
a police officer met him and said that Gwen was making a
statement. He was shown Randy's letter and confirmed it was
in his brother's handwriting. He told the local paper that both
he and Randolph were stubborn and would not give in to
each other. The next day he raised the question of money,
saying that he did not know Randy had been trying to sell
the Lonsdale Belt: 'Randolph was too soft at heart; too shy
and too trusting a man. He was, in his own way, still a perfec-
tionist. The kind of man who refused to sell his name . . .
He would have been well off if he had accepted just a few
of the offers by advertisers to use his name. And there were

all the people who owed him thousands, not hundreds of pounds.'[8]

Local reporter Rod Davies, who years earlier had promoted Turpin in a tournament to raise money for journalistic charities, traced the decline to the loss of his world title: 'After the second Robinson contest, far from being distant but polite to all but his closest friends, he became distant and none too polite.' Davies had played cricket at the training camp with Turpin before the Robinson fight. Before the Olson contest, Turpin had refused to open the door of his hut to him.[9]

Ronnie Pye, the boy Turpin and Mancini had been training, told the papers he was finished with boxing. Randy had told him, 'You and I are going to the top together. But when you are there you will not make the same mistakes as I did.'[10]

A fund was opened, with donations to be sent to the Mayor's Parlour. By the time of the funeral, it had reached £100, of which Lord Avon, who had been the Member of Parliament for Leamington at the time Turpin won the world title, had contributed £10. A collection at the funeral at the Holy Trinity Church raised £60 for the family.

Five hundred people are said to have attended the funeral. Turpin's former manager George Middleton sent a wreath in the form of a boxing ring, with a red R on a base of white carnations. To the distress of the family there were no stewards from the British Boxing Board of Control, although they sent a wreath. Representing the Board was merely a member of the Midland Area Council. After the funeral, he explained: 'Secretary Teddy Waltham very much wanted to be here to

[8] Warwick and Warwickshire *District Advertiser*, 18 May 1966.
[9] Rod Davies, 'The Turpin I Knew', Warwick and Warwickshire *District Advertiser*, 18 May 1966.
[10] Warwick and Warwickshire *District Advertiser*, 18 May 1966.

pay his respects to the memory of a great fighter. But there are still many details to be cleared up in London following the world heavyweight title fight and he could not get away.'[11] This was, of course, arrant nonsense. There was nothing to clear up. Waltham simply had no intention of appearing at the funeral of a man for whom he had had no time. Even assuming, and it is a big assumption, that he could not have spent half a day going to Leamington, he could have sent his deputy, Ray Clarke.

The vicar, the Rev. Eugene Haselden, said of Turpin's death: 'He was a simple and naïve man who needed friends to protect him from spongers. To our shame he was let down. Whenever a man's life ends like this, it is not his failure alone but the failure of the whole society, for we are inextricably bound together in the bundle of life.'

Of the funeral, Jack Birtley wrote: 'During the past few years I must have met thousands of people who claimed they were personal friends of the great "Leamington Licker". Especially among the boxing fraternity. Everyone in the fight game was Randy's pal. I wonder where they all were on Tuesday . . . In the years to come when the subject of Boxing Greats crops up in the pubs, in the cafés, in the factories, on the building sites or in the gymnasiums throughout the boxing-minded world, Turpin's name will be spoken of with justifiable pride.'[12]

By the time the adjourned inquest resumed in July, the fund had risen to just over £350, and there was talk that a boxing promotion which might raise as much as £1000 should be put on. However, Gwyneth Turpin wanted the fund closed, saying she was writing to the mayor, Councillor

[11] Jack Birtley, *The Tragedy of Randolph Turpin*, p. 145. The fight had been between Muhammad Ali and Henry Cooper three days earlier.
[12] Jack Birtley, Coventry *Standard*, 26 May 1966.

Leslie Freeman: 'I am very grateful to everybody who has contributed but I don't want it to go on. We are managing all right. If only the local people who owed Randolph money had been willing to come forward and pay there would not have been this tragedy. The fact that people owed him money was Randolph's only worry.'[13]

At the time, no one was seriously questioning the fact that Turpin had taken his own life after shooting his daughter in the head, because of his financial troubles. But where had all his money gone? Even allowing for the losses on Great Orme, he should have had thousands at his disposal. One suggestion was that he had never been paid properly. Many believed that Middleton had turned Turpin over, and some voiced this opinion: 'I wouldn't have trusted the man. Randy was always under the impression that Middleton paid the tax,' says Tom Price-Davies. 'Money didn't mean a lot to Randy. Only when he didn't have it. I believe that Middleton took the money for the tax and never paid it. I met Mrs Middleton at a boxing reunion in Leicester and we discussed the affair. She wouldn't admit that her husband was in any way to blame.'[14] On the other hand, Mosh Mancini will say no bad word against his former manager.

Another suggestion was that Turpin had garaged a large sum of money, said to be around £20,000, with friends or associates as a hedge against taxation, and had not been able to get it back. Much of it was said to come from the Robinson fights. In 1964, Turpin had written a letter, found after his death, in which he mentioned 'a gang which could be hired to dispose of people'. Then, after making an enquiring telephone call, he was badly beaten by four men, who left him with the parting words: 'Next time it will be your wife and kids.' After the visit he had abandoned his £20,000, if indeed it ever existed.'[15]

Jack Birtley wrote: 'Several people recalled Turpin being badly injured about that time but said that he had explained the cuts and bruises away by saying he had been attacked by a section of the crowd whilst wrestling in Wales.'[16] An attack by the crowd seems most unlikely. Instances of wrestlers being attacked are relatively rare and are usually the work of unbalanced individuals, rather than the crowd *en masse*.[17] It is singularly unlikely anyone would have attacked Turpin, who was always cast as the hero rather than the villain. An attack on the famous Turpin, however far he had slipped down the ladder, would surely have been reported in at least the local press. More importantly the wrestlers of the time would have known of it. The story would have spread through the ranks.

But Joe D'Orazio says: 'As for the beating up in Wales, I was working for Dale Martin Promotions doing their publicity and I never have heard of it. For a start Randy was popular. He'd never have worked up a crowd against him and we'd have heard.'[18]

---

[15] The story still persists. In October 2002 I received a letter: 'As for Randy Turpin they said (from a good source) he left a lot of money with a shady mob in London after the Ray Robinson fight. I suppose dodging tax. When he tried to get his money back he pestered for it and of course ended up dead.'

[16] Jack Birtley, *The Tragedy of Randolph Turpin*, p. 141.

[17] Sometimes it was the promoters who fell foul of the crowd. On 2 March 1968 the promoter of a tournament at the Community Hall, Grimsby, was attacked. Half the main event had failed to appear; the Red Devil was said by the more knowing spectators to be an imposter and the final straw had been when a wrestler who had appeared earlier on the bill was forced to make up the numbers and take part in the last contest. The promoter was chased by the crowd and had to be rescued by eight policemen and a dog. Grimsby *Evening Telegraph; The Times*, 4 March 1968.

[18] Conversation with author.

There is little doubt that something had been amiss with Turpin, and it was not merely to do with the council and income tax. He seemed to have been involved in some scheme with a local bookmaker. One former London villain recalls: 'I went up to see Randy just before he died. I went with a man from Hoxton about a corner. Turpin was a bundle of nerves about something. Nothing to do with us. We had a job to get him to come down from upstairs.'[19]

At the inquest, George Middleton was adamant that he was not one of those people indebted to Randolph. 'I didn't owe Turpin money,' he told the coroner. The jury was, however, curious, asking to whom a boxer's prize money was first paid. 'Everything was being dealt with straightforwardly by chartered accountants. All purses were dealt with by cheque, and transferred to Turpin's account after paying expenses. It is not correct to say that I owe him a large sum of money, or that I did not give him some of the money.'

According to the pathologist who conducted the post-mortem, to the naked eye there had been no signs of the brain damage, 'that one might have expected in the case of a professional boxer suffering blows in the ring'. Later disappointment was expressed by the Royal College of Physicians that more extensive tests had not been carried out.

According to Turpin's friend, Mosh Mancini, the night before Turpin's death they had been together, with Turpin happy and in the ring training young boxers. His brother Dick had also been with him and they had joked together.

There were also suggestions that Turpin had problems other than money. He had a chauvinistic attitude to extra-marital sex, and there had been persistent rumours that his

[19] Ibid.

youngest daughter Carmen, who did not then physically resemble her sisters, was not his child. Birtley wrote: 'She was in fact a cute little blonde-haired girl with dazzling blue eyes and a creamy-white skin. The three other Turpin girls were clearly half-castes, and their woolly black hair, deep-velvet brown eyes, and café-au lait skin left no guesses as to who their father was.' Birtley did, however, go on to give the lie to the rumours: 'But a Midlands doctor subsequently dismissed the suggestions that Turpin could not have been Carmen's father. He pointed out that while a white mother could often produce a throwback coloured child, it was equally possible for a white woman of a mixed marriage to bear a seemingly non-coloured offspring if the father also came from a mixed marriage. And bearing in mind that Turpin's mother was of white parents this seems quite feasible.'[20] Indeed in pictures of her as an adult she looks extremely like her father.

But such opinions came later. At the time, it was significant, said supporters of the suicide theory, that Charmaine, who had also been in the room when Carmen was shot, was uninjured. Some credence was given to this by Detective Chief Inspector Fred Bunting, head of the Mid-Warwickshire CID, who thought it significant that in Turpin's letter to his wife which began, 'My dearest Gwen', only two of the children had been mentioned. Furthermore, one person close to Turpin recalls: 'Randolph had a writing habit. When he was depressed he'd sit down and write letters to himself. After he died, a letter which has since been destroyed was found in which he said he felt cheated. He had believed Gwen was a virgin when he met her but she had a son by a Welsh

---

[20] Jack Birtley, *The Tragedy of Randolph Turpin*, pp. 140–1.

photographer. Whether this was true or his mind was going is another matter.'[21]

At the inquest Mancini said that on 16 May Turpin had been happy, laughing and joking with him and his brother Dick at the local gym. However, despite such evidence, the jury took only a few minutes to decide that Turpin had committed suicide.[22]

The Turpin brothers and sisters were never happy with the verdict. Years later, when the statue to Turpin was under discussion, Jackie Turpin told the local newspaper: 'I'm still unsure about Randy's death because there are a lot of questions which haven't been answered. He had his fair share of problems at the time, but he just wasn't a quitter – his boxing career proves that. It's possible he was murdered, but I'm convinced we will never learn the truth. It's a secret that's gone with him to the grave.'[23]

Peter McInnes questioned the suicide verdict on rather less evidence than he questions that of Freddie Mills. Again, as with Mills, there was the question of bullet wounds. Turpin had one to the left side of the head, just behind the eye and the other in the chest. The pathologist, Dr D. F. Barrowcliff, said that the head shot had possibly preceded the chest wound, which has led to speculation. McInnes states that Gwen said she did not know the gun was in the house, and

[21] Conversation with author.
[22] Those who believe that tragedies come in threes may point to the death of another of Britain's few post-war world champions, the flyweight Jackie Paterson, who died on 20 November 1966. He held the title from 1943, when he defeated Peter Kane, to 1948. By then he was having serious weight problems and had collapsed before the weigh-in of a championship fight against Dado Marino. He was then stripped of his title. He went to live in South Africa, but he was another ex-boxer who was beset by problems. He succumbed to drink and violence. It came as little surprise to hear that he had been stabbed in the throat in a brawl in a bar in Amanzimtoti, Natal.
[23] *The Leamington Spa Courier,* 5 July 1996.

that she did not hear the shots. Since there is no doubt that shots *were* fired, by Turpin or someone else, the implication can only be that she knew what was going to happen and was deliberately not listening. The fact that, as with Chrissie Mills, Gwen Turpin did not know of the gun, takes matters little further. At least in the case of Chrissie Mills she had apparently cleaned her husband's car shortly before his death and had not seen the rather larger rifle. Turpin knew perfectly well how to acquire firearms, as the 1954 case proves, when Turpin had bought a gun from an unnamed man and never registered it.

There is no evidence whatsoever for the suggestion that Gwen was hiding things.[24] Nor is there any evidence that Solomons had Turpin killed, although certainly the promoter knew men who would kill. In the spring of 1957 Bob Monkhouse had fallen foul of Dennis Hamilton, the syphilitic husband of Diana Dors. Hamilton suspected, quite correctly, that the pair were having an affair. Monkhouse recalls a call he received from Jack Solomons: "'Just to mark your card son, strictly *unter em tisch*, some bugger's out to do you a mischief. You know I've got one or two naughty lads fighting for me, not above upsetting the law, you follow. Well one of 'ems been offered a pony to duff you up, hospital job and he might have taken the job too, but for this customer saying he'd cough up a monkey to see you finished. Yeah. A beating's one thing but snuffing's another, so the lad came to me and I've come to you. Are you still there?'" Monkhouse did not rest easily until he heard of Hamilton's death in 1959.[25]

There is clear evidence that Solomons was connected both

[24] Peter McInnes, *Randy: the Final Complete Biography of Randolph Turpin*.
[25] Bob Monkhouse, *Crying with Laughter*, p. 133.

with the London underworld and indeed with the American mafia. As a boxing promoter, it would be difficult for him not to be. The 1940s and 1950s gang leader Jack Spot had effectively been his minder, but Spot had been well out of the way for a decade. Nor is there any evidence that Solomons ever employed the men he knew in an aggressive, as opposed to defensive capacity. Indeed, one thing that militates against the murder-by-Solomons theory, is that if it was indeed the promoter who had Turpin beaten up, why was he still writing to him asking him to negotiate the sale of the belts? Additionally, a fact against the murder theory as a whole, is that it was the youngest child who was shot, whilst her sister, who was at least a possible identifying witness, was unharmed.

Two weeks after the shooting, Gwen Turpin wrote in a Sunday newspaper: 'I think he wanted to take her [Carmen] with him because he had begun to look on the world as a place not fit for her to live in.'[26]

[26] *Sunday Mirror*, 29 May 1966.

21

Who Shot Freddie Mills?

Two questions must be answered about the death of Freddie Mills. The first is, was he murdered? The second is, if he was not, then why did he commit suicide? It is interesting how two camps have developed. Unsurprisingly, his family believes he was murdered, as do the boxing community as a whole, whose members are almost totally unwilling to accept his suicide. The police, on the other hand, believe that here was a man whose life, for a number of reasons, was becoming intolerable and that he killed himself. The underworld believes he killed himself specifically because he was 'Jack the Stripper', the name given to the murderer of prostitutes in the Hammersmith area, and was about to be arrested.

Chrissie Mills rapidly came to the belief that Freddie had been murdered. She may not have legally challenged the inquest verdict, but she soon did so outside the courts. She wanted an open verdict, and within a week *Sunday Mirror*

reporter Ronald Maxwell demonstrated, with the help of
Donnie McCorkindale, his wife and Leonard Pearce of the
gunsmiths Churchill's, that there was no way in which Mills
could have shot himself and ended in the position in which
he was found with the rifle where it was. McCorkindale
added: 'He had no really serious money troubles that we
knew of. I knew he was worried about the business and
about a month ago I asked him if he needed money. He told
me he didn't.'[1]

Later, Chrissie Mills would tell the writer and barrister
Fenton Bresler, 'If I live for a million years I will never
accept that Freddie killed himself.' According to Bresler,
Jack Solomons had spoken with her the day after
Mills' death, saying: 'If Freddie stood here and said to
me, "Jack, I shot myself," I wouldn't believe it. But I'm
warning you, be prepared. They may try to bring this in
as suicide.'[2]

Unknown to her at the time she first made her claims,
Chrissie would have had support from Professor David
Wingate, who was then the resident medical officer at the
Middlesex Hospital, and on duty when Mills' body was
brought in. He was alerted by a junior doctor, and also by
the casualty porter, who recognised the potential importance
of the situation. Wingate recalls:

I went along to casualty and Freddie Mills was lying on
a trolley. He seemed an enormous man. Glancing at him,
there was no obvious wound and he was dressed in a
suit. His eyes were shut and I couldn't see anything to

[1] Ronald Maxwell, 'Freddie Mills: New Evidence', *Sunday Mirror*, 8 August 1965.
[2] Fenton Bresler, 'Freddie Mills, a Puzzle', John Canning (ed.), *Unsolved Murders and Mysteries*, p. 87.

cause death until I pulled back his eyelids and there
was a bullet hole through one eye.

I think it is a weird way of killing oneself. It is a very
unusual site of election for suicide. The mouth or perhaps
the ear are more usual if you are going to try it yourself.
It is very difficult not to shut your eye when you squeeze
the trigger. Fairground rifles are notoriously inaccurate
and given the bad lighting in Goslett Yard it was even
odder.

Wingate, who was neither invited to the autopsy nor
required to give evidence at the inquest, was astonished by
the suicide verdict: 'I suppose suicide has to be top of the list,
but it requires a lot of nerve to look down the barrel before
you pull the trigger. It was such an unusual form of suicide
as to be implausible. But then, if I was being paid to top
someone, I wouldn't use a fairground rifle either.' Wingate
considers the most likely scenario was that Mills met someone
who took the gun off him and shot him. He therefore believes
there should have been an open verdict. 'The gun was discovered twenty minutes later, leaning in a doorway of the casualty department. Half an hour after that a detective wearing a
dinner jacket arrived and told me he would take over.'[3]

Chrissie Mills and her son Donnie McCorkindale were
convinced that Freddie was killed as an example by gangsters who were extorting a fortune in the mid-1960s from
club owners, allegedly under the benevolent eye of certain
West End policemen. But which set of gangsters? The Krays,
the Richardsons, the Triads, independent gangsters, a homosexual ring? From time to time, all have had their supporters.

[3] Conversation with author.

In every case except the last, the argument is that Mills was to be a high-profile example, targeted to ensure that club owners did not backslide in their protection payments. Chrissie Mills cited the case of an ex-wrestler whose club had been destroyed a fortnight earlier because he had refused to pay protection money. The reasoning also went that Freddie was known to take a nap regularly in his car and as such was an easy target.

Mike Hallinan, however, casts doubt on the story of the wrestler's club: 'I have spoken to Lou Ravelle [former body-builder, wrestler, gym owner], and asked him was the rumour true that he was approached and threatened with violence if he did not pay protection money? He replied, "Not true. I have never been approached by anyone to pay protection money."'[4]

Joe D'Orazio is another who does not accept the story: 'I can remember the only two wrestlers having clubs in Central London at the time were Paul Lincoln and Yuri Borienko. I seem to remember Yuri did have some trouble at one time during which his telephone was ripped off the wall. By whom I do not know.'[5] This hardly seems to amount to the total destruction cited by Chrissie, and other wrestlers say that the phone-ripping incident was a personal matter and not a case of Borienko being leaned on.

While serious incidents did certainly occur, the news-papers of the period tended to play up gang warfare and protection rackets, promoting contenders for control of Soho. The *News of the World* reported that recalcitrant club owners were sprayed with petrol whilst another man would stand by calmly striking matches until the protection money was

[4] Ibid.
[5] Ibid.

paid: 'One gangster is reputed to have 400 tearaways on his pay-roll.'[6] This was something of a ludicrous claim: the Krays at their zenith might have managed to muster fifty, including part-time hangers-on.

The claim that the Richardsons from south London were involved in Freddie Mills' death is an interesting one. It is raised by both Bill Bavin and Tony Van den Bergh.[7] In short, the theory goes as follows: John Lawrence Bradbury, a Richardson associate who lived with his wife and three children in Camberwell, was arrested in South Africa and sentenced to death in May 1966 for the murder of one Thomas 'Farmer' Waldeck. He appealed, but this was turned down on 25 November that year, although his sentence was commuted to life imprisonment. It was then suggested that Bradbury would help Scotland Yard in their drive against crime. It appears he had been interviewed by two Scotland Yard detectives in May 1966 and the information he gave them 'opened the way for the biggest crime sweep to be carried out in London'. For the crime for which he had been convicted, Bradbury had, he said, driven the killer to Waldeck's address, but that was all. He had done so because of threatened reprisals against his wife if he had disobeyed. Bavin then quotes a letter he received from Donnie McCorkindale in which he says he visited Bradbury in Pretoria Central Prison. The gist was that Bradbury had been skilled in the art of dispensing Mickey Finns. The drug he used made the victim extremely susceptible to suggestion, and Bradbury's accomplice would then have no trouble in getting him out of a club, and into less public surroundings,

[6] *News of the World*, 19 July 1964.
[7] This and future references to Bavin: Bill Bavin, *The Strange Death of Freddie Mills*; Tony Van den Bergh, *Who Killed Freddie Mills?*.

where they could 'work' without threat of interruption. Bradbury claimed that his unnamed accomplice was responsible for Freddie Mills' death.

In the winter of 1973, Bavin went to South Africa to see Bradbury. He was given the name of a second man, also in a Pretoria prison, who would tell him who killed Freddie Mills and why. Unfortunately when it came to it, he was not allowed to see either man.

There are difficulties for those who believe this theory. Even at first glance, the vague suggestions that the Richardsons were involved in Freddie's death would seem unlikely. For a start, they were not in the protection business, like the Krays were. They were basically businessmen who ran long-firm frauds. Nor were they ever suggested to have been prominent in the West End club scene. Really the nearest they had to a tie-in with a club were their social visits to the Astor Club off Berkeley Square, the home of the London criminal world, on a Friday night.

A closer look shows that the timing is all wrong. After a disastrous fight on 9 March 1965 at Mr Smith's nightclub in Catford, Dickie Hart was killed and subsequently most of the Richardson team was locked up. Of the survivors, the dangerous and volatile George Cornell was shot dead the next night by Ronnie Kray. True, Charlie Richardson was still at liberty, but he had more pressing matters, such as the release of his brother Eddie, on his hands. Apart from that, Richardson was no fool. The high-profile killing of a man like Mills would be particularly ill-advised whilst he and his firm were being investigated so closely by the police. Anyway, more crucially, it was simply not his game.

The names most often put forward in connection with the murder theory suggest that the anonymous gangsters were, in fact, the Kray Twins or their henchmen. Reggie and Ronnie Kray had taken over the control of many East End and central London clubs after the dispute between the previous London gang bosses Billy Hill and Jack Spot in 1955. With the Krays very much in the ascendancy, Hill, by then an extremely wealthy man, had effectively retired. Similarly, following the firing of his Paddington club, the Highball, in 1957, Spot had left for Ireland with his wife Rita and two young daughters.

By the early to mid-1960s, the Krays had an impressive collection of clubs and businesses from which they obtained a weekly income. They had forcibly taken over the once-fashionable Esmeralda's Barn in Wilton Place, as well as the Hideaway in Gerrard Street. They effectively controlled the upmarket North London Regency Club in Stoke Newington and took money from Benny's on the Commercial Road and Dodger's in Brick Lane. The Green Dragon in the Whitechapel Road, as well as its neighbour the Little Dragon, were others to hand over cash. In Soho, there was money coming from the Gigi and the New Life in Frith Street, as well as the New Mill Club in Macclesfield Street. Off Oxford Street, there was the Starlight Rooms. Money could also come from other protectors: they were paid a percentage of the money taken from the Astor and the New Bagatelle off Regent Street.[8] The Colony in Berkeley Square was paying a hundred pounds weekly and the Casanova off New Bond Street half that sum.[9]

There is no doubt whatsoever that the Krays were regular visitors to the Nite Spot. A photograph of Reggie Kray with

[8] Other protectors included Billy Howard, later styled as the Don of Soho, and Jerry Callaghan, from south London, who ran the Embassy Club.
[9] Ronnie Hart, in an unpublished account of his time with the Krays.

his wife Frances and other friends in the club shows Mills, a cigarette in his hand, with his arms around two of the men. In truth the club, and before that the restaurant, had always been a home for the Chaps. Gerry Parker, who for a time ran with Jack Spot in the 1950s, remembers: 'The food wasn't bad. Albert [Dimes] liked Chinese and you'd see him there occasionally.' One story goes that on one occasion Mills had a row with them and told them to leave. They did so, and it was after that he was killed.[10] Another version is one repeated by Chrissie Mills herself, in which a waiter told her about their presence. She immediately repeated this to her husband, saying: 'Those two! The Krays. The waiter, the one who never talks as a rule, has just told me that they are the heads of London's underworld, and that they would kill their own mother.' Mills is said to have patted his wife's hand, gone over to the men and to have repeated in turn what she had said. The two men, who Chrissie knew by name, looked round at her and then turned back to Mills. 'Don't worry Fred,' one of them drawled back with a wide grin. 'We wouldn't hurt you.'[11]

There have been efforts to portray Mills as some sort of holy fool who could recognise neither a gangster nor a prostitute from five feet, but they cannot be right. Mills had moved in West End circles for years and knew both the faces and the *mores* perfectly well. It was as if he had merely made an investment in his Chinese restaurant and Nite Spot. He was a hands-on proprietor. He knew other club owners and went to their clubs. When Bob Monkhouse was having trouble with Dennis Hamilton, not only did Solomons mark the comedian's card but so did Mills, telephoning him to say: 'I

---

[10] Conversation with Bill Sheeran, former member of the BBB of C.
[11] Jack Birtley, *Freddie Mills*, pp. 175–6.

saw Hamilton at the Astor, pissed as a fart but bloody dangerous. He's round the twist and that, I know, a nutter – but he'd got it in for you. I mean really got it in, no error. So watch your back, all right.'[12]

In support of the protection story is the one that in the club lighted matches were stuffed down the padding of a banquette, which had been cut. There is no doubt that the Twins could carry a grudge and that many of the underworld murders are not over money or territory, but over a so-called lack of respect. The murder of George Cornell by Ronnie Kray is a case in question, and Nosher Powell recalls some trouble he had with the pair at Isows around the same time:

They were improperly dressed. No collar and tie, plus at the same time they were pissed. I knew who they were. They was only welters. I'd have taken their heads off. Next night Charlie Kray walked in. 'What happened?' 'I'm not going into explanations, the club runs nicely, quietly.' 'You could have given them a tie.' 'Yes, but I couldn't have sobered them up.' For a time I'd leave the club at 3.30 a.m. After I'd locked the door I'd look left and right and then I'd leap into the road so I was away from shop fronts before anyone hit me. I'd do this six nights a week. I'd park in the Lex garage and I'd make sure the attendant came up with me. I'd get in, lock the doors and run the engine to get it nice and warm and I'd keep my eyes on the mirror to make sure no one was following me.[13]

[12] Bob Monkhouse, *Crying with Laughter*, p. 133.
[13] Conversation with author.

The Mills story surfaced on a regular basis. In November 1965 the *Daily Express* announced that the family was thinking of bringing a private prosecution for murder. Donnie McCorkindale was quoted as saying, 'My mother and I have never thought that Freddie killed himself. Now we have enough information not only to assure us that he did not kill himself, but also to convince us that we know who did kill him.' It was a statement later denied by Chrissie Mills.[14]

Three years after Mills' death, in 1968, Leonard 'Nipper' Read and his team arrested the Kray Twins, their elder brother Charles and a number of other men. Once this had been done Read was able to put together a case against the Twins for the murder of Cornell, as well as of another one-time member of The Firm, Jack 'The Hat' McVitie, this time by Reggie Kray. As a result of a letter from Chrissie Mills he also began to inquire into the death of her husband.

On 4 August, Read went to see Chrissie: 'Nothing would have given me more pleasure than being able to show that Freddie had not committed suicide. In those days there was much more of a stigma attached to the act than there is today. Moreover, if I could link the Krays to it my investigation would have a major boost. It would have been beautiful to have tagged this murder to them,' he recalled.[15]

But as far as he was concerned, the interview was a disappointment: 'She was pleased to see me and her attitude was, "Good, now something will happen." She was utterly convinced Freddie did not commit suicide, but as for hard

---

[14] Private prosecutions for murder generally bring grief only to the prosecutors. For a start the Director of Public Prosecutions can step in and quash the proceedings. Even if this does not happen, rarely, if ever, are they successful.
[15] Leonard Read and James Morton, *Nipper Read: The Man Who Nicked The Krays*, p. 258. Unless otherwise stated the other quotations by Read in this chapter are from the book.

facts, she could add little to what was common knowledge.' But Read also toured the West End speaking with the usual suspects and faces. All he could get out of them was, 'Oh guv, you know better than that.' One man had said, 'We don't make examples of other people. If somebody don't pay we break his legs not somebody else's.'

Read was by now leaning hard on the smaller fry of The Firm, who had been collectors and now were considering their positions and whether it would be preferable to be a witness or defendant. Again, he had no luck. The response, he says, was always the same: 'Freddie – no way. When the Twins went to Freddie's place they paid. They'd never nip him. They were boxers too. He was their hero. You can bet every time they went there they paid. No danger.'

Chrissie Mills was understandably gravely disappointed when Read told her he could find no evidence to justify a murder verdict. Read apologised for the disappointing news, 'However I have to look at it on the evidence and, based on that, I am sadly forced to the inescapable conclusion that he did, in fact, take his own life.'

So if it wasn't the Richardsons, and if the man who put them away said it wasn't the Krays, could it have been the work of an independent?

At the end of the dramatised television reconstruction of the Mills' story, *In Suspicious Circumstances*, Edward Woodward revealed that Jack Birtley, the writer, had received an anonymous letter saying that the killing had been carried out on the instruction of a man known in Soho as 'The Guv'nor', someone known to Mills. The writer of the letter had been offered the contract but, since he admired Mills, he had declined it. The theory was that the first bullet in the front nearside door of the car had been fired by Mills to scare off an attacker, but the Guv'nor had himself arrived later and had shot Mills. The writer backed up his credentials by saying that he had undertaken the contract killing of a prostitute known as Black Rita.

At the time there were two men who could claim the title of Guv'nor of Soho and it was certainly neither Ronnie nor Reggie Kray. The first was the ageing Billy Hill, and there is no evidence that he was ever seriously into protection. Hill was a thief and an organiser of high-class robberies, who by this time had effectively retired. The only person active in his place generally known as the Guv'nor was Billy Howard. As for the killing of Black Rita, this was a case from eighteen years earlier. Black Rita Green, or Driver, was shot on the first-floor landing of a house in Rupert Street on 8 September 1947. She was, by all accounts, a striking six-foot woman, the daughter of a former police officer who had been stationed at Bow Street. Two suggestions were offered for her death. The first was that she was a police informer; the second that she had been made an example for others after she had refused to co-operate with the Messina brothers, who ran vice in the West End at the time. The police rather took the view that she had been killed by a stranger with an aversion to prostitutes. There was also the story that she had a new boyfriend who was said to carry a revolver. It is curious that the man offered the contract for Mills should not have been able to offer a more recent example of his work.[16]

Even if, and this is by no means certain, Mills was paying straightforward protection money, it is extremely unlikely he

---

[16] One man who has been suggested as the killer of a number of prostitutes in the late 1940s, for business rather than personal reasons, is Edward 'Teddy' Machin, who worked with Jack Spot in the 1950s. Machin was shot and killed in a family dispute whilst out walking in Forest Gate on 23 May 1973. A man was charged with murder but received five years for manslaughter after a retrial.

was paying anything like as much as the very successful Colony Club. If he was, this would amount to around £5000 a year, admittedly a very considerable but by no means impossible sum, which does not account for the huge loss of his capital at the time and the liquidation of his property investments. One theory was that he lavished money on the dancer with whom he had fallen in love. Another is that he was a gambler. Chrissie Mills told Read that her husband was a 'regular but good one', but it is inevitably the case that the more one goes to the well of the table, the less one draws back. As Read points out, even the best have losing streaks.

Both Bill Bavin and Peter McInnes support the murder theory, indeed Bavin produced a twenty-four-point refutation of the suicide verdict, which can be summed up in sections. The first four points relate to Mills being an extrovert and in good humour on the last day of his life. Bavin claimed he was not a sufficiently convincing actor to keep things from his wife. Then there is the question of there being no note. Bavin also poses the question – why would a potential suicide ask how many people were in his nightclub? But the answer to that last point is simple: to find only a handful of people in one's club on a Saturday evening might well have been the proverbial last straw.

Bavin's second group of questions relates to his decision to use a firearm. Mills apparently had a phobia about firearms. Why shoot himself outside his club? How were there no fingerprints of his on the gun and why was it found out of his reach? There were only smudges indicating the use of gloves, which Mills was not wearing. Then there was the question of shooting himself in the eye, a suggestion that Bavin found unacceptable. Bavin also raised questions about borrowing the gun and returning it, as well as its condition. There was the question of how Chrissie Mills had never seen the gun, although she had cleaned Mills' car. Where was its third round? Bavin again raised the question of the threats of making an example. As for the apparent phobia, Mills had not displayed it when, as a young boy, he had shot holes with an air rifle in the family bathtub, and he had, of course, been in the RAF.

However, the real problem with the gun and the questions and doubts that arise from it, for those bent on establishing that Mills was murdered, is the witness May Ronaldson. If one accepts her evidence, then the murder theories become really extreme. They must presuppose that the killer knew Mills took a nap in his car in Goslett Yard and that he chanced on him with the gun in the car, took it off him, without a struggle, and shot him. It must have been a straightforward chance because had she not lent her car to her son, Chrissie Mills would have been at the club and Mills would not have been in the alley. So, if Mrs Ronaldson was correct, the coincidence of a stray killer happening upon the gun in Mills' car and taking the opportunity to shoot him with it, seems beyond acceptance. The only counter is that offered by Bresler, that Mrs Ronaldson was, for one reason or another, lying, and had been coerced into making the statement. A reason offered for this is that some of the stallholders at the funfair at Battersea were under protection from the same mob, and she was one of them. If so, why such an elaborate story of two visits when, for the purpose of a concocted story, one would have been so much simpler?

Read has dealt comprehensively with many of the questions raised by Bavin and McInnes. One of his points was that Mills, apparently fearful of guns, would not shoot himself in the eye. Read says that it could be argued with equal force that this would not be the favoured target of a gunman. 'There is no doubt that the eye as the site of injury is most unusual. There is something repugnant in most people's minds about putting a bullet through one's eye. Certainly the temple or mouth is the more usual target. I am sure, however, that the eye was not chosen as the site. I believe he chose to shoot himself in the forehead and, at the moment of pulling the trigger, jerked the weapon, causing the bullet to be deflected into the eye.' As for the absence of a suicide note, Read pointed out that he had investigated many suicides and that the majority had left no note.[17]

In his book, Peter McInnes writes of a chance meeting with Charlie Kray in the Fox Inn in Bournemouth, on the site of the terrace in which Mills was born, in the spring of 1975, shortly after Kray had been released from his ten-year sentence. McInnes questions why Kray was in Bournemouth and why, of all places there, he should choose The Fox as his drinker. The answer to the first is that the Krays had long had considerable interests in Bournemouth, where Bill Ackerman was one of their local representatives.

In any event McInnes was with Mills' old manager Jack Turner, and the three bought the rounds in turn, until McInnes confronted Kray with his 'unshaken belief' that the brothers must know who pulled the trigger and that if, as they insisted, Mills had been their friend, they would have done something about it. Words were exchanged and after

---

[17] Only a minority of people who kill themselves leave a message behind. In a 1953 survey it was probably around only 15 per cent. More people over sixty left notes and only around half of the notes in the survey referred to the reasons. See Dr E. Stengel, *Suicide and Attempted Suicide*.

McInnes left at 2.30 he was struck from behind, ending up in the casualty department. Some two days later he went back to the Fox, again with Jack Turner, and was handed an envelope containing ten pounds and a note which read, 'Sorry about that but don't you ever dare be such a silly boy again.'[18]

Rather dramatically, towards the end of his book, McInnes writes, 'Lest anything untoward should happen to my wife or myself as a result of what I have written in these pages of Freddie's biography, our Solicitor has already taken instructions. Such an event would, surely, provide final proof.' Fortunately it has not. McInnes and his wife have both outlived all three Krays.

What really does militate against the Krays being the killers, either personally or by proxy, is that over the last forty years not a single person has come forward to say that they know the man who carried out the killing, nor has there been any whisper of who it might be. The identities of the killers in many of the so-called unsolved gang murders of the period have been open secrets. But no name has ever been raised as the trigger-puller in the case of Mills.

If one does not accept the murder theory, then one is left with the suicide verdict. But the question then remains, why? Over the years many possible reasons have been advanced: that Mills was unable to cope with the blinding headaches from which he had been suffering; that his club was failing; that there were allegations of prostitutes on the premises, something which would bring shame to him and his family; that he was suffering from depression because

[18] Peter McInnes, *Freddie My Friend*, pp. 214–15.

of the break-up of a relationship with a young woman; that he was gay and unable to cope with the death of his lover, the singer Michael Holliday; that he had been arrested on an importuning charge; that he was being eased out from the BBC because of one, some or all of the above and could not cope with the loss of the limelight; that he was having to pay protection money to the Triads, to the Richardsons, to the Krays, to some other person; that he was nearly bankrupt.

It has remained a fascinating debate over the years. In 1990 a radio programme rehearsed the arguments, and Giles Smith reviewing the discussion for the *Independent* wrote:

> Desmond Lynam marshalled the facts of the case through a packed 25 minutes . . . 'Try this one for size,' he said wryly at one point, before wheeling on the notion that Mills was a depressed bi-sexual and involved in an affair with the singer Michael Holliday (Britain's Bing Crosby, who had been in Mills' club the night before his own suicide). It didn't fit. The DJ Pete Murray appeared from nowhere to remind us that Holliday was 'the number one crumpet man' and moreover 'never stopped trying to pull the birds'.[19]

The late actor Bob Monkhouse remembered a rather different Holliday:

> When I was in Neil Simon's comedy hit *Come Blow Your Horn* at the Prince of Wales Theatre in London Michael

[19] *Independent*, 13 March 1990.

Holliday used to come into my dressing room. He was very keen on pornography. In those days it was very lame and old-fashioned black-and-white flickering films. Ugly men with false moustaches and sleazy women with real moustaches. He was forever arranging get-togethers to watch them. He was another who had highs and lows. Some nights he'd stand in the wings and laugh louder than the audience. Other nights he'd slump in my dressing room and drink my booze. He'd be terrible company.

I'd say to Michael Crawford, who was playing my younger brother, 'Go and tell him he's great.' Crawford would say 'Sing *The Story of My Life*' and Holliday would perk up. Once there was some money missing from my dressing room. I'd left it in my trouser pocket and when I asked Harry, my dresser, he said, 'I think your friend needed it.' Quite a few who come from obscure backgrounds and achieve fame still go on doing petty thieving. Mike was underprivileged and felt he had a right to things. Some people think if you've left something lying about they can have it. There is no point in them asking, because you might say no. Mike was like that.[20]

The London criminal Frankie Fraser, a member of the Richardson gang, believes that the only reason why the official verdict of suicide was ever questioned was because of insurance:

Most companies wouldn't pay on a suicide policy in them days. That and it was still a bit of a disgrace. It hadn't

[20] Conversation with author.

long not been a criminal offence. His Chinese partner
[Andy Ho] had him over. Everything was on top. He'd
treat everyone who come in the club. It was quite nice in
them days. There were hostesses but not too prominent.
Michael Holliday had just died. He was gay as well. No
one admitted it in them days. Freddie was strongly fancied
for the towpaths. He'd been questioned. Rumours was
abounding in the underworld and rumours as strong as
that is sometimes right.

I saw him in 1946–7. I'd come out of Liverpool. He
had the heart of a lion. If only he'd had a bit more beef.
It's a sad story in many ways. He was used like a shut-
tlecock. Once McCorkindale was going down she
[Chrissie] was slipped into Fred.[21]

In Bavin's book, however, he maintains there was no insurance on Mills' life. The author Douglas Sutherland, who was
himself something of a man about town of the period, had
already placed an each way bet: 'In the underworld it was
acknowledged that it was not a Billy Hill job and one likely
put down to the Chinese Tongs – a deadly secret society
which specialised in assassinations – and a grudge killing
with a motive in the sinister ring of practising homosexuals
of which Freddie Mills was part.'[22]

The homosexual issue was also raised by Tony Van den
Bergh, who suggested there was a possible relationship
between Mills and Don McCorkindale, as well as talk of a
relationship with Michael Holliday. There is also a passage
in Jack Birtley's book that after Don's son was born in 1939:

[21] Ibid.
[22] Douglas Sutherland, *Portrait of a Decade*, p. 129.

'[his wife] claimed that McCorkindale began to make demands which upset her so much that the marriage gradually broke up'.[23]

However, Bavin dismisses the suggestion that Mills might have been a homosexual. Speaking with the police officer John du Rose he quotes him as saying, 'As far as I'm concerned, old chap, this sounds as ludicrous as the first rumour. He was the last fellow I'd ever begin to suspect in that direction.' Bavin then throws in his pennyworth: 'I said it was ridiculous, but I had to check it with you. I knew him for years and he was about the most masculine male I ever came across, wouldn't you agree?' And du Rose added, 'Wholeheartedly.'[24]

Bavin, though, had not seen Mills regularly before his death and there is little doubt that he had adopted show-business mannerisms. John Morris remembers he would say, '"Bye bye darling." You could see how some people said he had a gay tendency.' Dennie Mancini thought that, 'He was a bit soppy at the end. "Hello, lovely, how are you?"'

It has been suggested that Mills was being blackmailed over a homosexual liaison. If so, he was in a double bind. The authorities and courts were by no means sympathetic to men who found themselves paying money because of a homosexual relationship. When the Wolfenden Committee on Homosexual Offences and Prostitution reported in 1957, it quoted the case of a man A., aged forty-nine, who met B., aged thirty-five, in a cinema. They went to A.'s flat, committed

---

[23] Tony Van den Bergh, *Who Killed Freddie Mills?* p. 68; Jack Birtley, *Freddie Mills*, p. 122. In 1948 McCorkindale brought a petition for the restitution of conjugal rights and of malicious desertion in Johannesburg. Chrissie Mills cross petitioned. *Evening News*, 12 May 1948.
[24] Bill Bavin, *The Strange Death of Freddie Mills*, p. 75.

buggery and did so for the next seven years. B. then began demanding money and over a three-month period obtained some £40. A. complained and as part of a woeful statement to the police wrote: 'I sent the money because I thought from his letters that if I did not do so he would tell the people at the shop and where I live that I had had sexual intercourse with him.' The Director of Public Prosecutions recommended that no action be taken over the blackmail, but that both be charged with buggery. Each was charged with two specimen counts. Neither asked for matters to be taken into consideration; neither had previous convictions. Each received nine months' imprisonment.[25] Mills, in his position, had a great deal more to lose than A.

Could he not have gone to a friend in the police to have had the thing sorted out informally? One thing is certain – that in the mid-1960s there were some very odd senior officers floating around the club scene in the West End. It is a possibility, no more, that any blackmail was coming from a police officer. There was also the question of Mills' macho image.

There were even rumours that Mills had had a relationship with Ronnie Kray. Bill Ackerman claimed that he saw Mills and Kray together in the Society, a club in Jermyn Street, and later in other venues. 'They'd always sit side by side and they were just like a man and a woman together.' It was something Kray denied, saying that he would never have sex with a man, as opposed to a boy.[26]

Michael Howard writing about his father, the London

---

[25] Sir John Wolfenden, *Report of the Committee on Homosexual Offences and Prostitution* (1957) Cmnd 247, HMSO.
[26] Dan Slater, 'Kray Gay-Love Secret of Freddie Mills Death', *News of the World*, 5 April 1992. Kate Kray and Ronnie Kray, *Murder, Madness and Marriage*.

gang boss Billy Howard, has a long story about Mills and Michael Holliday. He maintains that one of his father's friends, the singer Dorothy Squires, asked Howard to come to her flat. The pianist Russ Conway had told her a story, told to him by Holliday, and she wanted advice. The gist of the tale was that Holliday had indeed had a homo-sexual affair with Mills and, both being bi-sexual, they had picked up girls for what were described as 'mild sado-masochistic acts on them for titillation before Mills and Holliday had sex with each other'. The girls were either club girls from the West End or, if they were not willing, then prostitutes.

In around 1959 on one occasion things had got out of hand and a girl had died. Mills had disposed of the body and then persuaded Holliday not to go to the police. Given that Holliday was at the peak of his career, this was not too difficult. According to Holliday, their relationship had then cooled but had revived in the early sixties. Holliday had, he maintained, insisted that the sado-masochism was merely acted out, but then *another* girl died. Her body was again disposed of by Mills. It was then that Holliday told Conway and asked for advice. Before it was given, Holliday committed suicide.

Billy Howard then arranged a meeting between Conway and a Metropolitan police officer at a Brighton hotel, before warning Mills that he seemed to have got himself into 'a bit of serious trouble' and that 'You are about to get your collar felt, so I'd arrange to have a brief on call.' As a West End club owner Mills had apparently been receiving protection from Howard, who thought he was entitled to advance notice on an impending arrest.

But fundamentally, this is, of course, a variation on the

version of the story in which the police mark Mills' card. It is also a story which is at best third-hand, and which none of the principals are alive to confirm.[27]

Bob Monkhouse, whose writing partner Denis Goodwin was a depressive, knew of Mills' moods:

> Freddie had a very dark side. Denis, my partner who committed suicide, felt a tremendous kinship with him and they palled around together. Denis had this unabashed glee and terrible moments of despondent mood exactly the same as Freddie. Denis said his depressions came after a successful show and Freddie that his came after a successful fight, because he felt he could never do any better.
>
> Freddie had male companions and he also consorted with a number of ladies on a casual basis. He'd try anything. With some people, when they become famous, they feel they have the right to have anything they want. I didn't see him do it but the story was that Freddie Mills was quite capable of whipping it out and saying, 'Wrap a smile round that.' He'd expose himself in front of anybody. He didn't bother to go into the gents'. I heard he was less interested in penetration, more in a Clinton–Lewinsky type of activity.[28]

Plenty of other sources support Monkhouse's impression of Mills. One, Nosher Powell, says that he was eventually caught out on the night of his death:

---

[27] Michael Connor, *The Soho Don*, pp. 92–4. Billy Howard's former wife Jan (who was with him at the time of Mills' death) is convinced that her son is wrong and that Mills was not paying protection to him. Conversation with author.
[28] Conversation with author.

Freddie would drive over Waterloo Bridge, down the Strand and into Wellington Street as a short cut to the West End. Whether he had to go to the toilet I don't know, but he stopped at a public urinal and he went in. There was a young fellow and Freddie propositioned him. Next, 'You're under arrest.' He was taken to Bow Street, charged with importuning and released. You could accuse him of murder or robbery and he'd hold his head up high, but to be charged with being a poofter was more than he could take. He walked up to the top of the road to an amusement arcade and said to the woman, 'Lend me a rifle'.[29]

If this is true then it throws some doubt on the evidence of Mrs Ronaldson, who would have possibly been open to a charge of assisting a suicide, had Mills borrowed the gun on the night of his arrest. It would, however, explain the comments in the newspapers about a six-hour time gap that night.

John Rigbey, then with the Flying Squad, confirms that in the 1960s, police officers were bought off on a regular basis. 'If someone was caught in a bog nodding and smiling then, provided it wasn't in the book, forty quid could square it. Once there was a charge then there was nothing could be done about getting rid of it completely.'[30] If Mills had been caught in a compromising position, then he would have been fair game for the numerous dishonest officers who were in

[29] Conversation with author. The story also appears in Dan Slater, 'Kray Gay-Love Secret of Freddie Mills Death', *News of the World*, 5 April 1992. Slater gives the lavatory as Chandos Place. He also says that a Superintendent Cooper and a Sergeant Smith often talked to him about it, with Cooper saying, 'If only Mills' old woman would keep her trap shut. We're trying to protect the man's reputation but the way she's going on we'll have to divulge the lot.'
[30] Conversation with author.

the Met at the time. There would also be questions about his club licence.

Then, of course, there were the headaches. Given the letter Bavin received from Mills' doctor, he clearly believed something was seriously wrong with him.

In November 1970, there was a flurry of activity after Michael O'Halloran, the Labour member of Parliament for Islington, announced that a constituent had given him the name of Mills' killer. Chrissie Mills said she was disappointed O'Halloran had not been to see her and that she was too upset to go to the reopening of the Royal Oak, Crawley Down, where the gloves from the Lesnevich, Harvey and Pol Gottaux fights were going on display, along with an oil portrait of Mills and some medallions. The inquiry came to an abrupt ending when it turned out that the claim had been made as a revenge by the man's former girlfriend.[31]

In May 1986 Donnie McCorkindale, then playing Don Lester in *Coronation Street*, said he believed that his step-father's killer was in Australia.[32]

[31] *The Times*, 19 November 1970; *Sunday Mirror*, 21 November 1970.
[32] 'I'll Get Man Who Shot My Dad', *Sun*, 10 May 1986.

22

Freddie Mills as Jack
the Stripper?

Over the years, the most persistent and certainly the most
sensational rumour has been that Mills was 'Jack the Stripper',
the serial killer of prostitutes in the Hammersmith area in
the mid-1960s. In one version of the story, Mills did in fact
leave a suicide note in which he admits the killings and which
found its way to the Police College at Hendon. It is a story
which has been vehemently denied. It is incredible that there
are whole swaths of the public willing to believe, on no real
evidence whatsoever, that Mills was a mass murderer. Nor is
it something which has diminished him in their eyes; on the
contrary it has rather enhanced him. It is a story which grew
into the status of urban legend. Not even Mike Tyson at his
best, or worst, has managed this.

The story goes that Mills knew the police were closing in
on him and killed himself to avoid capture. In some improved
versions he was actually tipped off by them, and told that

unless he committed suicide within a matter of hours, he would be arrested. So, is there any possible truth in such rumours?

The so-called 'Stripper' murders began when the body of a prostitute woman, the thirty-year-old Hannah Tailford, was found on 2 February 1964 on the towpath near Hammersmith Bridge. From a respectable home in Cumberland, she had come to London where she had worked under a number of names, including Anne Taylor and Teresa Bell. Most of her clothes were missing from her body, but her stockings were still around her ankles. She had bruising on her face and her knickers were stuffed in her mouth.

It seems she was mixed up in the porn business. Although she lived in West Norwood, she worked out of a flat in Victoria, and when the police looked there they found studio lighting equipment and a camera. Most prostitutes who are not actually working the streets keep a so-called black book – perhaps after black for blackmail – and that was missing. The police therefore thought she might have been killed to put a stop to blackmail. Curiously, because by then two more prostitutes had been found dead in the area, an open verdict was returned at the inquest. Since there was no evidence to show that Tailford was murdered, by June the case was no longer being treated as a crime.[1]

The body of the second girl was found at Duke's Meadows on 8 April, but the two deaths had not been linked. The girl was Irene Lockwood and she had certainly been strangled. Again, the police thought the reason for her death was that she might have been blackmailing her former punters. In

---

[1]   PRO MEPO 2 0 10.

1963 she had given an alibi for a man accused of murdering another girl – Vicki Pender – this time in Finsbury Park.[2]

The third girl to be found was Helen Barthelemy from Ormiston, East Lothian, who was discovered on 24 April, a little way from the river in a driveway near Swincombe Avenue in Brentford. She used to hang around the Jazz Club in Westbourne Grove, which had a large West Indian clientele. Four of her teeth were missing and a broken piece of one was found lodged in her throat. There were traces of paint spray on her body, which made the police think it might have been kept in a car-repair shop before being dumped. There was, however, no sign of a blow to the face. There were traces of sperm in her mouth and it seemed as though she had been orally raped or, more likely, had been fellating a man when she died. Now the police at last began to link the three murders. However, if one man had killed all three, it was looking likely that their original blackmail theory was wrong.

The next day Kenneth Archibald, a fifty-four-year-old care-taker, walked into Notting Hill police station and confessed to killing Irene Lockwood. He seemed to fit the bill for the crime. He worked part time in Kenny's, a basement drinking club, and a business card for Kenny's had been found in Lockwood's flat. Archibald retraced the evening of 7 April with the police, pointing out the pub in Chiswick where he had met and had a drink with Lockwood. He told the police he must have lost his temper 'and put my hands round her throat. She could not scream. I then proceeded to take her

---

[2] On 2 July 1963, Colin Welt Fisher received life imprisonment for the murder of Veronica Walsh, known as Vicki Pender, at her flat in Adolphus Road, Finsbury Park on 21 March 1963. The prosecution alleged both had been taking drugs. Lockwood had provided an alibi that Fisher had been at a hotel in Finsbury Park with her. She had not been believed.

clothes off and rolled her in the river. I took her clothes home and burned them.' The problem was that there was no way he could be tied to the murders of either Tailford or Barthelemy, so the serial-killer theory went out of the window. Nevertheless, the police had more than enough for a charge of murder to be brought, and Archibald was committed to the Central Criminal Court.

In those days, there was no great delay in bringing a case to court, and on 19 June Archibald was on trial at the Old Bailey for the murder of Irene Lockwood. However, he retracted his confession, explaining that he had been afraid after being accused of a theft at the tennis club where he was the caretaker. He had had six beers and then gone to the police station. The jury retired for less than an hour before they brought back a verdict of not guilty.[3]

Curiously, though, while Archibald was in custody, the murders stopped. The discovery of the next victim came on 14 July, when a chauffeur looking out of his flat window saw what he thought was a tailor's dummy and went to investigate. Mary Fleming, a mother of two, was found in a sitting position near a garage in Berrymede Road, Chiswick. She was naked and her denture was missing. Again someone had ejaculated in her mouth, and there were traces of paint spray on her body. She had last been seen alive at 1 a.m. on 11 July. It was apparent that the body had been kept for some time before being dumped.

[3] The dangers in bringing prosecutions based only on confessions were vividly demonstrated most recently in April 2003, when Leonard John Fraser was accused of the murder of Natasha Ryan in Queensland, Australia, in 1998. The prosecution rested on his alleged statement that he had smashed her head while she slept and dumped her body in a lily pond. During the trial, Ms Ryan emerged safe and well. She had been living with her boyfriend, hidden from public view. (*The Times*, 19 April 2003.)

Just before the body's discovery, there had been a near collision in Acton Lane, which adjoins Berrymede Road, when a motorist had to brake sharply to avoid a van coming out of a cul-de-sac. All that could be said about the van was that it was dark coloured. The assumption was that the body had been dumped out of the van.

There were no more incidents for over four months, until 25 November, when Margaret McGowan was discovered on a pile of rubble in a car park in Hornton Street, near Kensington High Street. Again, spots of paint covered her body and she had a tooth missing. She'd last been seen a month earlier. The previous year she had given evidence for the defence in the trial of Dr Stephen Ward, who had been charged with living off the earnings of prostitutes.[4] In her case, two small pieces of jewellery, a cross on a chain and a gold ring, had been stolen from her.

The last of the killings came at the beginning of 1965 when, on 16 February, the body of Bridie O'Hara was found behind a store-shed off Westfield Road, Acton. Brought up in Dublin, she now lived in Agate Road, Hammersmith. She had last been seen on 11 January when she visited the Shepherd's Bush Hotel, and it was thought she had been killed that night. Her wedding and engagement rings were missing. Now Detective Chief Superintendent John du Rose, known as 'Four Day Johnnie' for the speed with which he solved his cases, was brought in.

[4] The Stephen Ward trial was a great *cause célèbre* of 1964. It followed the disclosure that a nightclub hostess, Christine Keeler, had been involved simultaneously with both the Secretary of State for War, John Profumo, and Captain Ivanov, Assistant Naval Attaché at the Russian Embassy and an intelligence officer. Ward was charged with living off the immoral earnings of prostitutes, including Keeler and Mandy Rice-Davies. Put on trial on 22 July 1964, he committed suicide before the verdict of guilty was returned. See Christine Keeler and Robert Meadley, *Sex Scandals*.

Yet another girl, Susan Smith, was reported missing in the middle of March 1965. She spoke with a slight stutter and was known as Little Susan, or Goldie, because she often wore a gold-coloured dress. It was suggested that she might have been another victim. She had, according to the newspapers, 'often spoken to coloured men'. Du Rose was reported as saying that he thought the Stripper killed in ten-week cycles and another was approaching when her body was found.[5]

Soon after the discovery of O'Hara's body, the police issued a statement saying that they wished to interview a man who had recently lived in Hammersmith and who had a garage, in connection with the case. The *People* named the man, who then went to the police of his own accord and made a statement. The newspaper later published an explanation that there had been no intention to convey the impression that he was a suspect.[6]

All the murdered girls were small, and they all worked the Bayswater–Kensington beat. The scientists could tell from marks on their bodies that they had all been suffocated before their clothes were taken, and they were convinced that the girls had been kept in storage before their bodies were deposited in public places. They had all disappeared between 11 p.m. and 1 a.m., and they were thought to have been dumped between 5 and 6 a.m. The police were convinced that the killer worked at night, possibly as a nightwatchman. He also must have had somewhere to store the bodies.

Du Rose held a series of press conferences that were designed to put pressure on the killer. He announced that great progress was being made in solving the murders. A list of suspects had, he said, been drawn up and they were being

[5] *People*, 21 March 1965.
[6] Ibid., 21 February and 4 April 1965.

interviewed one by one. It was now only a matter of time before the killer would have his turn. In an early version of the ring of iron, additionally a police 'wall' was thrown around central London, and every vehicle in and out between 8 p.m. and 7 a.m. was noted. Three visits would secure a red flag for a special interview.

Then an apparent breakthrough was made. A sample which matched the paint flecks on the bodies was found opposite a paint-spray shop on the Heron Factory Estate in Acton. While the police were investigating the seven-thousand-odd people who worked on the estate, in June 1965 a married man from Putney killed himself. He left a note saying that he was unable to stand the strain any longer. There was no physical evidence to tie the man to the murders, but there was, so the police believed, sufficient circumstantial evidence. He had, for example, worked as a night-security patrolman for a company which operated small black vans with a white door flash. This matched the vehicle that was reported to the police after Mary Fleming's death. He was known to have had what could be described as 'legitimate access' to the Westpoint Trading Estate, where the body of Bridie O'Hara had been found. He had been due in court the day after his death on a charge of failing to stop after an accident. Du Rose was satisfied: on 1 July 1965 the decoy operation of policewomen posing as prostitutes was called off. No more murders that could be linked to Jack the Stripper ever took place.

As with the original Jack the Ripper, there is a suggestion that there were two other girls killed. One, Elizabeth Figg from the Wirral, was found dead on 17 June 1959 on the tow-path. Her shoes were missing, and it was some time before she was identified as living in a bedsit in Hornsey. In theory Figg is really rather out of the timescale of the murders positively attributed to the Stripper. Her death made headlines for a couple of days and it was believed that the name of the killer might be in the autograph book she kept in her handbag. Dr Ellis Stungo in the *Star* suggested the killing was the work of a 'manic depressive'.[7] Newspaper interest in the death soon fizzled out.

In his autobiography, du Rose wrote: 'It was assumed from the manner in which all these girls had died that their killer was a man of some strength and virility. He certainly wasn't satisfied with normal intercourse and in every instance the victims had slight marks on the neck apparently made by fingernails, either by the murderer, or by the victim in an attempt at self-defence. Some had injuries and very slight bruising as though pressure had been directed in the region of the nose and mouth.' All the girls had at one time or another suffered from some form of venereal disease, but du Rose did not believe the killings were by a man in revenge for being infected: 'Early in the inquiry I became convinced that the killer was a man in his forties with extremely strong sexual urges which, perhaps because of his age, were not easily satisfied normally. It is probably this physical difficulty that took him away from his wife and into the twilight world of the prostitutes. He knew that these women set no limits to the sexual acts in which they would allow their clients to indulge. In obtaining satisfaction he became utterly frenzied and at the moment of his orgasm the girls died.'[8]

Over the years, it has been suggested that the case was closed not because of the death of the man from Putney, but rather because of another suicide altogether. In his book *Found Naked and Dead*, Brian McConnell advances the theory

[7] *Star*, 17 June 1959.
[8] John du Rose, *Murder Was My Business*, pp. 103–4.

that the murderer was an ex-policeman who was not only a heavy drinker but also had bizarre sexual tastes and a life-time obsession with prostitutes. He calls the man 'Big John', saying he was brought up by a zealously religious family and was in the army before joining the Met in 1945. He married and stayed away from prostitutes and drink. He had left the force after being transferred out of, or rejected by the plain clothes division. He then returned to his old ways. Knowing the hunt was closing in, he turned on the gas taps at his home.[9] If this theory is correct, it is easy to see how the police of those, or any, days would not wish to suffer the embarrassment of naming one of their former colleagues.

However, even before his death, there had been persistent rumours in the underworld that the Stripper was Mills: 'Freddie Mills was the man. They didn't want him to be the culprit. He was part of the Establishment.'[10]

But what evidence is there against him? Absolutely none is the answer.[11] About the best that can be claimed is that he had a night job. If, however, Michael Howard's account of the confession to Billy Howard is correct, then the Stripper story becomes slightly less thin and the death of Figg comes into the equation. But another problem with Mills as the Stripper is that, if du Rose is correct, he did not conform to the ten-week cycle. Assuming for the moment that Susan Smith was another victim this would leave the killer to strike again around the first week in June. There were no more reports of women killed in similar circumstances and Mills did not die until the end of July.

[9] Brian McConnell, *Found Naked and Dead*.
[10] Anonymous, conversation with author.
[11] Yet the accusation continues to be made: 'Boxing Hero Freddie Mills "Murdered Eight Women"', *Observer*, 4 November 2001; 'Was a British Boxing Hero a Serial Sex Killer?', *Mail on Sunday*, 18 November 2001.

Purely on the timescale, the unidentified south London man fits the bill much better.

Nipper Read, who reinvestigated Mills' death, was horrified by the accusations that Mills could have been the killer: 'When I first heard this outrageous rumour I was lecturing at the Police Academy at Wakefield and I was horrified. These rumours were outrageous for there is no justification for any suggestion that Freddie was, in any way, a suspect in the investigation. I said then as I do now, with as much force as I can, that Freddie Mills was never, in any way, involved in this investigation.'[12]

In 2001, Martin Short and the former criminal James Evans put together a more plausible theory, even if there was no shred of evidence to back it – that the killer was Tommy Butler, the Scotland Yard detective who investigated the Great Train Robbery. In essence, their argument runs that Butler was born in Shepherd's Bush and therefore knew the area well. He was small, balding, unmarried and lived with his mother near Hammersmith Bridge. In April 1964, there had been an article in the *Daily Express* which suggested that the police were looking for a man they called the 'Solicitor' who was always prepared to pay prostitutes the substantial sum of forty pounds for the particular services he required. He apparently preferred small women. Evans and Short argue that, apart from the profession, this fitted the description of Butler. Late in his career, he took to scanning the beaches of St Tropez with a pair of binoculars, something which led to his arrest. He maintained he was looking for the escaped train robber Bruce Reynolds, and it is true that Reynolds was in the South of France around that time, but Short and Evans suggest Butler was a Peeping Tom. As a brilliant detective,

---

[12] Leonard Read and James Morton, *Nipper Read*, p. 191.

he would have known of traps laid for him by other officers. He might indeed have learned of any road blocks from one of his colleagues and taken steps to avoid them. As a senior officer, he was effectively above suspicion.[13]

In fact it is just about as arguable as the so-called case against Freddie Mills.

[13] Jimmy Evans and Martin Short, *The Survivor*, chapter 19.

23

'Battles' Rossi Meets Freddie Mills

Former Italian hardman, Robert 'Battles' Rossi, now in his eighties, may have the solution to the puzzle of the death of Freddie Mills. Rossi has had a long involvement with the underworld. Brought up in Clerkenwell, the traditional home of the Italian families who dominated London crime between the wars, he was a friend and employee of Billy Hill and criminals' criminal Jock Wyatt. In 1955, he served five years for assault on the former gangleader Jack Spot, which left the victim scarred for life. Rossi has always maintained that he was innocent. Later, he was acquitted of the murder of a Mrs Gold in Clerkenwell.

Rossi now lives in north London. He knew the Krays from the time he had been in prison with Ronnie:

Ronnie Kray, [George] Cornell and I were all in Winchester when I was doing the four years for Spot. Frank [Fraser]'s right: I was never on that. The reason

Spot put me in it was that he knew I was capable of marshalling people as retribution. What Spot did was unforgivable. A man like him should have known you lived by the sword, you died by it, not go running to the police. Ronnie, Cornell and me would walk round the exercise yard together.

When we were in Winchester I was the one who told the doctor that Ronnie was mad. I'd just moved to sewing mattresses rather than mailbags and Ronnie wanted a job along with me. I mentioned it to a screw and about a week later he got one. He didn't really talk to people apart from me. Then I got a pair of glasses and next thing he asks me if he should get some. What he does is have the fellow come into the mailbag shop with the tray of frames and he chooses one exactly like mine and asks if I thinks it suits him. A bit later I say I'm going to the film, what about his coming along? And he says no. He's got this slow sort of voice. I ask him why not and he won't tell me, then he says, it's because I'm going to have it put on him.

I told him I fucking well wasn't. What I wanted to do was finish my bird and get home. I wasn't like Frank Fraser who could turn a three-year sentence into a six-year with the trouble he got into. I was worried. I didn't want to get in a fight and here was this fellow, clearly something wrong with him mentally. For some reason I had to see the governor and there was the doctor as well with a screw with him. I said I wanted to speak to the doctor not about me but about Kray. I told him and the doctor asked if, off the record, I'd tell him if I was a 'bacca baron because he thought Kray was into me for money and I'd made him buy me the spectacles. I said I could get all the 'bacca I wanted. Anyway they put Ronnie in the hospital.[1]

Rossi maintains that after his release, over a period of time, he acted as an unofficial adviser to the Twins, particularly Ronnie Kray. The Twins had always had a serious interest in the south coast, where one of their representatives was Bill Ackerman. Then, in July 1965:

Ronnie came to me and said that Mills' partner, Andy Ho, wanted him [Mills] out [of the club] and that there was money in it for them if they got him out. They'd had an approach through Bill Ackerman. I said I didn't think it was a good idea. Freddie wasn't going to take any nonsense from them and he'd have hit them. Then they'd have had to up the ante, so to speak, and maybe it would have got out of hand.

I knew Freddie, and said I would go round and have a chat with him and I went to see him a couple of days later. At first he didn't seem to understand. He said was I saying that he should move out? I said that his partner had gone to people in the East End. I said, 'Your back's to the wall. Give a little or there'll be trouble.' I left him in an uncertain state of mind. He didn't say, 'Go and fuck yourself', but he didn't say he'd agree.

I said to Ronnie, 'Leave it four or five days. Then, if he says he'll go, you can tell the Chinese it was down to you and you'll earn a few quid. If need be do what you have to do.' But I didn't want any part of it.

Five, six, seven days later, all of a sudden he's dead in

---

[1] Conversation with author (and all Rossi quotes in this chapter).

the car. I went to Ronnie and asked what he'd done. I might have been seen coming out of the club and there'd be questions asked of me. Ronnie said it was nothing to do with them and I said, 'Are you sure?' And I believed him when he said he hadn't.

This does not, of course, quite square with the Twins' professed devotion to boxing in general and Mills in particular. Why would they go against him? Rossi claims it was simply business. There was money in it.

Suggestions of Triad involvement in Mills' death were first mooted by Tony Van den Bergh in 1991. At first they were dismissed as utter rubbish. He wrote that whilst he was researching *The Purse*, a documentary on punch-drunkenness, a Smithfield marketeer whom he called 'Big Den' told him that it was common knowledge that 'Mills was killed by a Chinese gang who wanted to take over his club. Everyone in the Market knows that.'[2] The theory was that a Tong organisation wanted a headquarters in Soho. The back of Mills' club was in shadows, and with its access from both Oxford Street and the Charing Cross Road, drug dealers would have been able to come and go with relative impunity. Mills had, according to the story, rejected several offers and, in the face of his continued resistance, he was killed. This story would require Andy Ho either to be part of the Tong, or to kow-tow to it.

But why Mills' restaurant? Surely there were any number of restaurants and clubs in Soho from which the Chinese could operate? After all, Gerrard Street is wall-to-wall Chinese restaurants and shops, as is the surrounding area. Could they not have operated from one of those premises? The answer

---

[2] Tony Van den Bergh, *Who Killed Freddie Mills?*, p. 187.

is that in the 1960s there was not a great Triad presence in Soho nor, for that matter, was there any great Chinese presence at all. For the purposes of crime the area was still an Italian-dominated one. There were Chinese shops and restaurants, but nothing like the number there are today. The argument that someone wanted a ready-made place from which to operate is just about sustainable, but it may have been more simple: no Triads, simply one man.

To criminals, members of the general public are expendable. Criminals will turn at the slightest provocation because of a slight – real or imaginary – and, if money is involved, professed friendships will fly out of the window.

No solution will please everybody, but Rossi's story may well be the answer. On the balance of probabilities, it seems that Mills had reached the end of his tether. Disregarding the story of his arrest for importuning, he was ill; he now had no great expectations in the entertainment world; he was in desperate financial troubles; and there were difficulties with his partner, Ho. He had gambled and either spent much of his money on a girl, or was being blackmailed, possibly both. The club was a black hole swallowing money that was not coming in.

Given the story from Deacon that Ho was loading money into boxes, it may well be that Freddie confronted him and in turn Ho looked to the Twins for help. The news from Rossi that the Krays, whilst they may not have made any overt move, were going to back Ho may well have been the last straw.

But if Ho did want the club for himself, all this did him little good.[3] The Nite Spot remained closed for a fortnight as

---

[3] In 1993, Peter McInnes contacted Andy Ho, who was then living in Surbiton. He spoke with the second Mrs Ho, who indicated that her husband would be pleased to talk to him as there was something 'he wanted to get off his chest'. They never met. Ho, who was already in poor health, almost immediately suffered a series of strokes. Peter McInnes, *Freddie my Friend*, pp. 227–8.

a mark of respect and then reopened. If it had been hoped that its new-found notoriety would bring in new punters, it was not realised. It closed finally within a week. It is not now possible to trace what happened to shares in the club, which were no doubt worthless. The company was dissolved on 6 December 1968 and its records have been destroyed. Some years later the premises became a Spanish restaurant.

None the less, despite all his troubles, how could Freddie Mills commit suicide when he had spent such a happy day with his wife and children? Inserted in his copy of Bill Bavin's book, *Nipper Read*, is a typed note. It reads: 'Commenting on the recent death (September 1991) of a woman who had thrown herself off Beachy Head, the coroner remarked: "She was in a relaxed, quite pleasant frame of mind, which is all too common in people once they have decided what they intend to do with their life."'

24

Where Have All the Boxers Gone?

Both the Mills and Turpin families survived the financial wrecks. Shortly after Mills' death, his wife was talking of having to cut back on food, and possibly emigrating to Tasmania. But then the troops rallied round. There was a gala night at the Prince of Wales theatre the February after his death with a host of stars, including Bud Flanagan, Dickie Henderson, the Beverley Sisters, Tommy Cooper, Sid James and Ted Ray. The BBB of C. helped to sell tickets; the programme sellers were the Playboy Bunny Girls. Immediately afterwards she spoke of emigrating but, when it came to it, Joggi Villa was saved and the hardworking Chrissie Mills catered for bed-and-breakfast clients.

But there was no night of the stars for Randolph Turpin's family, as there had been for Mills. The nearest they got was a benefit wrestling tournament in Birmingham on 15 June when Mitzi Mueller was matched with Naughty Nancy Barton.

After Turpin died, the local council generously announced that the family was not likely to be evicted in the near future and could stay on. But Gwen could not bear to go near the café and she and the children moved in with the Mancinis, who now had a council house. Maria had a Morris 1000, and she would drive Gwen first to Birmingham hospital to see her daughter, and then to Smethwick, when Carmen was transferred there.

For a time after the shooting it was feared that Carmen would die. Maria Mancini recalls: 'I took her [Gwen] over to Birmingham and the nurse said, "Here's your child's hair." She wouldn't have it so I took it. Jackie Turpin came with us. He hadn't been speaking to Randolph over a caravan which Randolph had put in their names. It caught fire and they claimed the insurance and never handed it over.'[1] Bulletins were issued for the next few days, but ceased when Carmen was out of danger. She recovered remarkably well and was home in two weeks.

As for the longer term, Maria remembers: 'I said I'd look for a bigger house and asked her to come in with me and share the expense. I went to see the building society manager. I'd been saving and Mosh had his business going and they lent us the money. £4,500 the house cost.' When it came to it, however, Gwen Turpin and the children did not move in with the Mancinis: 'We were just about to sign the contract when Gwen said "Maria, I have to take the children to Wales. Randolph doesn't want them to be with his family." There was a letter which was never read out but that is what it said. I never heard from her again. Peter Wilson arranged for the *Mirror* to pay her about £1000 for an article.[2] I think

[1]   Conversation with author (and all Maria Marcini quotes in this chapter).
[2]   *Sunday Mirror*, 29 May 1966.

that money made her feel good. She began to get paranoid. I nearly died to keep that family. I had double quinsies brought on from the strain.'

'Gwen was a survivor', recalls Orig Williams. 'There are people who, whatever happens, will never starve, and Gwen was one of them.'[3]

Turpin's precious Lonsdale Belt went back to Wales with Gwen, who sold it for three thousand pounds. In 1974, it was auctioned at Christie's and bought by a Birmingham businessman for ten thousand pounds. Towards the end of 2000, the belt was again put up for sale at the Birmingham auctioneers Fellows & Sons. It had been on offer before at £40,000 and now there was speculation that the Warwick District Council would bid for it. In the event, the price fell far short of the estimate when it was knocked down to a local businessman, Tony Baker, a former power lifter. 'I met Randolph when I was a boy and he's a legend to me. I didn't think I would get the belt, to be quite honest, and I'm overwhelmed,' he told the newspapers.[4] For a short time it was exhibited in the local art gallery. Later, Baker sold it.

Turpin's family was pleased the belt had returned to the Midlands, and they had been to view it at Fellows. Kath Turpin, Dick's daughter-in-law, thought, 'This will probably be the last time we will be able to see the belt. That's why I brought my four children and grandchildren along.' She had

---

[3] Conversation with author.
[4] *Birmingham Post*, 1 December 2000. On 12 October 1995 a pair of Freddie Mills' boxing gloves and two other pieces of memorabilia marking his 1942 win over Len Harvey – a belt from *Boxing News* and a silver cigarette case from Ted Broadribb – went for £1,610 at Phillips, the London auctioneers. The same year a GCSE candidate dealing with the set book *Animal Farm*, answering a question, 'Describe the life and death of Boxer and discuss his contribution to the rebellion', wrote of the life and death of Freddie Mills, his mother's background, his sparring with Gypsy Daniels and included the size of his underwear.

known Turpin only as an older man when he owned the café. 'It was only when he died that I realised he wasn't just a boxer but a great boxer and a big chunk of history was lost with him.'[5]

Efforts to have some form of memorial to Randolph in Leamington were repeatedly thwarted until a small blue plaque, paid for by local businessmen, was placed near the staircase in the town hall. Suggestions that there should be a Randolph Turpin Street were quickly knocked on the head. It was argued there was already a Turpin Court and a Randolph Street: 'The Councillors may feel this is enough,' said Trevor Ashbourne, the charter trustees' clerk, although whether the Turpin and Randolph referred to the boxer is extremely doubtful.[6]

Then came a long battle after a fund launched in July 1996 raised enough money to have a statue cast. However, neither Leamington nor Warwick – who had both rushed to embrace Turpin in his two-month reign as world champion – was now particularly keen to have the boxer looking down from a plinth on the citizenry. Alan Parton, chairman of the Warwick Society, was quite stern: 'There are members of this society who regard boxing as a barbarous sport and would object to the creation of a statue which glorified it. Others say while they would prefer a statue to the town's real heroes such as Thomas Oken, Richard Beauchamp or Guy of Warwick, if the townspeople wanted a statue of Randolph Turpin we should not oppose a popular choice. A few people over 60, who have spent their lives in Warwick, may remember Randy. But people under 60 and newcomers to the town will never have heard of him. Even

[5] Ibid.
[6] Leamington Spa *Courier*, 8 November 1996.

among sports enthusiasts he was famous for only one fight.'[7] Possibly, but Thomas Oken and Richard Beauchamp, let alone Guy of Warwick, are hardly household names, either.

There was a proposal that the statue of Randolph would be placed in the new shopping centre at Regent Court in Leamington, but that came to nothing and there were also rumours that the statue was being shuffled off to Warwick because Leamingtonians did not want it at all. A suggestion that the statue should be installed in the Pump Room at the Spa was ignored.

Adrian Bush, who commissioned the statue, believes that if it had not already been sculpted and ready at the foundry the councils would never have come to a decision on a site. In the end, it came to rest in the Market Square in Warwick, and was unveiled by Sir Henry Cooper in 2001, fifty years to the day after Turpin's victory over Sugar Ray Robinson. Earlier in the year, on 12 January, Turpin had been post-humously elected to America's International Boxing Hall of Fame at Canasota, New York State.

It was thought that thousands might attend the unveiling ceremony but, as at his funeral, only hundreds turned up. They included his three surviving daughters: Annette, Charmaine and Carmen. Charmaine told the newspapers: 'When I found out a statue to my father was being unveiled, I talked to my sisters and we agreed we had to be there. It is going to be an extremely moving, emotional and bitter-sweet occasion for us. Carmen realises it is going to be even

[7] Ibid., 4 May 2001. Oken's claim to fame was that as a sixteenth-century nobleman he provided money for his tenants to have bonfires in celebration of the feast of St John the Baptist. A straw poll of the workers in the Royal Leamington Spa Public Library failed to reveal any great knowledge of him, Beauchamp or Guy.

more difficult for her. But we are immensely proud of what our father achieved.'[8]

Turpin's son by his first wife, Randy Jnr, was also present: 'I feel very humble – I'm still a bit dumbfounded by it all. I'm very proud to be here and to have his name. It's just a shame I can't tell him myself how proud I am of him. The only shame is it has taken so long to properly honour him – it would have been nice if my father was here to see it himself. If he was, he would be a very proud man at this moment, but I'm sure he is looking down on us and knows what we have done for him.'[9]

The plaque on the statue reads: 'Randolph Adolphus Turpin (1928–66) Middleweight Champion of the World 1951. In palace, pub and parlour, the whole of Britain held its breath.'

Bournemouth finally stirred itself to pay tribute to Freddie Mills when a memorial slab was sculpted in marble by Sam Rabin.[10] It was unveiled on 8 September 1979. Along with Chrissie Mills and Donnie McCorkindale, among those present were Johnny Williams and Albert Finch, as well as Mills' old opponent Ginger Sadd. A number of boys from the Freddie Mills Club for Handicapped Boys, which had been founded shortly after his death, also came down from

---

[8] Leo Hickman, 'Boxing: When Randy Ruled the World', Birmingham *Evening Mail*, 10 July 2001.
[9] Leamington Spa *Courier*, 13 July 2001.
[10] Sam Rabin was born in Salford in 1906. He won a wrestling bronze at the 1928 Olympics. He boxed at the Ring, Blackfriars, and later became a professional wrestler. After attending the Slade School of Art, he was chosen in 1928 by Charles Holden to carve one of a series of stone panels on London Transport's headquarters. The other sculptors included Henry Moore and Eric Gill. Rabin was responsible for *West Wind* and Gill used a Rabin sketch for *South Wind*. He also worked on the sculptures on the *Daily Telegraph* building. He appeared in a number of films, including the 1935 version of *The Scarlet Pimpernel*, and later taught art, first at Goldsmith's and then in Bournemouth, where he died in December 1991.

London for the ceremony. The memorial was placed in the Winter Gardens and surrounded on three sides by wooden seats. Unfortunately it was out of general public view and over time was regularly vandalised. The Bournemouth Ex-Boxers' Association wanted it moved to near Terrace Road, where Freddie had been born, but the houses in that street were pulled down to make way for a car park. It was later moved to the Littledown Gardens Complex, where, scheduled to be moved back to the centre of the town when the Triangle was redeveloped, it was kept under a plastic wrap in the foyer. In November 1993, a blue plaque was unveiled at St Michael's School. It is in the playground to the right of the main entrance. To this extent at least Turpin has fared slightly better.

Where did all the champions and others who fought and worked with Mills and Turpin go? Mostly to relatively early graveyards, and mainly penniless. Beginning with the greatest, after his wrestling career, Joe Louis went into freefall. Always a womaniser, there was an extraordinary story that towards the end of his life he was introduced to a woman of Chinese origin in Texas. When he was not looking, she injected a drug into his buttock, and thereafter he was hooked. He later discovered that she was a prostitute owned by the Mafia, for whom she had made pornographic films. In his last years, he was of the firm belief that he was being followed by Mafia hitmen. He died on 12 April 1981.

Tommy Farr, one of only three men to go the distance with Louis during his eleven-year world-title reign,[11] had decidedly mixed fortunes. He had surgery on his eyes and

---

[11] The other two were Arturo Godoy and Jersey Joe Walcott.

as a result was not fit for active military service. In the 1940s, he ran a pub, the Royal Standard, near the railway station in Brighton, and a restaurant, Tommy Farr's Pantry. All went well for some five years until a fight broke out and Farr lost his publican's licence. He then became involved with horseracing, betting on his own horses, and it is estimated he lost around £25,000. He possessed prime property on the seafront at Hove which kept him a wealthy man, though, until a government property tax destroyed him financially. In 1950, it was back to the ring, partly for money and partly because he was confident he was still better than any of the current contenders. For a time, he did well, until he was unexpectedly knocked out in the second round by the almost novice Frank Bell at Carmarthen. He also lost to that perennial thorn in British flesh, Lloyd Marshall. Shortly before his fortieth birthday in 1953 he was stopped by Don Cockell in seven rounds at Nottingham. He retired, and for some twenty years wrote a boxing column for the *Sunday Pictorial*, but when that merged with the *Sunday Mirror* he was surplus to requirements. Absolutely at rock bottom, he found a job with an industrial paint company for which he worked for the next sixteen years. Towards the end of his life, he was a huge favourite at boxing dinners. Asked if it was his wife who was with him, he would reply, 'Well, if it's somebody else's I'm having a wonderful time with her.' He died in February 1985 at Shoreham, Sussex.

Chrissie Mills' first husband, Don McCorkindale, returned to South Africa after the war. In 1933 he had fought in America, putting himself in the world rankings with a defeat of Patsy Perroni. But he then injured his back in a contest with King Levinsky, who beat him badly, knocking him down six times. For a time he was involved with promotions at the Ring, Blackfriars. By 1966 he was suffering from arthritis and had, it was reported, lost his interest in boxing. It was said of him that, like Mills: 'He has always tried to serve the public by giving the best he has in him. He has never squealed or had any alibis when he has lost. He just grins and asks for more.'[12]

Jock McAvoy, whose real name was Joseph Bamford, killed himself on his sixty-third birthday in November 1971. Shortly after the war he contracted polio, which was sweeping the country, and was then confined to a wheelchair. But he was still as feisty as ever, and regularly attended tournaments at Belle Vue, Manchester where, on one occasion, he hit a reporter who annoyed him. In over one hundred bouts, he had never been knocked out. His daughter became a prominent show-jumper. The highly regarded Len Harvey never fought again after his defeat by Mills. He became a well-respected publican and died on on 28 November 1976. The genial Jack Petersen became a Cardiff councillor, winning the Plasnewydd constituency in December 1951. He served on the Boxing Board of Control for many years, eventually becoming its President. Gus Lesnevich died in February 1964, and Joe Baksi in August 1977, aged fifty-five.

As for Turpin's opponents, the great Sugar Ray Robinson fought on until he finally retired in 1965. In all, he had 201 contests, of which he lost a bare 19. He died on 12 April 1989. He was one of the few who, for years, kept his wealth and health. At the time of his death he had been suffering from heart disease for some time. He remained married to

---

[12] *Boxing*, 10 January 1934.

Ena Mae and was survived by her and their one son. 'He could move like a dancer and hit like a pile driver,' said his obituary in *The Times*.

In the latter part of his career Joey Maxim lost to both Bobo Olson and Willie Pastrano, before retiring after losing to Archie Moore. He moved to Nevada, where he became a cab driver, casino host and stand-up comic in Las Vegas. Towards the end of his life he retired to Palm Beach, Florida, where he died on 2 June 2001.

Carl Bobo Olson challenged the ageing Archie Moore for the light-heavyweight title on 22 June 1955 and, for his pains, was knocked out in the third round. He then lost his middleweight belt to Robinson in Chicago on 9 December of that year when he was knocked out in the second round. The next year the pair met again, this time in Los Angeles, and Olson lost in four.

He stayed out of the ring for a little over a year but then, as a heavyweight, he outpointed a fading Joey Maxim over ten rounds in Portland, Oregon. He trained down to light-heavy again and was in line for a challenge to Willie Pastrano when, in a final eliminator for the title, he was knocked out by Jose Torres in the first round. In 2000, he became the only Hawaiian to be inducted into boxing's Hall of Fame. During his retirement he worked both with troubled teenagers and in public relations, but before his death in January 2002 he had been increasingly incapacitated by Alzheimer's disease.

After the fiasco with Woodcock, Lee Oma redeemed himself. He won fifteen of his next seventeen fights and in January 1951 fought an eliminator for the world heavyweight title at the Madison Square Garden. He was stopped in the tenth round, but until then the critics had thought there had been little between the men.

Bruce Woodcock died in an old people's home in December 1997. After his retirement from the ring, he managed a few boxers for a time, but then he became a publican. A couple of years before his death, he stopped two men who were stealing from his allotment, which seems to be the nearest he got to his dream of owning a smallholding. In its obituary *The Times* thought he had been badly managed and had never recovered from the beating he took at Baksi's hands. The writer regarded the contest as a dreadful example of overmatching. Woodcock had been effectively blinded in his left eye by that contest. Not that that had stopped him boxing at the time. But over the years he became singularly disillusioned with the fight game and, whilst he acknowledged it had helped him escape from the Low Drop, and had put his son through college and provided a convent education for his daughter, he rarely spoke about his fights. In his autobiography he wrote, 'Bright lights, gay nights, champagne parties and pretty women are not for me.'[13] He was survived by his wife Nora.

Jack Gardner, Woodcock's conqueror, did not turn out to be the Great White Hope after all. He lost to, and then beat, Johnny Williams, before finally losing his title to Don Cockell. The Board of Control withdrew Gardner's licence on health grounds in July 1956. He became a farmer and died in November 1978, aged fifty-two.

Johnny Williams was another fighter consistently matched with heavier men. On the night of the second Woodcock v Savold fight, Broadribb had him paired with Pat Comiskey. Williams now weighed thirteen stone five pounds and was conceding two and a half stone. He outboxed the American

---

[13] Bruce Woodcock, *Two Fists and a Fortune*, p. 192.

for the first five rounds, but was then cut badly around the eye and the fight was stopped. He was a mere five weeks away from a fight with Jack Gardner in a final eliminator to meet Woodcock for the British title. Broadribb remembers: 'It is at those times that managers and fighters have to decide on the question of loyalties. All things being equal, I suppose we should really have called off the Gardner contest. As on the stage, where the show must go on, so we in boxing try to keep faith with the promoters, and that was the course on which we decided. So, I am sorry to say, Johnny faced his worst fight in anything but the frame of mind in which I wanted him to be for such an important occasion, and other circumstances surrounding the contest just made it more difficult than ever.'[14]

Unsurprisingly, Williams was determined to protect his eye. Gardner opened its cut early in the fight and then built up a decisive lead. Williams was pleading, 'Stop it, stop it' – Broadribb wondered whether he meant the bleeding or the contest. His boxer had a fine tenth round but it was the end. He slipped in the twelfth, jarring his spine, and was unable to throw another meaningful punch. He lasted until the end of the fight but when the decision was announced he collapsed. The press began to call for his retirement.

Broadribb took his new protégé to Harley Street, where a future operation was advised. In the meantime he sparred two rounds with Eddie Vann and his eyes stood up. He was matched on 14 November 1950 with the American George Kaplan, who opened up the left eye within the first ten seconds. Williams gamely battled on, and using his left hand

---

[14] Ted Broadribb, *Fighting is My Life*, pp. 126–7.

reduced his opponent to such a state that the referee stopped the fight in the seventh.

He was in the ring at Harringay again with Big Bill Weinberg and retired after taking heavy punishment. He had, it seems, put his spine out of alignment though he said nothing. He was unable to lift his arm. He was out once more against a man rated the best heavyweight in Europe, the black American Aaron Wilson, but he won on points over eight rounds. He then stopped Jo Weiden, the Austrian. Broadribb was understandably jubilant: 'All Williams needs to do now is to build up his strength and I am sure that in the evening of my career I shall steer him to bigger things.'[15]

Perhaps the saddest story of all is that of Tiberio Mitri, who knocked out Turpin for the European title. This blue-eyed, blond and baby-faced hero had married the glamour queen Fulvia Franco in 1948. She wanted to be a Hollywood starlet and they went to America, where Mitri lost over fifteen rounds to Jake La Motta on 12 July 1950. He had not trained properly, and in any event the Raging Bull was simply too strong for him. Within a year of defeating Turpin, he lost the European title and retired to become an actor, taking bit parts in films, and a painter. After a bitter divorce, he turned to heroin and his life spiralled downwards. In 1981, his thirty-year-old son died of an overdose, while his daughter by a second marriage died of an AIDS-related illness six years later. In his final years, suffering from Alzheimer's and Parkinson's, he frequented bars in Rome and was cared for only by a small local charity. It is thought that he forgot to take his medicine and, out of touch with reality, thinking he might take a train to his home town of Trieste, he wandered on to railway tracks where he was killed

---

[15] Ibid., p. 136.

by a train going at a mere 20 m.p.h. He simply ignored or failed to hear the warning signal, which was sounded three times.

Charles Humez, Turpin's opponent in the final eliminator before he fought Olson, was not defeated by another European for five years. Then, in September 1958, he was being badly beaten by Gustav Scholz of Germany when he was stopped with a deep cut over his right eyebrow in the twelfth round. On his retirement, he also turned professional wrestler, appearing in England at various venues on promotions by Paul Lincoln. He died in November 1978 following a stroke at the age of fifty-two. 'They don't make them like Humez any more in Europe,' wrote Graham Houslar in *Boxing News* a year later.

Mills' manager Ted Broadribb died at his home at Horsham in 1967. Turpin's manager George Middleton died, aged eighty-six, in hospital at Leamington Spa at the end of December 1990. 'He didn't know a left hook from a fish hook', said Peter McInnis, but others remembered him more kindly. Turpin's early trainer, Ron Stefani, died in hospital in 1999, also aged eighty-six. When Turpin turned professional, he wanted his father-figure to remain his coach, but Stefani preferred to stay at grassroots level in the town he loved. To do so, he worked as a foreman and dispatch rider for Automotive Products in Tachbrook Road, Leamington. Stefani's daughter Joyce Golding said: 'Randolph was from a poor family and my father wanted to give him a good start in life – he treated him like a son. When Randolph won the world title my father was over the moon, but when he committed suicide he was absolutely devastated.' Ron retired from the local boxing scene in 1976, but, unlike many, he remained an avid armchair follower until his death.[16]

[16] Duncan Gibbons, 'Boxing Legend's Mentor Is Dead', Coventry *Evening Telegraph*, 29 October 1999.

Jack Solomons, 'Mr Boxing', as he was described on his death by Sikrumar Sen, the boxing correspondent of *The Times*, was never again the force he was when he promoted Mills and Turpin. He lost his control of boxing in a coup organised by the businessman and promoter Jarvis Astaire in 1963. The Southern Area Council, a powerful body, was a financially interested council run by Solomons. Before the Annual General Meeting at which members of the council were re-elected, Astaire lobbied members, with the result that Solomons' faction was voted out, to be replaced, un-fortunately from Astaire's viewpoint, by another clique led by Harry Levene, Solomons' old rival.

Astaire would say later: 'Quite frankly, I didn't want to be in a position where my so-called loose acquaintances were in power. I didn't want anybody in power. So I used my influence to take my friends out and replace the council with people not financially interested in boxing. I had to talk them into it. I remember saying to Mickey Duff, the matchmaker, "Mickey, you've had to be nice to Solomons' stooges all these years. Why do you want to be nice to someone else now? Because he's yours for one beer, but he'll be somebody else's for two." Mickey saw the point and I said the same to a number of other people.'[17]

Boxing itself was in decline. The great arenas were closing their doors to the sport – Harringay had gone and so had Earl's Court. The future, such as it was, was in the small halls and the so-called 'dinner shows', with the major promotions in London more or less reserved for the Royal Albert Hall and the Empire Pool, Wembley.

In 1965 Solomons founded the World Sporting Club,

[17] Russell Miller, 'Iron Fist in a Velvet Wallet', *Sunday Times Magazine*, 7 October 1973.

which promoted dinner shows. But his rivals had Joe Bugner, who later fought Ali for the world heavyweight, whereas Solomons' drawing card was the hard-punching Irishman Danny McAlinden, who later became British heavyweight champion. McAlinden recalls: 'The most money I made from a fight was £10,000. It was always "The Big One's the next one." I was fighting the same people as Joe Bugner but not for the same money.'"

It was the same old story as it had been for Mills. McAlinden had a good punch and a great heart but as a heavyweight he was too small. He barely made six foot. He was also mismatched: 'Solomons put me in with Morrie Jackson, who was six foot five and weighed seventeen stone. He said, "He's a heavyweight, just a human being." Jack was never hit on the chin in his life. I put him down in the first round, he put me down in the second, but I thought, I can take it. It was the first time I was ever stopped. Roland Dakin was the referee and I don't think he should have stopped it so quickly.'[18]

Solomons died on 8 December 1979, survived by his wife. He left 45 per cent of his shares in the World Sporting Club, along with £200,000, to his long-time friend Kay O'Dwyer who had been the constant companion of the singer Donald Peers until his death in 1973. There was also a bequest to set up a charitable trust of £20,000 for boxers who had fallen on hard times. He left a penny in his will to the British Boxing Board of Control. It was paid and, much to the chagrin of Simon Block, the present General Secretary, Ray Clarke, then the incumbent, threw the coin down the sink. Solomons left the rest

---

[18] Conversation with author.

of his estate to his wife. She died two weeks after her husband.

Asked for a comment on the death of his great rival, the promoter Harry Levene merely gave the date and venue of his next show.

The much-loved Dick Turpin died in Leamington Spa on 7 July 1990. After his retirement from the ring, he worked at Flavells, a local company. He had been in poor health for some time. Of the funeral, the local newspaper wrote:

> What a wretched pity that the district's municipal authority did not see fit to pay its respects as well. Warwick District Council was not officially represented; a floral tribute was not received; no councillors made their independent presence known to the family. Dick Turpin was a man whose honour will be forever upheld by his sporting achievement. He would not have asked for, nor expected, the local authority to recognise after his death what they shamefully refused to recognise throughout most of his life.[19]

Kath Turpin died in 1992 at the age of sixty-five. In her younger days, she had wanted to go into the ring herself, but was forbidden by her mother and would certainly have fallen foul of the Board of Control had she tried. At one time there had been talk of matching her in a bout with Alex Buxton's sister. Instead, she sparred with her brothers.

None of the Turpin sons did as well in the ring as their fathers had done. Randy's son, Randolph Jnr, was a very

[19] Leamington Spa *Courier*, 20 July 1990.

useful junior amateur but not a greatly successful professional. Dick's son, Howard, had only a short career in the
ring. The best was Jackie's son, Jackie Jnr, who continued
the family tradition by becoming 'Boxer of the Year' in the
1970s. 'He had the fastest hands I ever saw,' said Danny
McAlinden,[20] and many would agree with him. Unfortunately,
like his father, he was vulnerable to a head punch. Towards
the end of his career, he was badly beaten by the American
Frankie Lewis, and in his next contest was knocked down
sixteen times. There was talk of him starting special neck-
strengthening exercises, but his licence was withdrawn before
he could, and he followed his uncle onto the wrestling circuit.

Gwen Turpin lived near Prestatyn in north Wales. At
various Pat Dwyer promotions in Wales and the north-west,
he would often introduce the Turpin girls from the ring. In
spite of everything, Turpin's daughter Charmaine spoke affec-
tionately of her parents: 'He was a hands-on dad. My dad
couldn't have chosen a nicer woman. I think he chose my
mother because of the way she was brought up. They had
such a nice family life.' Of her father's death, Carmen said,
'I honestly don't think we'll ever know the truth. I don't think
he could have done that to me.'[21]

In its obituary of Mills, *The Times* said: 'No one would
ever call Freddie Mills a boxing purist. He lunged, swung
and swept in against all his opponents with all guns firing
and seemed to care little about the risk of taking counter-
punches. But his courage and strength were nigh inex-
haustible.'[22] In fact, no one ever had a bad word to say about
the hail-fellow-well-met, the seemingly happy-go-lucky Mills.

[20] Conversation with author.
[21] *Randolph Turpin* film.
[22] *The Freddie Mills Story* film.

His daughter Susan said: 'It really is irrelevant whether it was suicide or whether he was killed, as some people think that he was. Whatever happened it will never bring him back. I'm just glad for the time I spent with him and I'm so happy I was able to have that sort of person as my father.'[23]

The epitaphs for Randolph Turpin are not so unanimous. He was not popular with the press, who found him moody and, because of his deafness, increasingly uncommunicative. The boxing writer and broadcaster Harry Carpenter thought he was 'too rich too soon and he had too little personality'.[24] Perhaps, however, Randolph's boyhood friend Ernie Halford best sums up his life and career: 'All I would ask, you try to appreciate the marvel of a kid from the background we shared getting as far as he did.'[25]

Towards the end of his life Turpin wrote a short poem:

> So we leave this game which is hard and cruel
> And down at the show on a ringside stool
> We'll watch the next man, just one more fool.

[23] *The Times*, 26 July 1966.
[24] Harry Carpenter, 'The Randy Turpin Story', *Daily Mail*, 30 October 1959.
[25] Letter to author.

Bibliography

Books

Anderson, D., *Ringmasters* (1991) London, Robson.

Baker, M., *The Rise and Fall of Gwyrch Castle* (1998) Rhyl, Mark Baker.

Barrington-Dalby, W., *Come in Barry* (1961) London, Cassell.

Barrow, J. L. Jr and Munder, B., *Joe Louis: The Brown Bomber* (1988) London, Arthur Barker.

Bavin, B., *The Strange Death of Freddie Mills* (1975) London, H. Baker.

Bean, J. P., *Bold as a Lion* (2002) Sheffield, D & D Publications.

Bettinson, A. E. and Outram, T. W. (eds), *The National Sporting Club: Past and Present* (1901) London, Sands & Co.

Birtley, J., *The Tragedy of Randolph Turpin* (1975) London, New English Library.

——*Freddie Mills, His Life and Death* (1977) London, New English Library.

Booker, P., *'The Ring' Blackfriars* (1999) London, London Ex-Boxers' Association.

Booth, J. B., *Old Pink 'Un Days* (1924) London, Richards Press.

——*'Master and Men'; Pink 'Un Yesterdays* (1927) London, T. Werner Laurie.

Broadribb, T., *Fighting is My Life* (1952) London, Frederick Muller.

Brunt, S., *Facing Ali: The Opposition Weighs In* (2002) Toronto, Knopf Canada.

Butler, F., *Randolph Turpin . . . Sugar Ray Robinson: their Story in pictures* (1951) Norwich, Jarrold & Sons.

——*The Good, the Bad and the Ugly* (1986) London, Stanley Paul.

Canning, J. (ed.), *Unsolved Murders and Mysteries* (1987) London, Michael O'Mara Books.

Collins, N., *Boxing Babylon* (1999) London, Robson.

Connor, M., *The Soho Don* (2002) Edinburgh, Mainstream.

Daniels, D. M., *The Mike Jacobs Story* (1950) New York, Ring Bookshop.

Deakin, F., *Tommy Farr* (1989) Stone, Crescendo Publications.

Deghy, G., *Noble and Manly* (1956) London, Hutchinson.

Downes, T., *My Bleedin' Business* (1989) London, Robson.

Duff, M. and Mee, B., *Twenty and Out* (1999) London, Collins Willow.

du Rose, J., *Murder Was My Business* (1971) London, W. H. Allen.

Evans, J. and Short, M., *The Survivor* (2001) Edinburgh, Mainstream.

Farr, T., *Thus Farr* (1989) London, Optomen Press.

Francis, G. and Fife, G., *Trainer of Champions* (1998) Edinburgh, Mainstream.

Frederick, O., *Battling Bruce* (1947) London, Bertrand Snelling.

Gee, T., *Up to Scratch* (1998) Harpenden, Queen Anne Press.

Hauser, H., *The Black Lights* (1986) New York, McGraw-Hill Book Co.

Henderson, E., *Box On* (1959) London, Phoenix House.

Ingle, J., *The Jimmy Ingle Story* (1984) Co. Kerry, Brandon Books.

Keeler, C. and Meadley, R., *Sex Scandals* (1985) London, Xanadu Publications.

Kelly, P., *The Barmaid's Tale* (1996) London, Little, Brown.

Kent, G., *Boxing's Strangest Fights* (1991) London, Robson.

Kray, K., with Kray, Ronnie and Bruce, M., *Murder, Madness and Marriage* (1993) London, Blake.

La Motta, J., with Carter, J. and Savage, P., *Raging Bull* (1980) London, Bantam.

Legge, H., *Penny a Punch* (1981) Christchurch, Curtis Publications.

——*Four Punches More* (1987) Christchurch, Curtis Publications.

Lewis, M., *Ted 'Kid' Lewis* (1990) London, Robson.

Lewis, N., *Britain's Gangland* (1969) London, W. H. Allen.

Lonkhurst, R. B., *Man of Courage* (1997) Lewes, Book Guild.

Louis, J., with Rust, E. and A. Jnr, *My Life* (1978) New York, Harcourt Brace Jovanovich.

McConnell, B., *Found Naked and Dead* (1974) London, New English Library.

McIlvanney, H., *McIlvanney on Boxing* (1996) Edinburgh, Mainstream.

McInnes, P., *Randy: The Final Complete Biography of Randolph Turpin* (1996) Chippenham, Caestus Press.

——*Freddie My Friend* (2001) Chippenham, Caestus Press.

McRae, D., *In Black and White* (2002) London, Simon & Schuster.

Mills, F., *Twenty Years* (1950) London, Ivor Nicholson & Watson.

——*Battling for a Title* (1954) London, Stanley Paul.

Monkhouse, B., *Crying with Laughter* (1993) London, Century.

Moore, A., *The Archie Moore Story* (1960) London, Nicholas Kaye.

Morton, J., *East End Gangland* (2001) London, Warner Books.

——*Gangland: The Early Years* (2003) London, Time Warner Books.

Mullen, H., *Heroes and Hard Men* (1989) London, Stanley Paul.

Oakley, A., *Blue Blood on the Mat* (1971) London, Stanley Paul.

Odd, G., *Boxing: The Inside Story* (1978) Feltham, Hamlyn.

Powell, N., *Nosher* (1999) London, Blake.

Read, L. and Morton, J., *Nipper Read: The Man Who Nicked the Krays* (2001) London, Little, Brown.

Robinson, J., *Claret and Cross-buttock* (1976) London, Allen & Unwin.

Robinson, S. R., with Anderson, D., *Sugar Ray* (1970) London, Putnam.

Scott, F., *Weigh In* (1974) New York, Thomas Y. Crowell Co.

Skeham, E. M., *Rocky Marciano* (1977) London, Robson.

Solomons, J., *Jack Solomons Tells All* (1951) London, Rich & Cowan.

Stengel, E., *Suicide and Attempted Suicide* (1964) Harmondsworth, Penguin.

Sutherland, D., *The Mad Hatters* (1987) London, Robert Hale.

——*Portrait of a Decade: London Life 1945–1955* (1988) London, Harrap.

Taub, M., *Jack Doyle: Fighting for Love* (1990) London, Stanley Paul.

Tremlett, G., *Little Legs: Muscle Man of Soho* (1989) London, Unwin Hyman.

Van den Bergh, T., *Who Killed Freddie Mills?* (1991) London, Constable.

Watson, N., *Matt Moran's Shamrock Gardens* (1988) Stoneclough, N. Richardson.

Wilson, P., *Ringside Seat* (1949) London, Rich & Cowan.

——*More Ringside Seats* (1959) London, Stanley Paul.

Woodcock, B., *Two Fists and a Fortune* (1951) London, Hutchinson.

Selected Articles

J. C. Batt, 'Murder: A Psychiatric View' in *The Criminologist*, Spring 1972.

Blue-Bird's Eye, 'Gus Lesnevich World "Cruiser" Ace' in *Boxing News*, 11 April 1947.

Tom Brimble, 'He Made Boxing History' in *Boxing News*, 24 November 1948.

Fred Burcombe, 'King Randy by His Brother Jackie' in *News of the World*, 28 July 1991.

Dave Caldwell, 'Broadribb Was the Greatest Manager' in *Boxing News*, 6 December 1968.

Bert Callis, 'Freddie Mills in a Playful Mood' in *Boxing News*, 29 May 1946.

Harry Carpenter, 'The Randy Turpin Story' in *Daily Mail*, 30 October 1959.

Rod Davies, 'The Turpin I Knew' in *Warwick and Warwickshire District Advertiser*, 18 May 1966.

Peter Earle and Charles Sandell, 'Was Freddie Mills Murdered?' in *News of the World,* 22 September 1968.

Keith Ellis, 'Lucky Jack Solomons' in *John Bull*, 20 and 27 June 1953.

Peter Forbes, 'It's Time You Cleaned up Your Club, Mr Mills' in *People*, 5 July 1964.

Desmond Hackett, 'The Great Untamed' in *Daily Express*, 1 December 1972.

Len Harvey, 'They Must Look After Randy' in *Boxing News*, 22 August 1951.

W. L. Hoban, 'What Does Constitute an Ace Trainer?' in *Boxing News*, 4 June 1952.

Charles Hull, 'Devonshire Club Reminiscences' in *Weekly Sporting Review*, Christmas and New Year 1948–9.

Jersey Jones, 'So Long, Mike' in *Ring*, July 1949.

Charles Lesemann, 'Harry Greb, the Human Windmill' in *Boxing News*, 16 April 1954.

Jack Macadam, 'England's Mike Jacobs Is Fishmonger Jack Solomons' in *Ring*, January 1946.

Peter McInnes, 'Knight of the Roped Square' in *Boxing News*, 26 September 1958.

Harry Markson, 'The Mike Jacobs Story' in *Empire News*, 5 July 1953.

Ronald Maxwell, 'Freddie Mills: New Evidence' in *Sunday Mirror*, 8 August 1965.

Russell Miller, 'Iron Fist in a Velvet Wallet' in *Sunday Times Magazine*, 7 October 1973.

Freddie Mills, 'From Boxing Booth to World Champion' in *Empire News*, 2 January 1949.

——'My Great Fights' in *Sunday Graphic*, 31 October 1958.

Murder Casebook, Volume 33, 'Jack the Stripper'.

Andrew Newton Jnr, 'Pen Picture of "Nipper" Pat Daley' in *Boxing News*, 26 December 1940.

——'More about "Nipper" Pat Daley' in *Boxing News*, 16 January 1941.

Gilbert Odd, 'Booths Breed the Best' in *Boxing News*, 30 April 1947.

——'Sweet Taste of Glory for Handy Randy' in *Boxing News*, 7 September 1959.

Sugar Ray Robinson, 'My Fighting Life' in *Empire News*, 10 June 1951.

John Sampson, 'My Broken Romance with Randy: The Truths' in *Empire News*, 15 November 1953.

Ted Scales, 'British Boxers as I See Them' in *Ring*, January 1936.

Nat Seller, 'Champions are My Business' in *Empire News*, 6 March 1955.

Jack Solomons, 'I Believe in Turpin' in *Everybody's*, 14 November 1953.

Randolph Turpin, 'The Women in My Life' in *Empire News*, 31 March 1957.

——with Sam Leitch, 'With Hate in My Heart' in *Sunday Pictorial*, 15 April 1962.

Tony Vairo, 'How I Put One across Harry Levene' in *Sunday People*, 18 March 1962.

Billy Williams, 'The Turbulent Turpins' in *Ring*, October 1953.

Television Programmes

Dave Hannington, *The Freddie Mills Story*, 1975.

Franco Rosso and Gordon Williams, *64 Day Hero*, 1985.

In Suspicious Circumstances, 1992.

Eryri Productions, *Randolph Turpin*, 2001.

Freddie Mills' Professional Record

1936

Mar	25	Reg Davis	W KO	3	Bournemouth
Apr	20	Stan Nelson	Drew	6	Bournemouth
Oct	14	Jack Scott	W KO	1	Bournemouth
Oct	28	Stan Nelson	W rsf	2	Bournemouth
Nov	11	Slogger Wilson	W KO	7	Bournemouth
Nov	17	George Heskett	Drew	6	Weymouth
Nov	25	Fred Lennington	W KO	4	Bournemouth
Dec	9	George Bradby	W KO	1	Bournemouth

1937

Jan	6	Billy Brown	W KO	1	Bournemouth
Jan	20	Teddy Warren	W KO	2	Bournemouth
Feb	3	Harry Frolic	W rtd	7	Bournemouth
Feb	17	Jack McKnight	W pts	12	Bournemouth
Mar	3	Red Pullen	W pts	12	Bournemouth
Mar	17	Jack McKnight	W pts	12	Bournemouth
Apr	14	Jack Alder	W pts	12	Bournemouth
Apr	28	Harry Lister	W pts	12	Bournemouth

May 5	Albert Johnson	W pts	12	Bournemouth
Aug 14	George Davis	L KO	10	Poole
Oct 8	Harold Kid Anthony	W KO	1	Paignton
Oct 20	George Davis	L pts	12	Bournemouth
Nov 3	Billy Fuller	W KO	7	Bournemouth
Nov 17	Jim Greaves	Drew	12	Bournemouth
Dec 1	Fred Clements	W rtd	6	Bournemouth
Dec 15	Jack Lewis	L pts	10	Bournemouth
Dec 17	Ginger Dawkins	Drew	12	Paignton

1938

Jan 5	Ginger Dawkins	W rsf	8	Bournemouth
Jan 19	Jim Greaves	W rsf	12	Bournemouth
Feb 2	Billy James	W rtd	2	Bournemouth
Feb 16	Ted Barter	W rsf	6	Bournemouth
Mar 2	Harry Vine	W rsf	9	Bournemouth
Mar 16	Tommy Taylor	W pts	12	Bournemouth
Mar 30	Jack Lewis	W pts	12	Bournemouth
Apr 13	Charlie Parkin	W rsf	3	Bournemouth
Apr 27	Charlie Parkin	W pts	12	Bournemouth
Aug 1	Moe Moss	W KO	5	Bournemouth
Oct 7	Fred Clements	W rsf	6	Portsmouth
Nov 9	Seaman Long	W KO	3	Bournemouth
Nov 14	Tom Curran	W pts	10	Brighton
Nov 23	Yorkie Bentley	W KO	6	Bournemouth
Dec 7	Butcher Gascoigne	W pts	12	Bournemouth
Dec 14	Dave McCleave	L pts	12	Bournemouth

1939

Jan 4	Yorkie Bentley	W rsf	7	Bournemouth

Jan	18	Paul Schaeffer	W pts	10	Bournemouth
Feb	1	Johnny Blake	W rtd	6	Bournemouth
Feb	20	Butcher Gascoigne	L pts	12	Gt Yarmouth
Mar	1	Eddie Maguire	W pts	10	Bournemouth
Mar	13	Nat Franks	Drew	12	Plymouth
Apr	12	Elfryn Morris	L pts	10	Bournemouth
Apr	26	Charlie Parkin	W pts	10	Bournemouth
May	3	Dave McCleave	W KO	1	Bournemouth
June	14	Ginger Sadd	L pts	10	Bournemouth
July	21	Charlie Parkin	W KO	1	Plymouth
Oct	28	Dave McCleave	W KO	3	Southampton
Nov	7	Eddie Maguire	L pts	10	Southampton
Nov	27	Eddie Maguire	Drew	10	Southampton
Dec	26	Elfryn Morris	W KO	6	Bournemouth

1940

Mar	17	Jim Berry	W pts	10	Coventry
Apr	10	Ginger Sadd	W pts	10	Eastbourne
Apr	17	Stafford Barton	W rtd	7	London
May	22	Ben Valentine	W rtd	3	Bournemouth
Aug	8	Jock McAvoy	W pts	10	Liverpool
Sept	7	Ernie Simmons	W rtd	6	Newcastle

1941

May	26	Ginger Sadd	W rtd	9	Leicester
May	31	Trevor Burt	W rtd	1	Pontypool
June	8	Jack Hyams	W rsf	4	Liverpool
June	30	Jack Powell	W rsf	1	Reading
Aug	5	Tom Reddington	W pts	10	Leicester
Sept	1	Jack Hyams	L dsq	3	Leicester

Sept 29	Tommy Martin	W rsf	5	London
Nov 3	Jim Wilde	W KO	3	London
Nov 28	Tom Reddington	L pts	10	London
Dec 8	Jack London	W pts	10	London

1942

Jan 26	Tom Reddington	W rsf	9	London
Feb 23	Jock McAvoy	W rtd	1	London
	(Final eliminator for British Light-heavyweight title)			
June 20	Len Harvey	W KO	2	London
	(British and Empire Light-heavyweight titles)			
Oct 23	Al Robinson	W rtd	6	Manchester

1943

May 22	Al Robinson	W KO	2	Leeds

1944

Feb 16	Bert Gilroy	W rsf	8	London
May 25	Al Delaney	W KO	5	London
Sept 15	Jack London	L pts	15	Manchester
	(Vacant British and Empire Heavyweight titles)			

1945

Feb 7	Ken Shaw	W rsf	7	London

1946

May	14	Gus Lesnevich	L rsf	10	London
		(World's Light-heavyweight title)			
June	4	Bruce Woodcock	L pts	12	London
Aug	13	John Nilsson	W KO	1	Brighton
Nov	5	Joe Baksi	L rtd	6	London

1947

Jan	20	Willie Quentemeyer	W KO	2	London
Feb	17	Enrico Bertola	W KO	5	London
Apr	29	Nick Wolmarans	W KO	8	Johannesburg
June	3	Lloyd Marshall	L KO	5	London
Sept	8	Pol Goffaux	W rtd	4	London
		(Vacant European Light-heavyweight title)			
Nov	28	Stephan Olek	W pts	10	Manchester

1948

Feb	17	Paco Bueno	W KO	2	London
		(European Light-heavyweight title)			
Apr	20	Ken Shaw	W rtd	1	London
		(Final eliminator for British and Empire Heavyweight titles)			
July	26	Gus Lesnevich	W pts	15	London
		(World's Light-heavyweight title)			
Nov	6	Johnny Ralph	W KO	8	Johannesburg
		(British and Empire Heavyweight title)			

1949

June 2 Bruce Woodcock　　　L KO　14　London
　　　　(British and Empire Heavyweight title)

1950

Jan 24 Joey Maxim　　　　　L KO　10　London
　　　　(World's Light-heavyweight title)

Randolph Turpin's Professional Record

1946

Sept 17 Gordon Griffiths　　　W rsf　1　London
Nov 9 Des Jones　　　　　　W pts　6　London
Dec 29 Bill Blything　　　　　W KO　1　Birmingham

1947

Jan 14 Jimmy Davis　　　　　W KO　4　London
Jan 24 Dai James　　　　　　W KO　3　Birmingham
Feb 18 Johnny Best　　　　　W rsf　1　London
Mar 18 Bert Hyland　　　　　W KO　1　London
Apr 1 Frank Dolan　　　　　W rsf　2　London
Apr 15 Tommy Davies　　　　W KO　2　London
Apr 28 Bert Saunders　　　　W pts　6　London
May 12 Ron Cooper　　　　　W rsf　4　Oxford

May 27	Jury VII	W pts	6	London
June 3	Mark Hart	W pts	6	London
June 23	Leon Fouguet	W KO	1	Coventry
Sept 9	Jimmy Ingle	W rsf	3	Coventry
Oct 20	Mark Hart	Drew	8	London

1948

Jan 26	Freddie Price	W KO	1	Coventry
Feb 17	Gerry McCready	W rsf	1	London
Mar 16	Vince Hawkins	W pts	8	London
Apr 26	Albert Finch	L pts	8	London
June 28	Alby Hollister	W pts	8	Birmingham
Sept 21	Jean Stock	L ret	5	London

1949

Feb 7	Jackie Jones	W ret	5	Coventry
Feb 27	Doug Miller	W pts	8	London
Mar 25	Mickey Laurent	W ret	3	Manchester
May 3	William Poli	W disq	4	London
June 20	Cyrille Delannoit	W rsf	8	Birmingham
Aug 22	Jean Wanes	W ret	3	Manchester
Sept 19	Roy Wouters	W rsf	5	Coventry
Nov 15	Pete Mead	W ret	4	London

1950

Jan 31	Gilbert Stock	W pts	8	London
Mar 6	Richard Armah	W ret	6	Croydon
Apr 24	Gustave Degouve	W pts	8	Nottingham
Sept 5	Eli Elandon	W KO	2	Watford

Oct	17	Albert Finch	W KO	5	London
		(British Middleweight title)			
Nov	13	Jose Alamo	W KO	2	Abergavenny
Dec	12	Tommy Yaroz	W disq	8	London

1951

Jan	22	Eduardo Lopez	W KO	1	Birmingham
Feb	27	Luc Van Dam	W KO	1	London
		(European Middleweight title)			
Mar	19	Jean Stock	W rsf	5	Leicester
Apr	16	Billy Brown	W KO	2	Birmingham
May	7	Jan de Bruin	W KO	6	Coventry
June	5	Jackie Keogh	W rsf	7	London
July	10	Ray Robinson	W pts	15	London
		(World Middleweight title)			
Sept	12	Ray Robinson	L rsf	10	New York
		(World Middleweight title)			

1952

Feb	12	Alex Buxton	W ret	7	London
Apr	22	Jacques Hairabedian	W KO	3	London
June	10	Don Cockell	W rsf	11	London
		(British and Empire Light-heavyweight title)			
Oct	21	George Angelo	W pts	15	London
		(British Empire Middleweight title)			

1953

Jan	19	Victor D'Haes	W KO	6	Birmingham
Feb	16	Duggie Miller	W pts	10	Leicester

Mar	17	Walter Cartier	W disq	2	London
June	9	Charles Humez	W pts	15	London

(European Middleweight title)

Oct	21	Carl Olson	L pts	15	New York

(Vacant world Middleweight title)

1954

Mar	30	Olle Bengtsson	W pts	10	London
May	2	Tiberio Mitri	L rsf	1	Rome

(European Middleweight title)

1955

Feb	15	Ray Schmit	W disq	8	Birmingham
Mar	8	Jose Gonzales	W KO	7	London
Apr	26	Alex Buxton	W KO	2	London

(British and Empire
Light-heavyweight title)

Sept	19	Polly Smith	W pts	10	Birmingham
Oct	18	Gordon Wallace	L KO	4	London

1956

Apr	17	Alessandro D'Ottavio	W rsf	6	Birmingham
June	18	Jacques Bro	W KO	5	Birmingham
Sept	21	Hans Stretz	L pts	10	Hamburg
Nov	26	Alex Buxton	W rsf	5	Leicester

(Light-heavyweight title)

1957

June 11	Arthur Howard	W pts	15	Leicester
	(British Light-heavyweight title)			
Sept 17	Ahmed Boulgroune	W rsf	9	London
Oct 28	Sergio Burchi	W rsf	2	Birmingham
Nov 25	Uwe Janssen	W rsf	8	Leicester

1958

Feb 11	Wim Snoek	W pts	10	Birmingham
Apr 21	Eddie Wright	W rsf	7	Leicester
July 22	Redvers Sangoe	W rsf	4	Oswestry
Sept 9	Yolande Pompey	L KO	2	Birmingham

Index